Lucie Morris-Marr is a Walkley Award-winning journalist, twice Highly Commended as Journalist of the Year at the British Press Awards. After moving to Australia as Associate Editor of *Marie Claire*, she went on to report for the *Herald Sun* and the *New Daily*. She is the author of *Fallen: The inside story of the secret trial and conviction of Cardinal George Pell*. She is also a bowel cancer advocate and patient mentor. She lives in Melbourne with her family.

'Impassioned, informed and well documented, *Processed* brings to light the dangers of a processed food often eaten daily.' **Matthew Evans, chef, food critic and author of *On Eating Meat***

'*Processed* is a brilliant work of investigative journalism. It is a firecracker of a book! Using robust research and compelling storytelling, Lucie Morris-Marr tears down the false idols of processed meat.' **Tracey Spicer, multiple Walkley Award–winning journalist**

'Lucie Morris-Marr is one of the best and bravest journalists in Australia. When writing about professional or personal experiences, her prose should not be missed.' **Derryn Hinch, media personality and former federal senator**

'*Processed* is like sitting down with a familiar friend as they help unravel a complex subject. [It] is a richly detailed, stunningly researched book that demystifies the system around the way we produce our food, market it and sell it to an unwitting public.' **Ms Ronni Salt, journalist, political-social commentator and author**

'With her lived experience and passion, Lucie Morris-Marr lifts the lid on the secrets behind the common meat products in our fridge. It is a must-read for anyone concerned about health and longevity.' **Melanie Schilling, TV presenter on** *Married at First Sight* **and bowel cancer advocate**

'Thought-provoking and at times terrifying, *Processed* will make you stop, think and change the way you eat.' **Paula Joye, journalist and author**

'From one bowel cancer patient to another, what an incredibly insightful book so wonderfully written.' **Gemma Farquhar, bowel cancer patient and advocate**

PROCESSED

How the processed meat industry is killing us with the food we love

LUCIE MORRIS-MARR

ALLEN&UNWIN
SYDNEY•MELBOURNE•AUCKLAND•LONDON

The content presented in this book is meant for inspiration and informational purposes only. The purchaser of this book understands that the author is not a medical professional, and the information contained within this book is not intended to replace medical advice or to be relied upon to treat, cure or prevent any disease, illness or medical condition. It is understood that you will seek full medical clearance by a licensed physician before making any changes mentioned in this book. The author and publisher claim no responsibility to any person or entity for any liability, loss or damage caused or alleged to be caused directly or indirectly as a result of the use, application or interpretation of the material in this book.

First published in 2025

Copyright © Lucie Morris-Marr 2025

All rights reserved. No part of this book may be reproduced or transmitted in any form or by any means, electronic or mechanical, including photocopying, recording or by any information storage and retrieval system, without prior permission in writing from the publisher. The Australian *Copyright Act 1968* (the Act) allows a maximum of one chapter or 10 per cent of this book, whichever is the greater, to be photocopied by any educational institution for its educational purposes provided that the educational institution (or body that administers it) has given a remuneration notice to the Copyright Agency (Australia) under the Act.

Every effort has been made to trace the holders of copyright material. If you have any information concerning copyright material in this book please contact the publishers at the address below.

Allen & Unwin
Cammeraygal Country
83 Alexander Street
Crows Nest NSW 2065
Australia
Phone: (61 2) 8425 0100
Email: info@allenandunwin.com
Web: www.allenandunwin.com

Allen & Unwin acknowledges the Traditional Owners of the Country on which we live and work. We pay our respects to all Aboriginal and Torres Strait Islander Elders, past and present.

 A catalogue record for this book is available from the National Library of Australia

ISBN 978 1 76106 621 4

Except where otherwise stated, all images are from the author's collection
Index by Garry Cousins
Set in 11.5/18 pt Sabon LT Pro by Midland Typesetters, Australia
Printed and bound in Australia by the Opus Group

10 9 8 7 6 5 4 3 2 1

 The paper in this book is FSC® certified. FSC® promotes environmentally responsible, socially beneficial and economically viable management of the world's forests.

For Kieren Gaul
1969–2023
My brilliant and brave bowel cancer comrade

Dishes containing processed meat often form part of a country's culinary heritage and can have a special place in people's hearts . . . Research shows that processed meat increases your risk of developing cancer, with the evidence strongest for colorectal cancer, but this is not always understood by the public.[1]

Rebecca Taylor, Head of Policy and Public Affairs,
World Cancer Research Fund International, February 2023

Contents

Foreword		xi
Introduction	Intensively caring about ham	xiii

PART ONE

Chapter 1	In plain sight	3
Chapter 2	Toxic bites	29
Chapter 3	Swallowing the bait	56

PART TWO

Chapter 4	Club billionaire	89
Chapter 5	Take away this	123
Chapter 6	Gut instinct	160

PART THREE

Chapter 7	Meat me in the cells	191
Chapter 8	Salty sorrow	206
Chapter 9	Painful reality	214

PART FOUR

Chapter 10	Memory addicts	233
Chapter 11	Recipe for disaster	249
Chapter 12	Beyond the snag	288
Afterword	Transplanted	322
Acknowledgements		343
Notes		348
Index		364

Foreword

by Professor Denis Corpet

Lucie Morris-Marr's book *Processed* is moving and inspiring, accurate and informative, in parts sad, and also funny.

For more than twenty years I researched how food could cause cancer, focusing on meat and colon cancer. I remember in 1996 when a PhD student and I fried bacon every day to test it in rodents: it smelled so good that I couldn't help but have a taste before mixing it in the rats' food. I was working full time with the help of ten to fifteen other scientists, to understand how common foods could cause cancer, to try to prevent it before it starts. When dealing with intersecting complexities (the chemistry of cured meats, gut digestion and fermentation, stool chemistry, colon mucosa carcinogenesis), it is difficult to prove what is happening scientifically. I retired ten years ago, having published 25 scientific articles on the topic.

At the end of my career in October 2015, a WHO expert group was hired by the International Agency for Cancer Research, where I served as a co-chairman. The WHO concluded that consumption of processed meat is a primary cause of cancer. *Oui, les charcuteries* were classified in the same group as asbestos and tobacco smoking. However, this groundbreaking news did not change how bacon, ham, sausages and saucisson are produced or consumed. Shockingly, for the meat industry, the regulatory agencies, and even consumers, it was business as usual with processed meat.

This is why Madame Morris-Marr's book is so important. She has done her research well and the science is sound. I also learned some new things, particularly about the big meat industry, the Australian way of life, and the incredible determination of a mother struggling to survive cancer and to change the world for the better. I also learned that processed meat is implicated in diabetes, dementia, arthritis, leukaemia and brain tumours in children.

Kieren Gaul, a friend of the author who died recently of his cancer, said, 'Make the most of your short stay on this planet. Leave a little more love than you take.' To which I'd like to add, 'Try to change the world by truth-telling on important matters.'

This is clearly what Lucie has done in her book, and I loved it. *Bonne lecture!*

Denis Corpet, Professor of Food Safety & Human Nutrition
Research Centre in Food Toxicology, National Research Institute
for Agriculture, Food and the Environment (INRAE)
French National Veterinary School, University of Toulouse, France

Introduction

INTENSIVELY CARING ABOUT HAM

A sharp, irritating and piercing beeping noise wakes me rudely. *Is it the doorbell?* I'd better get up. *Why isn't the dog barking? What time is it?*

I try to move but I feel weighed down. I realise I'm trapped. I look and see I'm being held in place by multiple tubes and wires. I'm sore, groggy, confused.

Luminous strip lighting on the ceiling above is making me squint, but I can just see an empty fluid bag hanging above me on a metal trolley. The alarm is going because it needs refilling, but I don't comprehend that yet, or understand.

I've forgotten I'm in intensive care. The sequence of events then starts to slowly re-emerge in my mind. Oh so slowly.

I'd been wheeled in late the previous evening for a mammoth twelve-hour operation to remove eight metastatic tumours from my liver. Sigh. It's all coming back to me.

They had to open me up from chest to groin to carry out the 'multiple wedge resection', but thankfully it had been successful, I'd been told by the smiling yet exhausted surgeon who spoke to me gently in the recovery room.

'The team had to order pizza just to get through the day,' he'd laughed, trying to cheer me up.

As I begin to take in my surroundings and accept the limits on my current reality, I wish with all my soul I could be at home with my two children. But I'm thankful to be alive, to have made it through my second high-risk liver operation and my fourth surgery in three years.

If cancer is indeed a battle, as it's so often described, then I felt like I was nursing my wounds in the trenches after a desperate and brutal push forward over the top. I try to turn my head to the right, in the direction of the nurses speaking loudly during the morning staff changeover, where they are obliged to repeat my entire cancer history, stretching back to the early niggles and pain that led to an innocent jaunt to the emergency room, then to months of misdiagnosis, then onwards into the dark abyss of a shock diagnosis in late 2019.

The nurses smile over at me as they keep talking. They are now discussing how I've already undergone more than a thousand hours of aggressive chemotherapy. It's never a quick handover for the lady in bed four.

I attempt a weak smile back, realising my head can't fully manoeuvre due to the many wires leading to a tube in my neck.

And then I see it. On a grey tray perched next to my bed is a ham sandwich. It's the type of processed-meat sandwich for sale in service stations and shops the world over, packaged up in cardboard and plastic.

The fact that I'm supposed to be on a fluid-only diet for several days at least isn't what starts to rile me as I stare at the thin, pink, fatty slices of ham poking out from within the flimsy white bread.

Despite being on a multitude of hardcore pain medications, and sedatives from the night before to help me sleep, I feel so angry. I can't help it.

I call over one of the nurses. 'Whoever is in charge of the catering here, I will need to speak to them,' I say in a slight, weak whisper, in a tone that belies my furious mood.

She looks startled. Intensive-care patients tend to have other things on their mind—mostly surviving, sleeping and, at most, vaguely looking at their phone for a distraction from the difficult and arduous nature of postoperative recovery. Sometimes we only nod. Words are rare.

Why has a ham sandwich caused a patient like her to feel so distressed in intensive care? the nurse must be thinking. *This patient is not even supposed to be eating yet.* She furrows her brows and puts her hand on her hips. *This patient is clearly trouble*, her expression says.

She's got that right.

———

And so it comes to pass that a few days later, a sheepish, diminutive catering manager—let's call him Hospital Harry—comes to visit me in the ward. I'm sitting in a chair for the first time since the operation, looking out at the tall gum trees outside being rocked by a winter Melbourne gale, still sore and pale but feeling stronger. Thanks to the drugs and the general haze of the previous days, by the time he appears I have totally forgotten about my request for his company.

'I've come about the ham sandwich,' Hospital Harry says, looking tense and worried, his fingers nervously touching the collar of his neat white shirt.

'What ham sandwich?' I reply, confused. Then the dire memory of the 'lunch' perched next to all the beeping machines comes back to me.

'Oh, yes . . . sorry, I remember now,' I begin. 'I'm sure you've got a really difficult job, it's just I'm both a patient and a journalist and I've been doing quite a lot of research for a book on processed meats. So . . . I want to ask you a question.'

'Sure,' Hospital Harry says, shifting uncomfortably on his feet in the doorway.

'Did you know that some experts say processed meats, and particularly some of the preservatives in them, have proved to be carcinogenic and are known risk factors in causing bowel cancer?'

'Um, no . . . not really,' he admits quietly.

'Do you know why I'm a patient in this hospital?'

'Um, no,' he says, folding his arms across his chest, defensively.

'Stage-four bowel cancer,' I say bluntly, letting the words hang in the air, without any kind of follow-up to make the landing more comfortable.

'I'm . . . really . . . um . . . sorry about that,' Hospital Harry says. 'But we have to cater for so many different diets in this hospital and we do offer a large menu of choices.'

'I get that,' I say. 'I know it must be hugely complicated with so many different dietary needs, but this is a hospital treating a lot of cancer patients. So don't you think it's wrong to be serving food that has been proved to play a role in actually causing cancer? I don't know that it definitely caused my own bowel cancer but I hope you can understand that I don't want to ever eat it again now I know eating processed meat is one of the risks?'

He looks down. 'Um . . . we're very restricted as we have to order the food in. It's not made fresh on site, you see . . . so the ingredients aren't even chosen by us.'

So here was the catering manager of this busy private hospital in Melbourne playing the blame game. Shifting responsibility. Passing the buck.

I was just half alive, early in the recovery stage, but you can't switch off being an investigative journalist. It's a calling, especially when you have cancer and see bad decisions playing out right in front of you. You question the things we may just accept and take for granted—even when you don't officially have the energy.

But giving a bowel cancer patient a ham sandwich right after a massive operation to try to save their life from bowel cancer seemed not only ridiculous but offensive.

Dude, I felt like saying, *you don't know who I am, but you really don't want to be giving me ham.*

xvii

PROCESSED

The hapless Hospital Harry had literally just found himself slammed into the introduction of this book, like crispy bacon squeezed tightly into a fluffy white bap.

I had found myself—not by choice, it has to be said—to be well placed and well qualified to question the status quo regarding that ordinary-looking ham sandwich. It was a sandwich that represented something far bigger than a snack or a light lunch; it represented an entire greedy processed-meat industry, presided over by billion-dollar multinational companies and a huge dollop of We Don't Give a Damn Mustard.

Don't get me wrong: even I wasn't fully aware of the dangers of processed meats before my cancer journey. But I had woken up. I had been shaken up by my own pain and suffering, and by detailed research that made my hair stand on end.

Something was amiss. And it matters enormously. Why? Because the average Australian meat-eater consumes a massive 17 kilograms of processed meats every year, with our nation falling in the top 25 countries in the world whose people gorge on various forms of processed pork, beef and other meats.[1] It also matters because according to the 2022 ranking by World Cancer Research Fund International, Australia is the number one country globally for cancer rates in both men and women.[2] Out of those 15,000 Australians per year are being diagnosed with bowel cancer. Some of those cases are due to inherited risk factors, but the majority are not.

I started to see how buying mystery-mixed ham and cured meats from the deli means you are shopping amid a backdrop of a long and dark history in which wild guesses, bullied governments and industrial-scale greed are firmly wrapped up with your charcuterie favourites.

Yes, I'm aware these are bold statements to make and it's devastating to anyone who loves a cheeky Domino's BBQ Meat Lovers pizza or likes adding chunks of ham hocks to soup. Processed meats are heavily ingrained in our culture and daily lives.

But I began to see that there was a glaring gap in public awareness around the mass consumption of processed meats—in particular sausages, ham, salami, pepperoni, hot dogs and bacon—which are embedded in Australian culture and in many other cultures, especially in Europe and the United States. Actually, there was something more cavernous than just a gap. There was a mass deafness, a culture of ignoring the obvious because it just didn't suit anyone involved.

But let's get one thing straight—the major issue with processed meats is their deliciousness. They are not easy to give up. I get it. I smell bacon as it's sizzling in a pan and I want a slice. Bacon famously turns many of the most determined vegetarians back to meat eating.

Believe me, my resolve has been challenged. But it's not just because I miss the salty taste, the 'umami' savoury flavour or the convenience of processed meats, which can last for weeks in the fridge. It's more complicated than that, and it involves neglect and manipulation—as we shall see later.

It's also a whole lot to do with memories. And love, actually.

PROCESSED

I want to take you on this journey with me as I investigate this pepperoni orgy, exploring the science, our food history, and our social lives, rituals and celebrations.

I'm determined to find out exactly who and what might be encouraging us to remain skewered to health risks as those smoked sausages cook away on our backyard barbecues. Let's find out why our health and environment ended up being fried up and roasted by powerful marketing campaigns, and controlled by international companies, billion-dollar bacon barons and their cashed-up shareholders. We'll have a bit of fun on the way, too. I can promise you that.

And yes, I'm well aware that there are multiple potential risks with a lot of foods we consume: ultra-processed products, mercury in fish, hormones in dairy products, and pesticides in some fruits and vegetables. I could have chosen to focus on any of these. Red meat alone has a lot of health risks.

But this out-of-control modern-day processed-meat feast is personal. The strong potential link between processed meats and a bowel cancer journey like mine makes my blood run cold. I'm not a doctor, scientist or dietician so with their help I want to learn more, to nail down the facts and share them far and wide. I'm prepared to knock down doors in search of the truth, in the same way I once asked for a cardinal to be woken up from his bed in the Vatican to answer some important questions for a front-page story.

But don't be alarmed: this book isn't an evangelical call to make you turn vegetarian or vegan. There are plenty of other books out there about that.

INTENSIVELY CARING ABOUT HAM

It's also important to state that my attitude to processed meats isn't coming from a place of naive privilege or judgement. Born in 1975, I was brought up with my younger brother by a single mother, in a semi-rural village in Hampshire, England. As Thatcher's Britain struggled under the weight of miners' strikes, electricity shortages, poll tax riots and the Falklands War, times were very tough for millions economically.

My mother often only had enough money to cook a small Fray Bentos tinned meat pie to share between the three of us, along with frozen peas and a packet of powdered potato mixed with warm long-life milk.

She also didn't have her own car at times, so she bought what she could afford from the limited offerings at the local corner shop. Preserved meats such as bacon meant we had tasty food in our fridge that could last. My mother later got a degree and remarried but at the time she was just doing her best. Public awareness of the possible health impacts of mass-produced foods was also then close to zero.

So I totally understand that sheer economic survival sometimes trumps a more wholesome, fresher and healthier choice. That's the nature of food insecurity. And I know it because as a small child I lived it.

So what you choose to buy or eat and why is not my calling or my business. Your body, your rules. But hunting out facts as purposefully as a terrier down a rabbit hole is, especially if there are gaps in public awareness that need to be filled.

After reading this far, I expect you've started to get hungry. So go to your favourite cafe and order that bacon and egg roll with your latte, if you feel like it. Put a slice of salami from the fridge on your cracker with your cheese and a slice of pickle.

Wrap that cute little piglet sausage in its tiny stretchy bacon blanket and kiss it goodnight, too, if you have to, before you bake it with the spuds and eat it with gravy on Sunday. You might not want one again by the end of this book, or maybe you will. It won't be for me to judge. That will be your call. See you on the other side . . . well, that's if I manage to stay the fuck alive.

Are you ready?

Let's go.

PART ONE

Chapter One

IN PLAIN SIGHT

> In 2019, a diet high in processed meat was responsible for 34,000 deaths [globally].[1]
>
> The Global Burden of Disease Study, 2019

Some enchanted evening

It's a balmy, clear night in rural Queensland as more than 500 guests gather in the Kingaroy Town Hall forecourt and are offered cocktails as they mingle.

Crowds this size aren't too common in a farming town this small and this remote; after all, it's 218 kilometres from Brisbane and a 141-kilometre drive to Gympie. Next stop from Kingaroy: thousands of kilometres of national parks, inhabited by wallabies and very few humans.

But the event is marking the start of a much-anticipated annual festival. Indeed, the event tonight is devoid of smoked-salmon canapés or mini goat's cheese pastries—or even peanuts, which the town famously produces in abundance—because every single guest is here to help celebrate the festival theme: bacon.

PROCESSED

Platters of the salty meat are offered to the hungry guests at what is described aptly as a 'Wine & Swine' evening.

The great and the good are in attendance, including Queensland's tourism minister at the time, Stirling Hinchliffe, happily mixing with the rugged young farmers as they chat excitedly about the many bacon-themed events due to take place over the following two days.

Locals are delighted to hear the infectious laugh of a handsome celebrity chef in the crowd too. Talented Spaniard Miguel Maestre, who has made Australia his home, is totally on board with the cured-meat theme. He's just launched his own processed-meat brand on sale in Woolworths, which includes Chorizo Migsy Sticks and Beer Salami. All the packaging is adorned with Maestre's smiling face, along with ingredient labels that include 'Preservative (250)'.

During the next couple of days, Chef Miguel will be taking part in cooking demonstrations and tastings, and maybe even catching a glimpse of the highly popular BaconFest beauty pageant for female contestants. Crowds will also be treated to the appearance of 'BaconMan'—a fella posing as a juicy rasher, dressed in a pink-and-white-striped costume.

Yes, 2023 Kingaroy BaconFest, brought to the town by sponsor SunPork Fresh Foods, has got it all. It's one gigantic, crispy orgy of cured pork.

'What you put on your kitchen table matters,' an update from the organisers says on their Facebook page, encouraging locals to buy Australian pork-based products. 'It matters to Festivals like ours, businesses like theirs and hardworking, honest farmers working for a living like all of us.'

But like most things that are related to bacon or processed meat, BaconFest missed what else matters too: the inconvenient truth. The elephant in the room, stomping around the edge of parties that nobody sees. Or wants to see.

The facts no one says out loud. The facts some may not even know. The facts so many stakeholders would prefer we didn't know.

Because—let's face it—it would spoil the party.

An heir of hunger

Just under twenty years before this bacon soiree, in September 2004, the early autumn season of mists and mellow fruitfulness turned out for a special chapter in the gilded life of George Garfield Weston.[2] The debonair Oxford and Harvard-educated member of the Weston family, one of the best-known and richest men in England, enjoyed a *Succession* moment.

His family, originally from Canada, founded George Weston Limited in the 1930s and later invested in British food businesses leading to the founding of Associated British Foods in 1994.

According to The Sunday Times 'Rich List' in 2023 the family's net worth was estimated to be £14.5 billion, making them the seventh wealthiest family in the UK.[3]

It was announced in that autumn that George, one of six children of Garry Weston who passed away in 2002, would take over Associated British Foods after the CEO at the time, Peter Jackson, decided to stand down. George was just 40 years old.

While the brands owned by Associated British Foods included beloved staples of British life—Silver Spoon (sugar),

Sunblest (bread) and Twinings (tea)—the company also had a big appetite for processed meat. More pertinently, it had a lust for buying up smallgoods companies in Australia that produced the nation's hugely profitable and beloved bacons, salamis and hams. These were companies with long histories, having begun as corner-shop butchers established by immigrants to the English colonies, often as far back as the 1800s. The newly crowned heir—Gilded George, I will call him—would soon personally take this 'Hungry Hippos' business approach even further.

By 2004, Gilded George had already gained solid experience in the expansion of the cured-meat business Down Under. For two years, in his thirties, he had headed the company's subsidiary company George Weston Foods (GWF) in Australia and New Zealand.

In 1965, GWF had bought out Watson Foods, which had been started by William Watson in Fremantle in 1895, and supplied food for the armed forces and the UK during World War II.[4] GWF went on to acquire other Australian smallgoods businesses including Watsonia, Don, Melosi and Chapman's, and its multi-million-dollar acquisitions of the nation's smallgoods companies didn't end there. Soon after Gilded George took over running Associated British Foods, he oversaw the purchase of two WA smallgoods brands, Adelphi and Globe, strengthening its market share in the country dramatically.

There would be a bit of trouble ahead, though, for Gilded George amid this meaty shopping spree.

Devastated and tearful workers came out of Don KRC's Altona plant in Victoria in July 2008, knowing they would be out of employment by 2010 as a result of a decision to cut 640 jobs.[5] Up to 420 workers, many in their fifties, were told they were going to be made redundant, and another 220 positions would be cut at Watson Foods' Spearwood factory in Western Australia. The company said the local jobs had to go because it was centralising its manufacturing base in Victoria.[6]

The news came just months after the company had purchased KR Castlemaine, another smallgoods producer based in central Victoria. Now the newly formed Don KRC operations would be based at a sprawling factory in the historic town of Castlemaine with young, ambitious Gilded George as its proud father.

Not that Gilded George lived anywhere near the Victorian town, or indeed even in Australia. The CEO based himself in a vast, sprawling, historical mansion in the leafy village of Chalfont St Giles, in the pretty English county of Buckinghamshire. He lives in this picturesque area of the UK with his elegant wife Katharine, daughter of British diplomat Sir Antony Acland, with whom he has four grown-up children.

In a 2013 report in London's red-top tabloid *The Mirror*, complete with the headline 'UK Greed List: The champagne lifestyle of the fatcat bosses', it was stated that George's pay packet was over 200 times higher than the average salary for his staff.[7] In 2022, it totalled £2.286 million (A$4 million), including base salary and annual bonus.[8]

In the meantime, at the end of their shifts at the Don KRC mega-factory, I've been told by a current employee that the hundreds of workers are allowed to use 'generous' staff discounts at the on-site shop. 'They also recognise staff doing it tough

PROCESSED

financially and each week there is a batch of free product in the shop,' the insider said.[9] Free packs of salami, bacon, pepperoni and other smallgoods are happily stuffed into bags and car boots by employees to be eaten for dinner, or to place in their children's lunch boxes the next day. Most of the cured-meat products made at Don KRC, bar a very small 'Naturals' range,[10] have something in common: they have sodium nitrite, also known as preservative 250, listed on their ingredient labels.[11]

As for the sacked Altona and Spearwood employees, many of whom came from non-English-speaking backgrounds, and at least one of whom had been with the company for 50 years . . . well, they were left to find new jobs.

At the time of the mass redundancies, the WA secretary of the Australasian Meat Industry Employees Union, Graeme Haynes, told a reporter of the upset it caused. He said, 'It's left a bit of a sour taste in our mouths.'[12]

Setting the stage

As we pulled out of the underground hospital car park in Malvern, Melbourne, my husband and I both fell into a dazed silence.

I know the date. I'll never forget it: 7 November 2019. Everything in my life until that point would now be known as 'BBC'—Before Bowel Cancer.

A few minutes earlier I'd leaned forward and put my head in my hands as a neatly suited bowel cancer surgeon confirmed my worst fears. Following the discovery of a large mass in my colon a few days before, a biopsy had revealed it was indeed cancerous. But there was more devastating news; the results of a subsequent CT scan showed the cancer had spread to my liver.

'You have at least four or five lesions . . . so . . . I'm afraid that means it's officially stage-four bowel cancer, but . . . um . . . don't worry, I'm pretty sure it's all treatable,' he told us, perhaps in a kind attempt to make the bad news good for the weekend.

All I thought I knew about the words 'stage four' was that it meant the cancer was terminal. I would find out later that some stage-four patients do beat the odds and can even be cured, but in that moment I thought that I might not have long to live. I headed into an unstable spin. Christmas was just weeks away. *Will it be my last? What about the children?*

As we walked through the labyrinth of long, grey-walled hospital corridors I gasped for air and just tried to keep my feet moving. My husband halted briefly and had to take a moment to lean against a wall to compose himself. I put my arm around him.

'It's okay,' I said. 'You know I'm tough. I can fight this.' In reality I was unsure whether this ambitious goal was even possible. I just needed to do everything I could not to tumble into a terrifying abyss that I feared would be so dark, so deep, that I'd never find my way out.

As we drove away from the hospital, past people in cafes sipping lattes and laughing with friends, I felt utterly disconnected.

My diagnosis had come hurtling out of a clear, blue springtime sky like a random meteorite, smashing into my life and threatening my future. *How was the world still spinning on its axis?* This is what shock feels like. It's like your brain and thoughts are having a heart attack that no one can see.

It was Spring Racing Carnival week in Melbourne. Pretty pink, yellow, white and red roses were blooming in front gardens, and flowering cherry blossom trees lined garden fences as we drove past. I usually loved this time of year, when the city that had been my home for nearly ten years came alive in nature and in spirit.

The only thought that held still in that moment of internal chaos was that I was desperate to get on to Google. Anyone would be—especially a journalist, I suppose.

'What are the causes of bowel cancer?' I typed into my phone as we drove towards our home in Bayside, where we would have to break the news of my diagnosis to our children, then aged just nine and eleven, instantly shattering their childhood innocence and sense of security.

There were several main risk factors and causes, it seemed. I went through them one by one. Was I aged over 50? No. Was I obese? A few extra kilos like many mums, yes, but obese? No. Did I smoke? Never. Did I have a close relative with bowel cancer or a genetic risk? No. Did I have a diet low in fibre and high in ultra-processed foods? Not at all; oats, fruit, legumes and vegetables were part of my daily regime. Was I active? Definitely. Was I a regular drinker? Perhaps one or two glasses of pinot noir on a Friday. I'd had stressful times in my career as a news reporter but that was it.

Naturally, this brief initial search simply left me confused. *Why me? Why now? At 44 years old?*

'What the hell!' I blurted out, breaking the silence in the car and briefly startling my husband, pale and in shock himself, as he turned into our street.

As the weeks went on and I began my intensive treatment, I would have more time to read quietly alone, as my working life as a freelance journalist and author screeched to a halt, as did my ability to be a mother. The publicity events, writers' festival appearances and speeches for my first non-fiction book, which investigated child abuse in the Catholic Church, had all been quickly cancelled.

And I felt like my whole identity had been cancelled too. I was now a seriously sick cancer patient with my life on the line. Not a journalist, an author or even a mother. I often couldn't do the school run or make meals or do chores. If I was able to manage a shower and getting dressed, that was a good day.

Lost in my own fast-shrinking world, I dug deeper into other possible links to bowel cancer. To my horror, I discovered that—according to many scientific studies—if you regularly eat red and processed meats, such as frankfurts, bacon and salami, you are risking your health and your life. There is a strong bowel cancer link, and other suspected health impacts, particularly with processed meats.

You may have read various media headlines over the years and may already know this. But perhaps you are like I was at the time, and are not fully aware of the risks, especially being so young and not even considering bowel cancer as a remote possibility.

For quite some time, as I absorbed all this information, I looked back over my life, trying to remember everything I'd ever eaten. *I'm not really a huge consumer of processed meats*, I said to myself, over and over. I'd never liked the look of those plastic packets of ham and usually preferred chicken, cheese or salmon. But then I really started to think about it more deeply. I certainly had the time.

I thought about the occasions I'd asked for a side of bacon at brunch, or told the workers at the deli counter to 'please slice the prosciutto extra thin, because it's just so delicate and delicious that way!'. I remembered how when I made a big batch of veggie soup, I'd often fry up a few pieces of chopped bacon to add to it, to inject that complementary meaty, earthy taste.

I thought about how I'd loved carving the little diamond-shaped patterns into the mammoth leg of ham I cooked every Christmas Eve, pushing cloves into the gaps and covering it in demerara sugar, red wine and cinnamon. Sigh.

Gosh, I always loved slices of that ham in the days that followed, just like you might do every year. Cold in salads, or between sourdough with chutney. In truth, over the decades I'd probably eaten quite a few kilos of that salty Yuletide ham.

Then I thought back with a growing sense of dread to all those trips to Bunnings and how I would be occasionally lured in by those tempting, sizzling snags neatly packed into a single white slice of cheap bread. Oh, the soft, caramelised onions. The mustard. A warming, satisfying late lunch for the whole family, for the price of a few gold coins. Bargain.

In short, I ate processed meats, just like most 'generally health-conscious' modern mums do in our busy family lives.

Was it possible, just maybe, that occasionally eating these processed meats in my otherwise healthy diet may have been the cause of my bowel cancer? The thought was horrendous. The idea that I may have brought the pain and suffering on myself, let alone my family, made it even harder. Finding another possible reason outside my own control would have been far easier.

And there I was, trapped in bed on a chemo pump for 48 hours every two weeks as the world went on without me. As my husband and children went out to work and school, because life has to go on. That's just the reality. Dear friends dropped off meals and flowers. I got so many cards. But at the end of the day, sickness involves endless hours of being alone. That's just the nature of it. It's lonely. But its silver lining is that it also gives you time to reflect, without distractions. The time to research. To read. To reflect some more.

I started poring over studies and reports in the following months and years, uncovering facts that I realised the meat industry would much rather you didn't know.

Why? Because I found out the Australian processed-meat industry, also known as the smallgoods market, is currently worth $4.3 billion per year and employs more than 10,000 people.[13] So there's a lot at stake in this valuable, salty chain—for major supermarkets, famous fast-food franchises, net profits and share prices.

I soon realised, with growing clarity, that what the many stakeholders in the processed-food business probably don't want us to know are the results of an extraordinary analytic study, involving nearly half a million adults, published back in 2013.

It concluded that 'men and women with a high consumption of processed meat are at increased risk of early death, in particular due to cardiovascular diseases but also to cancer'.[14]

I read this line over and over. It made me gasp as I lay alone on the sofa one day, recovering from a chemotherapy session.

The report, titled 'Meat consumption and mortality', also estimated that 'a reduction in processed-meat consumption to less than 20 grams per day per person would prevent more than 3 per cent of all deaths'.

Finally, the report's authors advised: 'As processed meat consumption is a modifiable risk factor, health promotion activities should include specific advice on lowering processed meat consumption.'

Within just two years the report's findings were backed up with another remarkable study. The Global Burden of Disease Study found the number of total deaths (including those from heart disease, diabetes and various cancers) that could be put down to a diet high in processed meat in 2013 was an astonishing 644,000. *What the hell.*

This damning figure from this study, funded by the Bill & Melinda Gates Foundation, wasn't just plucked from thin air with vague guesses. It reflected the work of more than 1000 researchers in more than 100 countries. It was a solid, valid study and sparked concern globally.[15]

'Apparently soda isn't nearly as deadly as bacon, ham, and hot dogs,' remarks the respected author Dr Michael Greger in his 2015 bestselling book *How Not to Die*. He points out that, worldwide, four times more people die from consuming processed meats than die from illicit drug use.

Just two years after the Global Burden of Disease report was published, another explosive report from the World Health Organization (WHO) made global headlines. The review by WHO's International Agency for Research on Cancer (IARC), released in October 2015, said that eating processed meats like hot dogs, sausages and bacon can cause colorectal cancer in humans, and red meat is also a likely cause of the disease. It also linked the consumption of red meat with pancreatic and prostate cancers.[16] (It's important to note that, globally, the disease is named colon cancer, bowel cancer or colorectal cancer.)

The IARC wasn't making these bold statements based on flimsy evidence. Far from it. It had, in fact, examined 800 studies during a gathering of 22 top health experts. The meat industry could hardly dispute its rigour.

In its review, the IARC classified processed meat as 'carcinogenic to humans' and added it to the Group 1 list of carcinogens. This means there is 'sufficient evidence' of cancer links. Group 1 includes at least 120 substances, elements and compounds, with tobacco, asbestos and radiation among them.[17]

When you consider the amount of bacon or pepperoni the average meat-eater consumes, the report is hard to comprehend. Yes, that rasher of bacon next to your fried egg is considered by the WHO in the same line-up as deadly baddies like asbestos. It doesn't mean that processed meats are considered *equally* bad alongside all other carcinogens, but the potential health issues mean they have landed in the same deadly bracket.

Scientists have even narrowed down the fact that in 2019 34,000 bowel cancer deaths per year worldwide were attributable to diets high in processed meat.[18] This may not be on the same scale as tobacco smoking, which is linked to about one million cancer deaths per year, but 34,000 people is eleven times the number of people who were killed in the September 11 terrorist attacks in New York.

I felt my anger rising further. Sometimes I had to take breaks in my reading, because all this was making the chemo-induced nausea worse. Of course I would never be able to know for certain what sparked my own cancer, but I was determined to keep researching.

According to the WHO, each 50-gram portion of processed meat eaten each day increases the risk of colorectal cancer by 18 per cent. To make it simpler, a 50-gram portion would be just one hot dog or a couple of rashers of bacon. It may sound alarmist but experts argue the public need to know; 'For an individual, the risk of developing colorectal cancer because of their consumption of processed meat remains small, but this risk increases with the amount of meat consumed,' says Dr Kurt Straif, Head of the IARC Monographs Programme. 'In view of the large number of people who consume processed meat, the global impact on cancer incidence is of public health importance.'[19]

A possible link between processed meat and stomach cancer was also found in the IARC review. Many other health risks are being established year by year, as we shall see later.

What about red meat you may be asking? Is that still okay? Well, red meat—including beef, lamb and pork—wasn't classed in Group 1 with processed meats. Instead, the IARC declared it as 'probably carcinogenic' and placed it in the Group 2A list, joining items like glyphosate, the active ingredient in many weedkillers.

It certainly wasn't the best day for meat-lovers. Or for the many authors of Paleo-diet and keto-diet books for that matter.

The outcome of this IARC report? Gasps and tears from all corners. The news outraged agriculture groups, and prompted animal-rights activists People for the Ethical Treatment of Animals (PETA) to offer free vegan-diet starter kits.

It wasn't surprising, of course, that the meat industry closed ranks and produced all sorts of defensive, deeply strategic sound bites. For example, the Canadian Meat Council, which represents huge meat companies such as Maple Leaf Foods and the Canadian branches of Cargill Ltd and JBS, rejected the findings as 'simplistic'. In the meantime trade group North American Meat Institute said the IARC report 'defies common sense'. What it defied, of course, was the industry's concern with profits. So much so they would also soon fund their favoured scientists to declare in reports nitro-preservatives were safe.

In Australia, the meat and farming industry is a powerful force, representing billions of dollars in investment and taxes, and thousands of jobs. Staying on the defensive, Australian food producers argued that processed meat provides essential protein, vitamins and minerals.

Unsurprisingly, Australia's agriculture minister at the time, Barnaby Joyce, immediately tried to play down the report. Joyce was at the time the deputy leader of the National Party, a party that traditionally represents graziers, farmers and regional voters. He said that he didn't think Australians should be concerned. How and why he made this snap conclusion was unclear.

But with Australians well known for being among the biggest consumers of meat in the world, the agriculture minister perhaps could have vowed to at least investigate properly, to find out the facts first and perhaps order an official review. Instead, he decided to brutishly brush off the extensive research by the leading health body in the world and make his own rapid conclusions.

'If you got everything that the WHO said were carcinogenic and took it out of your daily requirements, well, you are kind of heading back to a cave,' he told ABC Radio National. 'If you're going to avoid everything that has any correlation with cancer whatsoever—don't walk outside, don't walk down the streets in Sydney. There's going to be very little in life that you actually do in the end.'

Comparing meat to cigarettes as a carcinogen, said Joyce, was a 'farce'. 'I don't think that we should get too excited that if you have a sausage you're going to die of bowel cancer, because you're not.' Well, thank goodness Joyce had such an insight, one that the WHO didn't see for themselves.

In the meantime, Australia's new chief scientist Dr Alan Finkel was asked for his reaction, telling reporters in Canberra that 'moderation is probably the best approach'.

Despite the headlines, the share prices of most meat companies saw little change in the days following the report. Finance experts globally had already weighed in with their view, dismissing the idea that the bad publicity around processed meats would affect the market and investor confidence.

'I'm not expecting that report to be a big issue going forward,' Brian Weddington, a vice president of Moody's Investors Service told Reuters. 'I think there's still going to be a lot of hot dogs sold tomorrow.'[20]

In the end, it was only the cancer charities that tried their best to spread the message. Here in Australia the website of the Cancer Council stated; 'About 2600 cases of bowel cancer diagnosed each year in Australian adults can be attributed to eating red and processed meat.' Yet their audience, of course, was likely to be made up of those already diagnosed, so reaching millions of other people to encourage them to change their diets was close to impossible.

Have you ever seen this very clear World Health Organization diagram in your local butcher or deli? Have you seen it displayed at your doctors' surgery? I think we already know the answer to that.

WHO classification of red and processed meats

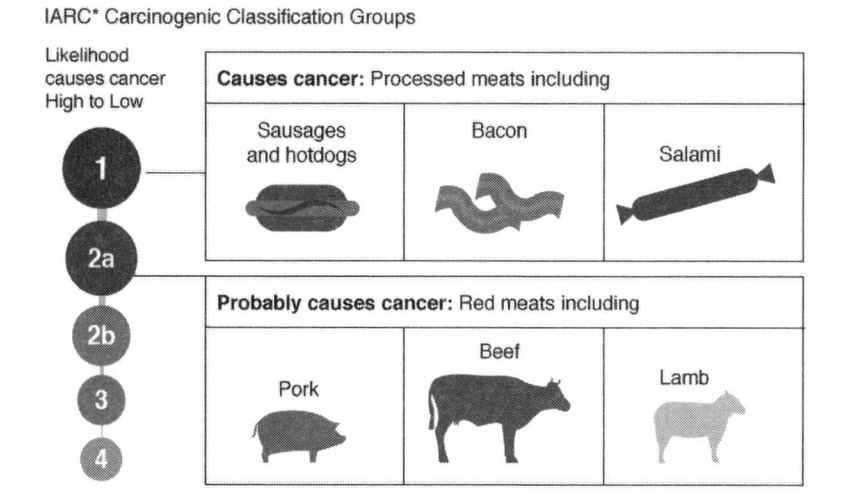

IARC* Carcinogenic Classification Groups

Likelihood causes cancer High to Low

1 — **Causes cancer:** Processed meats including
- Sausages and hotdogs
- Bacon
- Salami

2a
2b — **Probably causes cancer:** Red meats including
- Pork
- Beef
- Lamb

3
4

In the text of their website the charity Cancer Research UK highlights the studies which have shown that eating processed meat increases the risk of bowel cancer.[21] 'It is estimated that around 13 out of 100 bowel cancer cases (around 13 per cent) in the UK are linked to eating these meats,' the charity states. 'Processed meat is any meat that has been treated to preserve it and/or add flavour.' If this same statistic applies to Australia this would mean out of the approximately 15,000 new cases per year around 2000 would be due to processed meats. So that's five Australians per day.

It can't be denied that headlines were certainly made at the time of the WHO report, and that chatter and pushback were prompted. Media do love a food-scare story, after all.

'Perhaps no two words together are more likely to set the internet aflame than BACON and CANCER,' one journalist wrote in *Wired*. As journalist and food writer Bee Wilson reflected later in a feature for *The Guardian*, it was, briefly, a watercooler moment: 'You couldn't miss the story. It was splashed large in every newspaper and all over the web . . . Health scares are ten-a-penny, but this one was very hard to ignore.'[22] But, in Australia and New Zealand and many other countries, generally ignored it was.

Australia's Cancer Council has a warning on their own website, saying that processed meats increase your cancer risk. It reads: 'Cut out processed meats altogether or keep them to an absolute minimum. Processed meats include bacon, ham, devon, frankfurts, chorizo, cabanossi and kransky.' Despite this, have you seen any government health campaigns giving the public this extremely important dietary advice? Have processed meats been banned in school canteens or by sporting bodies after youth team games? The answer to both is a firm no. That much is clear.

Thankfully I would soon experience a serendipitous moment in a Sydney cafe early in 2021, lunching with my Allen & Unwin publisher, Elizabeth Weiss, along with Rebecca Kaiser, the company's editorial director. I told them how I was keen to write a book on the subject of cancer, but hadn't yet nailed down the angle.

'Is there anything you don't eat?' Elizabeth asked as we looked over the menus.

'Only processed meats . . . just because of their link with bowel cancer,' I replied.

She paused for a moment and placed her menu on the table.

'Do you know what?' she said, leaning forward. 'That's the way into it. I think the public needs to know more about this processed-meats business.'

Confessions of a bacon troll

I have a confession to make. As my research deepened, now armed and dangerous with a signed book deal, I became an undercover 'polite troll' of sorts on processed-meat groups on social media platforms.

It was strangely entertaining at times, yet worrying and sad all at once. One site on Facebook is called Bacon Addicts Anonymous and has more than 116,000 members, mostly based in the US. The posts, which include videos of homemade recipes, quotes and ideas, always have an excitable tone. 'Have you ever had "pig candy?"—it's bacon with brown sugar on top while fryin' in the oven!! I make it for xmas gifts!' one group member wrote.

Another member responded: 'Well god love ya brother! That'd be a great way to prepare. I wish bacon was my middle name! Happy eating friend!!'

At other times, the posts are simple and to the point.

'When you have a bad day and have so much pain bacon is the cure,' wrote one member, alongside a picture of a pile of crispy bacon on a plate. Her picture prompted 133 comments of enthused agreement.

A few times I threw in a little comment of my own in response, just to test the mood. As you can imagine, they didn't usually go down well.

'Oh bacon, it's delicious yes but do you ever worry about the link with processed meats to cancer?'

That comment was akin to setting off a hand grenade. These enthusiasts were nothing less than enraged.

'I think you will find my dear that bacon IS NOT a processed meat!!! It's a cut!! It's pure MEAT!!'

Despite the angry response, it was a useful exercise. It revealed what I had already suspected: there is a lot of confusion about what processed meats actually *are*. Another phrase I hear quite often is, 'I don't eat the cheap, nasty ham, I buy slices of proper ham—like ham off the bone.'

So here we go, to be absolutely clear. Processed meats are meats that have been modified through methods such as salting, curing, fermenting and smoking. It's the actual processing of these meats that can lead to the formation of harmful substances, which then have a whole range of negative effects on health. But here's the key point to make very clear: the addition of certain chemical preservatives, which yes, are nearly always used for 'ham off the bone' too, can then make those effects worse. More on these later.

During the Covid-19 pandemic, researchers at the University of Oxford did an interesting survey on what meats were considered 'processed' by people around the world. The engagement activity was called 'Don't Go Bacon My Heart' and it ran for a month, reaching 335 people internationally. To answer the questions, the survey displayed photos of sixteen types of meat and asked participants to select which of these were 'unprocessed' or 'processed'.

The researchers then gave participants the WHO's definition of processed meat and checked how they classified meat products depending on where they were purchased or consumed. They found that regular meat-eaters have a greater understanding of which meats are classified as processed than those who eat meat only once a week or less, but that most people generally have a good understanding of what processed meat is. The research did, however, find some confusion around some types of meat, and concluded that nutrition researchers can improve how they 'communicate research on processed meat by considering 1) how some foods are consumed in different settings and cultures, 2) how often people eat meat, and 3) the audience's demographic'.[23]

In Australia and New Zealand, Food Standards Australia New Zealand (FSANZ) clarify processed meat as 'a meat product containing no less than 300g/kg meat, where meat either singly or in combination with other ingredients or additives, has undergone a method of processing (other than boning, slicing, dicing, mincing or freezing), and includes manufactured meat and cured and/or dried meat flesh in whole cuts or pieces'.

I also came across the term 'comminuted meat', which is categorised under processed meat and means an edible product resulting from the separation and removal of most of the bone from attached skeletal muscle of livestock or poultry.[24] It also defines products which are minced, ground and mashed. Pure 'n' simple it ain't. Anyway, for the fine folks of Bacon Addicts Anonymous—or to anyone else—here are some examples of processed meats, which have *all* been altered in form, salted, cured, smoked or subject to added preservatives. Most of them are made from pork, some are from beef, and some are from poultry including chicken and turkey.

Processed meats include—but are not limited to—the following products:

- bacon
- sausages
- pancetta
- turkey bacon
- pork or beef hot dogs
- chicken or turkey hot dogs
- frankfurts
- cocktail frankfurts
- jerky
- biltong
- smoked speck
- smoked brats
- wiener/Vienna sausage
- kransky
- prosciutto
- chorizo
- salami
- devon/luncheon meat
- strasbourg
- bologna

- mortadella
- meat pâté
- pepperoni
- pastrami
- Wagyu beef bresaola
- twiggy sticks
- kabana sticks
- smoked pork hocks
- corned beef
- Spam (and canned meats in general)
- luncheon ham
- honey ham
- champagne leg ham
- ham off the bone
- formed ham.

Yes, sorry, it's basically including all the many, many varieties of ham.

And as a reminder, meats that aren't considered processed, even though they have been cut into convenient portions, include chicken, lamb, pork, beef, goat and so on. That's not to say they don't have their own health risks (related to animal feed, hormones and antibiotics), and they are often the main ingredient in processed meats.

Sometimes other products get classed as processed meats, such as:

- meat pies
- sausage rolls
- chicken nuggets
- crumbed chicken products such as tenders and schnitzel
- burgers
- beef mince (if preservatives are added).

If you have any frozen chicken pies, tenders or nuggets in your freezer, take a quick look at the ingredient list. Often they only contain 50 per cent meat and are bulked out by a massive list of other ingredients, including water, salt, gums and soy protein. Yes, this means they're processed, and they have been created from a sloppy raw mix, even if they declare boldly that the product uses '100% chicken breast!'.

For this book, however, I decided to focus my investigation on the processed meats that are more closely linked to bowel cancer and other health impacts. They are the tasty, salty ones in your fridge that appear on that long list. The bacons. The hams. The hot dogs. The salamis. The twiggy sticks. Unlike chicken products or the minced-type processed foods, these are the cured, salted and preserved meats which are causing the most alarm.

Since the 2015 report by the IARC, many other health organisations have issued warnings about the health risks of processed meats, including the American Cancer Society and the American Institute for Cancer Research. Yet millions around the world continue to eat processed meats with wild abandon amid aggressive marketing campaigns by supermarkets and fast-food chains.

Yes, there is also an upward trend of plant-based diets, foods, products and lifestyles. Unfortunately, this doesn't seem to be affecting the upward trajectory of the processed-meat market. My proof? In 2022 the global processed-meat market was valued at US$500 billion and is expected to reach the extraordinary figure of US$700 billion in 2028.[25]

It seems that nothing can prevent the world's intense love affair with salted and cured meat, despite wars, economic sanctions in several countries, higher commodity prices and interrupted supply chains, which have hiked up prices for goods and services across the globe. The WHO did its best but the headlines alone clearly weren't enough.

Still, the studies on the dangers of processed meat continue to flood in. In October 2022, the University of Oxford warned how even one slice of processed meat per day could increase the risk of colon cancer. The research was conducted by professor of epidemiology Tim Key and his team, and was based on around half a million British participants aged between 40 and 69.

According to the team's findings people who consumed 76 grams of processed red meat a day, such as a large hot dog, had a 20 per cent higher chance of getting bowel cancer than people who ate a third of that amount, amounting to just one slice of ham. They found this risk then increased by 20 per cent for every further 25 grams—a single rasher of bacon—of processed meat.

The results clearly even alarmed the research team. 'A small amount of processed meat appears to have the same carcinogenic effect as a large amount of red meat,' Professor Tim J. Key stated.

The advice moving forward for the bacon-loving Brits? No more than 70 grams of red and processed meat per day should be eaten. 'Our results conclusively suggest that people who eat red and processed meat four or more times a week have a higher risk of developing bowel cancer than those who eat red and processed meat less than twice a week,' Dr Key added.

It was a damning report but one which again didn't seem to infiltrate public awareness or a move to change. Yes, there have also been occasional media stories that raised the issue. In June 2023, Paula Goodyer wrote in the *Sydney Morning Herald* and *The Age* about healthier alternatives to processed meats. 'By the end of this year, we'll have chewed our way through around 5.5 million pigs, often in the form of ham and bacon—and you have to wonder why,' she wrote.[26]

Why indeed?

But the problem remains; processed meats are winning. They are profitable and popular. Vast swathes of the population love processed meats, whether they are cured, salted or marinated. They are tasty, relatively cheap and oh so convenient for picnics, quick dinners, lunch boxes and grazing platters.

I felt it was time to find out exactly how these processed meats were produced, and how they become so potentially deadly.

The foreboding soundtrack was already playing in the background. I braced myself for a mixtape of culinary low notes.

Chapter Two
TOXIC BITES

The everyday consumption of nitrite-containing
bacon and ham poses a very real risk to
public health.[1]

Professor Chris Elliott, Director, Institute for
Global Food Security, Queen's University Belfast,
December 2022

Behind the candelabra

'Mum, have you seen this? Is this really how ham is made?' my thirteen-year-old daughter asks, passing me her phone.

It is mid-2023, and what has caught her attention is a TikTok video with the headline comment 'What in the world, watch till the end, this can't be real'.

The video, posted by the account @thatafricanchick2, shows workers in a processed-meat factory, dressed in what look like hazmat suits, preparing a sloppy, pale-pink mixture and placing it in a giant mixing bowl. The workers then pour the mixture into individual metal trays around 20 centimetres long and 10 centimetres deep.

The contents of the metal trays are then cooked in ovens; the resulting firm 'ham' is then put through a slicer and revealed to resemble a type of ham with a thin brown crust.

The viral clip generated nearly 30,000 comments, mostly of outrage, and more than 300,000 impressions among the popular social platform's users all over the world.

Naturally, it's hard to verify where or when the video was taken, but the post served to deliver a young generation of TikTok users (and, more pertinently, eaters of processed meat) an important lesson: that many cheap and mass-produced 'formed hams' are indeed made in a similar way. Formed is also another description for manufactured meat, which means meat is just one of the 'ingredients', but must be no less than 660 grams per kilo.[2]

Yes, it is all incredibly revolting and shocking.

'You mean to tell me that pink stuff is ham? I thought that mix was pink yoghurt,' one TikTok user commented.

'Could be turkey,' another replies. 'Oven roasted turkey slices is [sic] the same. All nuggets and frozen burgers and lunch meat are made from trimmings and made into a paste.'

The result of this viral video? Thousands of young people all over the world having their eyes opened to a very real but often misunderstood part of the production of many types of processed meat. It's something the meat industry makes a concerted effort to keep away from the final marketing packages you see in the supermarkets. For good reason.

Take the words 'champagne leg ham', for example. It's a product made by Australian meat company Primo and sold in many of our major food stores, including Coles, Woolworths and IGA. The name has a marvellous, confident ring to it, doesn't it? I can tell you now it has nothing to do with a bubbly drink from the Champagne region of France.

It's true that the production of ham is of French origin and it was the Gauls who first became known for the salting, smoking and curing of pig about 2000 years ago. They would apparently enjoy eating ham at the beginning of a meal to whet appetites for more food, or at the conclusion of a huge feast to induce thirst.

Back then, in a time devoid of fridges, the ham may have been neatly sliced, salted, smoked pork, perhaps with added herbs and spices, but today's supermarket 'manufactured meat' ham slices are utterly packed with additives, salts and preservatives. According to the ingredients of a pack of Primo champagne leg ham, it includes:

Pork, Water, Acidity Regulators (326, 325, 262), Cure [Salt, Mineral Salts (451, 450), Sugar, Antioxidant (316), Preservative (250), Dextrose (Maize or Tapioca)], Natural Flavours. Naturally Wood Smoked.

Because Primo isn't obliged under Australian law—via the FSANZ and its code—to fully explain these ingredients or use their full names on the packet, let's blow this pack of 'champagne leg ham' wide open. Happy to oblige.

First, despite the impression the description gives of 'leg ham', the pork isn't just sliced from one leg of a pig, and neither is it from one animal. Far from it. It's made from more than one pig and it's made from meat that has been mechanically recovered. Basically, ham of this kind is often what is left on the bone after the rest of the meat has been used for other products.

'All of the little bits that are left over on the bone will be blasted off with high-pressure water,' Carrie Ruxton, a dietician affiliated with the UK meat industry, told *The Guardian* in 2015.[3]

Unless it states 'leg' on the label, major meat companies don't release the exact body parts or bones used to gain the other pork 'meat', but industry insiders have confirmed generally nothing is wasted; so there could be bits of flesh, muscle and fat playing a part in the delightful mix. Water and other ingredients are then added into this stomach-churning amalgamation of minced up pork. The 'acidity regulators' used in this champagne leg ham in particular are sodium lactate (326), potassium lactate (325) and sodium diacetate (262).

I was especially startled by the inclusion of sodium diacetate, as I had seen it mentioned in relation to farming. On further investigation, I found out that it is indeed a registered 'fungicide and bactericide' that is used to help store large amounts of grain. In general terms, it comes under the umbrella of 'pesticide'. The chemical can irritate the eyes of farm workers so much that they are advised to use protective eyewear.

Here in Australia, butchers or meat manufacturers can purchase sodium diacetate for around $250 for 25 kilograms.[4]

I then looked up what Primo lists as 'Cure', including sodium pyrophosphate (451) and potassium tripolyphosphate (450). These two additives help to keep processed meats moist, avoiding spoilage. However, one study from 2012 found when sodium phosphate is used as a food additive it can impact health differently from natural phosphates.[5] Reason being it's absorbed differently and high levels of phosphate may raise death rates among the general public, as well as for those with kidney or heart issues.

It doesn't end there. Researchers even linked high phosphate levels to early ageing and vascular damage. As a result they advised people to eat foods with naturally occurring phosphates, rather than foods with added sodium phosphate. 'The public should be informed that added phosphate is damaging to health,' the study's authors stated. 'Furthermore, calls for labeling the content of added phosphate in food are appropriate.'

So far, so disturbing. But it gets worse. In our ingredients list, after the inclusion of ascorbic acid (E number 316), also described as an antioxidant, we then arrive at 'Preservative (250)'. This is sodium nitrite, which is the true bad boy in the sloppy mystery mix, and it's officially classed as a poison. Yes, *poison*. It gets added to processed meats, mixed with salt, in either a watery brine form or as a dry power. This is the most troubling snake in the grass—or, rather, the paste. I decided to do a deep dive into that chemical later.

Finally, though, we come to 'Natural Flavours' and 'Naturally Wood Smoked' as our last ingredients in this 'champagne' megamix. Some passionate campaigners have raised concerns that even so-called 'natural flavours' may not be exactly natural. But as long as companies are using flavours that are permitted by FSANZ's Food Standards Code, they do not have to list them on their ingredient labels.

PROCESSED

'You can contact the company and ask them what their flavour(s) consists of, but they're not obligated to tell you,' says the website of Australian campaign group Additive Free Lifestyle, launched by two Tasmanian sisters, Tracey and Joanne Fry, who have since published a cookbook and produced a podcast. 'It's a loophole in the system that allows companies to hide ingredients without the consumers knowing. We're not saying that this is always the case, but it does beg the question.'

The sisters argue consumers can't be certain these 'natural flavours' are the healthier choice. 'It's a shame that we have no idea what we're eating and being misled by purchasing products listing "natural flavour" thinking it's the better choice . . . Who knows? Because we have no idea what is in it, therefore no idea what we're eating!!'

Companies have a massive array of permitted flavouring substances to choose from. 'There is no limit on the number of ingredients they can use in their "flavours" in any one product.'[6]

So there you have it. This churned-up slop of doom is then cooked, cooled, thinly sliced and packaged for human consumption. Or, rather, inhuman consumption, in my view.

So that pack of champagne leg ham, which you may well have innocently and trustingly placed in your shopping basket many times for decades, is a horrendous culinary mix that is more chemistry than cooking. To summarise: it's the manufactured meat of possibly multiple animals, with at least five chemical additives—which may pose health risks and one of which is used as a pesticide—topped off by the addition of a controversial nitro-preservative. Then, finally, they chuck in the mystery mix represented by two words: 'natural flavours'.

Sadly, it soon became clear that these are standard ingredients in many mass-produced formed hams or 'manufactured meat' hams in Australia and New Zealand—and all over the world.

So, what does the law say? I wondered. *Is this vague labelling even legal?* According to FSANZ, 'all representations made about food are subject to fair trading laws and food laws in Australia and New Zealand which prohibit false, misleading or deceptive representations'.[7]

I don't think the labelling of this ham product and similar versions seems 'fair'. What's your view?

It won't be a surprise to find out that mass-produced salami isn't much better. Whether it's made from chilled beef or pork, or both, it is chopped, ground, then mixed with spices, starter culture, sodium chloride and, yes, those questionable nitro-preservatives. It's then stuffed into the desired shape or mould, before slowly fermenting from anywhere from one to six weeks, or more. It is finally dried and sometimes heated.

Coles and Woolworths sell many salami products made by Don KRC. The company, which uses the marketing slogan 'Is Don. Is Good.', makes its products at Gilded George's supersized factory in Castlemaine, Victoria. According to the Don KRC website, it produces 21 different types of salami, from slices of Calabrese and mild Hungarian, to sausage-shaped versions including a popular one you may have tried called 'hot Hungarian salami'. Underneath the description on the package are the words 'Authentic taste. IS DON. IS GOOD. Made to share.'

PROCESSED

It also says, 'GLUTEN FREE: No artificial colours or flavours.' The reason I find this last part of the description so misleading is that while there might not be artificial colours or flavours, this is an ultra-processed product containing other artificial elements. Once you turn over the roll of salami, the back label starts to give the true picture.

FERMENTED MANUFACTURED MEAT—HEAT TREATED: Ingredients: Meat including pork, salt, skim milk powder, chilli, lactose (milk), spices, dextrose (maize), maltodextrin (maize), antioxidant (316), flavour, starter culture, sodium nitrite (250), sodium nitrate (251), dehydrated vegetable, herb extract, smoked. CONTAINS MILK. MAY CONTAIN SOY.

There is a growing number of bespoke charcuterie firms in Australia and New Zealand that may have a slightly better process and may not use quite so many ingredients or nitro-preservatives. But it's the mass-produced products that make up the majority of salami eaten by Australian consumers finding their way into the nations' fridges—and stomachs—via the supermarket giants. And companies owned by the likes of Gilded George have the nerve to literally market these products as 'good'—and to offer them at reduced prices to their employees to take home to their families. Yet, in my view, mass, cheaply produced salami is one hideous culinary nightmare. And it's certainly very different from its purer origins in southern Europe.

Even most of the smaller Australian companies that are making inroads into this popular market still rely on nitro-preservatives. Take, for example, Sydney's bespoke Papandrea smallgoods brand. In their description of their 'free range black garlic salami', they seduce consumers with promises of 'sweet caramelised flavours' and 'a good dose of umami magic'.

Umami, of course, is that addictive, savoury, meaty flavour and one of five core human tastes. But despite this alluring, oh-so-aspirational, middle-class message—not to mention the fact the black garlic is apparently 'specially prepared ... on Victoria's Mornington Peninsula', the ingredients state 'sodium nitrite' is the preservative used:[8]

INGREDIENTS: Free Range Australian Pork (93%), Salt, Black Garlic (1.9%), Dextrose (Maize), Spices, Antioxidant (316), Sodium Nitrite (250), Starter Culture.

It sort of takes away some of the promised 'magic', doesn't it?

The cheapest pack of sausages you can find in any major supermarket would be another case in point. Here's another prime example of how the processed-meat industry loves to try to make their worst seem like their best.

Originally, the sausage was made out of necessity, a way of preserving meat in times of plenty, to eat in leaner, more challenging times, such as winter, when food was more scarce and there was no refrigeration. The fact that it was tasty and easy to cook while making efficient use of an animal and could be seasoned and shaped accordingly meant sausage became a beloved classic.

PROCESSED

It would be placed in pantries next to other staples such as potatoes, legumes and flour.

Today's mass-produced sausages, however, are a far cry from the early varieties, which, in my view, at least had some actual nutritional benefits.

Take the Coles 'Simply' brand of 'thin BBQ sausages', which, the package states, are 'made with Australian meat'. The package label also states that there are 'no added hormones'. Just for good measure, anyone buying this 24-pack of sausages is informed the meat is from 'RSPCA approved farms'. It all sounds very aboveboard, Coles. Good effort. Oh so tempting, right?

But this is half the story. The ingredient label is really just rows of abbreviated hints that distract us from what really, truly lurks within these mysterious fingers of raw 'meat'.

> INGREDIENTS: No Added Hormones Australian Beef (58%), Water, RSPCA Approved Chicken (15%), Rice Flour, Salt, Bamboo Fibre, Thickeners (401, 412), Mineral Salt (451), Preservative (223 (Sulphites)), Hydrolysed Maize Protein, Dextrose (Maize), Acidity Regulators (330, 270), Vegetable Powders (Onion, Garlic), Spice Extracts, Firming Agent (509), Spices, Antioxidant (Paprika Oleoresins), Rosemary Extract.
> ALLERGY ADVICE: Contains Sulphites. May contain milk, soy.

Yes, I'm afraid the making of these sausages could quite easily make another viral TikTok. It would have involved yet more vats of gluey, pink-tinted sloppiness. They are also a surprising mix of both beef and chicken. And there are many of the same sort of additives we found in the mass-produced ham mix, plus the following additional delights:

- potassium tripolyphosphate (451)
- sodium alginate (401)
- guar gum (412)
- citric acid (330)
- lactic acid (270)
- calcium chloride (509).

Compare the texture of a high-quality butcher's sausage with the contents of one of these cheap, mass-produced sausages and you will notice a clear difference.

Naturally, some Australian consumers have families to feed on very tight budgets and I will never judge them for purchasing these products. Needs must. But I find it outrageous that producers like Coles are marketing these additive-laden products as if they are somehow healthy and pure, with the labels mentioning 'no hormones' and 'RSPCA approved'. Those 'pluses', in my view, are completely cancelled out by the full list of ingredients.

I believe this is potentially misleading for the consumer. Just to add to this already shady situation, it's important to point out that traditionally sausage is made of cuts of pork that are ground up with fat, curing agents such as salt, breadcrumbs and seasoning. The fact that traditional sausages are cured however means they are still placed in the processed-meat sin bin and they have their own health risks. But they are not ultra-processed like these supermarket sausages, which masquerade as a healthy and fresh food product with the help of an array of distracting statements. There are also growing fears about the 'forever chemicals' which experts warn are entering foods during the modern-day mass production process in factories. CNN reported in 2024 how a new study found 3600 chemicals leach into our food, especially during the processing, packaging and storage stage.[9]

The one preservative most fresh-meat sausages don't often tend to include is sodium nitrite. But hot dogs often do. And in Australia these US-style snacks are gaining popularity in cinemas, play centres and theme parks. It makes me wince when I attend my daughter's dance competitions, where hundreds of teen girls are performing, and one of the only lunch options in the small on-site cafes is often hot dogs. Snags of any kind are no longer on my family's menu, and I get upset when my children come home from school to say there was a sausage-sizzle event, or that they have been given sausages at barbecues or after sporting events as a matter of course. The sausages are never high-quality butcher sausages, but are the cheap, low-quality versions full of additives and sulphites. Yet these beloved sizzles are considered as Australian as Vegemite or Tim Tams—and as unstoppable as the rising sun.

Another product the food industry tends to try to promote as something oh-so-pure is bacon. Apologies in advance. I know bacon is beloved the world over and this is a touchy subject for many. Never mind the old adage 'Don't mention politics or religion'—I've discovered that mentioning bacon in conversation is a high-risk activity. You can lose friends over it, if you're not careful.

In a podcast series for bacon lovers called *The Sizzle*, host Phillip Sellers likens bacon to cultural icons such as 'the hot dog, apple pie, jazz—maybe even rock 'n' roll'. He goes on: 'Above all, however, bacon is sensual, sexy—it's really sexy, has a sexy texture. Sweet, salty, pleasantly smoky on the palate. And it has aroma—it's savoury, alluring, it's tempting. Oh man. Bacon . . . Even more tantalising is the sound, the sizzle, like a lover whispering a sweet nothing.'[10]

During the pandemic, an article reported that, in the UK, a bacon sandwich was the second-most-eaten snack by working-from-home (and eating-from-home) Brits. A bacon and egg roll is also a beloved breakfast choice of millions of Australians— at home, at work, while camping or in a cafe. And bacon is a popular ingredient for lunch and dinner. Or for any hour of the day or night.

The problem is what really goes in to making the most popular bacon in Australia is only included as a careless whisper on its ingredient label. Major brands, I found, usually add the following to their meat: water, salt, sugar, mineral salts, antioxidant and, yes, here it comes again—preservative 250, or sodium nitrite.

It was time to pursue a highly specific angle of my investigation into a controversial aspect of the processed-meat industry. Nitro-preservatives were now in my firing line.

On the shelf

It's been sitting there for over a week, that packet of streaky bacon you've had in the fridge, but you're looking forward to frying it up on the weekend with some eggs. And there's that sausage-shaped, vacuum-packed salami that you can't even remember buying, but you're saving it for a picnic if the weather warms up.

You can't store or extend the life of fresh meat in this way, or for a long time—unless you freeze it, of course. So when it comes to processed meats, a key motivation for the food industry is to extend the time in which they can be transported, warehoused or left on a supermarket shelf. To do this, they use preserving methods that massively extend the time before their products go off. Preservatives are essential to profits.

Processed meats are also marketed to the consumer for their handy ability to be stored for long periods, and the consumer appreciates it. Indeed most meat-eaters—including myself, before my bowel cancer diagnosis—have appreciated this convenient aspect for our entire lives. If you take a look at the best-before dates of bacon or salami, for example, you have anywhere from four to eight weeks before you need to put it in the bin, as long as you keep it in the fridge. As British investigative food journalist Joanna Blythman states, 'the need of food processors to postpone the evil hour when their products start showing their age trumps public health concerns every time.'[11]

One of the more well-known concerns with all processed-meat products, of course, is their high levels of sodium and saturated fat, which come with their own array of health risks. We'll explore these later.

It's the frequent and murky use of the common nitro-preservatives in meat, however, which I started to discover is largely being overlooked here in Australia.

The preservatives fall into two main groups.

Sulphites (often used in fresh-meat sausages)

Sulphur dioxide (220), sodium sulphite (221), sodium bisulphite (222), sodium metabisulphite (223), potassium metabisulphite (224), potassium sulphite (225), potassium bisulphite (228)

- Sulphites are a naturally occurring mineral and have several uses in the food industry but when it comes to processed meat they are most commonly added as a preservative to fresh-meat pork and beef sausages. However, because some sulphite-sensitive people, many of whom also have asthma, may react to sulphites with allergy-like symptoms, it is required by law in Australia and New Zealand that a warning is included under the ingredients.

Nitro-preservatives (often used in cured meats, e.g. bacon, ham, salami, frankfurts)

Potassium nitrite (249), sodium nitrite (250), sodium nitrate (251), potassium nitrate (252)

- I discovered that this group of nitro-preservatives are mixed with salt (sodium) and referred to as nitrites/nitrates, are used by meat industries the world over to prevent the growth of harmful fungi and bacteria (such as listeria, salmonella and *Clostridium botulinum*), while also improving the flavour, colour and texture of processed meats that are cured, smoked, canned or fermented. These include ham, bacon, pepperoni, salami and so on. In short, they are the reason these products are pink (and not a pale

grey or brown) and don't cause harm with potentially fatal microorganisms.
- It should be noted that some traditional deli products—such as Parma ham, Bayonne ham, certain Corsican charcuterie meats and certain Spanish chorizos, for example—don't have nitrites added, but they are in the minority. Interestingly, ever since the Parma Ham Consortium decided in 1993 to ban nitro-preservatives it's been said not a single case of botulism has been detected in the 8–9 million raw hams they produce every year.[12] Despite growing links in multiple reports and studies between nitro-preservatives in processed meats and potentially fatal health impacts, there are currently no warnings about them on labels in Australia or New Zealand (or in most other countries).

Thousands of years ago, it was simply salt that was used to cure meat; saltpetre, a crude form of potassium nitrate, known as 'wall saltpetre', was then discovered and first used in ancient India and China where it was scraped from rocks and caves.[13] Today's synthetic nitro-preservatives, most commonly sodium nitrite, are used in processed meats because they are cheap and effective. I decided to examine the detailed, disturbing history of that later.

'Nitrate' and 'nitrite' are compounds made of oxygen and nitrogen—a large component of the atmosphere and present in soil. An article in *The Guardian* made clear the interchangeability between the synthetic compound sodium nitrite (E250), along with sodium nitrate (E251) and potassium nitrate (E252).[14]

'The latter two are both naturally occurring minerals—although they can be industrially synthesised—and have been used in meat curing for centuries, to give it colour and protect it from deadly bacteria. Other bacteria, during the curing process or in our mouths when we chew the meat, convert the nitrates into nitrites—which is why, collectively, these additives are often referred to simply as nitrates or nitrites.'

Here's a key point: studies show that nitro-preservatives are not carcinogenic in their pure form, but under certain conditions they can be transformed to be potentially deadly. They can give rise to free radicals, in particular nitric oxide (NO), and when these react with the components of meat (especially with iron, and with amides or amines in meat proteins), it leads to the production of certain carcinogenic compounds. Scientists call these *N*-nitroso compounds, which include nitrosamines.

So, just to be clear: these potentially harmful compounds appear as a result of the interaction between nitrites and the meat itself.[15] Here's how it works: after we digest the meat nitrosamines are broken down by the liver and can damage DNA leading to mutations causing cancer to develop. Most pertinently these nitrosamines can damage cells in the bowel and, as we shall see, could possibly be the cause of other serious health risks. Worryingly for anyone already fighting cancer, nitrosamines may also cause the growth of existing cancerous cells and tumours.[16] So that's another reason to stop giving cancer patients ham sandwiches in hospitals.

In short, these preservatives which give products an appealing pink colour, prevent harmful bacteria and extend their shelf life massively, come with risks. Not 100-per-cent-guaranteed health impacts, for sure. But established risks. And when it comes to 'risks' of cancer in particular, I now take this incredibly seriously—because I know firsthand how truly horrendous the treatment experience is, let alone the very real potential to lose your life.

So what does sodium nitrite ($NaNO_2$)—the most common nitro-additive in our processed meats—even look like? It's a white crystalline powder that resembles kitchen salt. It has no odour, and dissolves in water. It can be added to a processed meat mix in powdered form, or injected into meat, or added to water to create a brine or 'pickle' as it's known in the meat industry. As well as being used as a food preservative, I discovered, to my horror, that it is added to antifreeze for car radiators, and used to prevent pipes and tanks from corroding. It's also an ingredient in many dyes, pesticides and pharmaceuticals.

Naturally, it's extremely important to avoid potentially fatal food poisoning from meat. But sodium nitrite's major downside—to say the least—of a cancer risk made me feel dismayed. The saying 'robbing Peter to pay Paul' comes to mind.

Yet food manufacturers find it hard to let go of nitro-preservatives. Without nitrites, processed meats would turn brown quickly, making them far less appealing to consumers. The meat would have to be sold within hours, not sit on shelves or be transported long distances. Some smaller meat businesses use celery powder and other organic compounds to cure meats because it's a 'natural' source of nitrates, although the health implications of natural versus synthetic sources are a topic of ongoing research and debate. There are also concerns over some people being allergic to celery powder or extracts.

A 2020 academic review demonstrated that, in preparing meat products, 'the addition of plant extracts helps to achieve a product quality similar to that achieved using sodium nitrite alone', but noted that further research was needed to determine the quantities of plant extracts to use.[17] Another recent study pointed towards the possible use of green tea polyphenols and grape seed extract for their ability to preserve dry cured bacon safely in particular, but concluded the results were not yet certain.[18] So we just don't know yet if using natural sources will take out the health risks of processed meats, or whether the risks will be the same.

Additionally, regulations and guidelines regarding the use of natural curing agents like celery powder can vary between countries.

In Melbourne, a high-quality butcher in my local area of Bayside talked me through how he cures his own bacon, showing me the measurements he uses written on a large Tupperware box.

It read 'Bacon Cure' on the side with another label reading '1125g salt, 125g cure'.

'The cure is a sodium nitrite mix we buy because I'm not legally allowed to buy nitrite by itself, but I still have to be so precise to make sure I don't add too much,' he said. 'It makes me so nervous I even use a highly accurate jeweller's scale to weigh it out.'[19]

What about organic alternatives then instead?

'We don't know how much to put in, it's too much of an unknown,' he said. 'Some butchers are chucking in large amounts but I don't want to take the risk.'

PROCESSED

When I asked if he had any nitrite-free bacon for sale he went to his freezer and pulled out a packet of frozen bacon which had been cured simply with salt. Granted, it was much paler than the pink offerings in his large fridge displays, but otherwise it looked the same. (Later, I took the block of frozen rashers and with a sharp knife easily shaved off a few slivers to cook for my delighted children.)

'I only made this batch because someone requested nitrite-free,' he said, 'but they never collected it.'

Hang on a salty minute. So it was possible, then, for butchers—and indeed producers, suppliers and supermarkets—just to freeze nitrite-free bacon and display it in that form, avoiding the established risks of nitro-preservatives and unknown risks of organic preservatives? And this method could perhaps even apply to other cured meats too? It seemed to me to be such a simple solution for the industry to explore considering the health impacts at stake.

But the butcher pointed out the catch, the crack on the icy lake, as he saw it. 'The sodium nitrite means our bacon in the shop can last for six weeks, and anyway I don't think people would go for frozen bacon,' he sighed.

Why though? Frozen wouldn't be a problem, this was Melbourne and the cold never bothered us anyway.

My new meaty confidant begged to differ: 'Consumers are very much used to the fresh meat bacon in fridges and the pink colour. They are also used to it then lasting a long time in their own fridges at home.'

In other words, without these cheap chemical preservatives, the processed-meat industry would face major problems. They might not be able to make billions of dollars a year. Part of the smallgoods industry may even collapse. As we shall see they are well aware they are facing a growing crisis, one which threatens the status quo.

And *that's* their primo concern.

A little book of horrors

If you're still yearning for your favourite charcuterie at this point, you might not want to read what I went on to find in Meat & Livestock Australia's *Guidelines for the Safe Manufacture of Smallgoods*.[20] For any smallgoods manufacturers in Australia, this guide—complete with a front cover showing a pile of pink and orange meats—contains all the rules and recommendations for making processed meats.

And here lies the proof that nitro-preservatives are being added as the norm, even while the guidelines openly flag their dangers. The guide's second edition, published in 2015, clearly states that in the wrong doses, 'chemicals such as nitrite' are 'toxic or poisonous when too much is ingested'.

'The quantity of ingredients added is crucial to the health of consumers,' it states. 'For example, if sodium nitrite and sodium chloride are mixed up and nitrite is added at the amount meant for sodium chloride, the dose could be lethal. A fail-safe system of batching up ingredients and additives is needed.' When manufacturers use bags of premixed additives, amounts can be more easily controlled. But problems can arise if these ingredients are weighed out individually by staff who are not fully trained in how to weigh out ingredients.

So here it is: my raison d'être, skewered into the heart of this whole project. The raison d'être that made me down tools to dedicate three years to researching and writing this book. There are actual poisons added to processed meats that increase our risk of developing cancer.

And yes, it's all above board and official, according to our regulatory bodies. According to FSANZ's Food Standards Code, nitrate is permitted to be added to slow-dried cured meats, and 'fermented, uncooked processed comminuted meat products' to a maximum level of 500 milligrams per kilogram. Nitrite can be added to commercially sterile canned cured meats—up to 50 milligrams per kilogram—and to cured meats, dried meats, slow-dried cured meats, 'processed comminuted meat, poultry and game products' to a maximum level of 125 milligrams per kilogram. The standards also specify the maximum amount of combined nitrates and nitrites allowed in processed meats.[21]

Yes, this means the nitrites in the meats are in relatively small quantities. Yet, along with a growing number of health experts, I felt strongly that consuming such a dangerous poison—even in tiny, tiny amounts—could not be 100 per cent safe. How could the processed-meat industry guarantee that? It still enters your mouth, your stomach, your liver, your colon and your bloodstream. As a bowel cancer patient still needing extremely difficult treatments to survive, I was relieved processed meats had been off my family's menu for some time. This all felt so wrong. I could feel it in my bones.

Angry exchanges

As I carried on researching and reading, often fuelled by the energy-inducing steroids I was given to combat chemotherapy side effects, I found there were issues around nitrites that were causing confusion.

First, there was a point about nitrites in meat specifically that defenders of processed meat seemed to be missing. They argued that it didn't matter that nitro-preservatives were used in processed meats because nitrates and nitrites also occur naturally in vegetables. So, if they're in vegetables anyway, these people argued, surely they were safe in meat?

In one of the many outraged responses to the IARC's shock report in 2015—the one that linked processed meats to an increased cancer risk—author and podcast host Elizabeth Benton set out to explain why she believed hot dogs were not a cancer risk at all. On an episode of her podcast *Primal Potential* called 'Does Bacon Cause Cancer?', Benton told listeners just how incensed she was at the idea that processed meats could be bad for anyone's health, and argued that the WHO was in fact misleading the public over the cancer risks.

'Let me blow your mind a little bit more,' she told listeners. 'The number one source of nitrites in the human diet? Vegetables. Arugula, butter lettuce, four servings of celery or beets. Right? All these things have more nitrites than 467 hot dogs . . . When we talk about hot dogs and bacon, there are limitations on the total amount of nitrates allowed in these things.'

Let's just say that Benton got herself into a little bit of a pickle. What she left out of her research scope was the precise reason *why* nitrates and nitrites in processed meats are considered a higher cancer risk compared to those in vegetables.

As I noted earlier, it's their combination with amines in meat to form nitrosamines, which can damage DNA and cells, among other dangers. Vegetables typically contain lower levels of these amines, reducing the potential for nitrosamine to form.

So, in short, it's the way nitrates are used in processed meat, and how they react, that leads to them go on to become cancerous, unlike nitrates in vegetables.

In recent years there have also been health scares regarding high levels of nitrates in drinking water in certain parts of the world, where water supplies may be polluted by farming or industry. However, there just haven't been enough studies to make confident conclusions about risks from consuming nitrates from drinking water.[22]

If nitrates and nitrites are so controversial, you must be thinking, *how are food companies getting away with adding them into our processed meats?*

The meat industry argues that processed-meat products contain less than 100 parts per million of nitrites, and as a result there is 'minimal' nitrosamine formation within the food. It's the word 'minimal' that isn't good enough, in my view, for troubling reasons we shall explore later. Talking of troubling, I would soon discover a 'smoking gun' of sorts, in the form of an industry review paper compiled in 2020 by researchers employed by the Commonwealth Scientific and Industrial Research Organisation (CSIRO).[23]

It was published by Meat & Livestock Australia (MLA), an independent organisation which regulates standards in the industry and works closely with the government.

At the start of the 38-page document, titled 'Review of emerging (food industry) clean technologies for potential high value red meat opportunities', it's made clear the research was joint funded by Meat & Livestock Australia and the government.

Just keep that in mind, because the attitude within the text which follows is rather revealing.

They start by admitting two major problems facing the industry: the increased competition from plant-based meats and the fact red and processed meats have been 'subjected to negative press', including being classified by the WHO in 2015 as a carcinogenic risk to humans 'due to additives such as nitrites'.

They even state processed meats, in particular, are being 'targeted' which I find a rather misplaced turn of phrase, along with the word 'subjected', considering the context.

This vernacular sounds a little defensive, don't you think? As if the innocent, misunderstood processed meats stand wrongly accused of a crime.

I couldn't help but notice, as I read on, they also never actually accept the WHO findings, or state concern for the health of the consumer as a priority. Their concern in the report rests on the changing desires of the consumer amid a growing 'clean label' trend—and how they can adapt to drive sales.

'... the meat industry needs to address these clean label issues in order to maintain their customer base and ensure the continued growth and viability of the industry,' the report states.

PROCESSED

Tackling 'cooked sausages' (hot dogs) and 'deli meats', which generally come with nitro-preservatives as standard, they discuss the idea of using a combination of natural ingredients and emerging food industry technologies.

For example, they suggest high-pressure processing (HPP) and high-pressure thermal processing (HPTP) would be effective at destroying any 'harmful microorganisms' such as listeria and salmonella.

This all sounds like an excellent set of solutions but the researchers then note the potential industry challenges in switching to clean label ingredients, including the 'costly' research and development required, as well as 'reputational risk'. They also flag that changing to natural preservatives could hinder overseas exports if those ingredients are not yet approved in certain countries.

'Due to its multi-functional purpose (preservation, colour, flavour and antioxidant), nitrite is not easily replaced in meat products, however the desire for its removal remains topical,' the report states.

Topical? Urgent more like. It's been a few years now since the review was published and, sadly, as we shall see later, nitro-preservatives are currently very much included in many processed meat products in Australia.

What's taking them so long? The government and meat industry are clearly aware of the risks and that changes to production methods could save lives. Or is the whole idea in the too complicated and too expensive basket? The current defence from many meat companies is that as well as using small amounts they also add in ascorbic acid (vitamin C), which they claim aids in keeping processed meat pink and the flavour stable but also apparently 'helps' stop the nitro-preservatives from forming the nitrosamines.

So, let's get this straight. The use of nitro-preservatives is partly justified because the food industry uses another ingredient, ascorbic acid, to hopefully—*hopefully*—carry out war games in your digestive system. Every time you eat processed meat with these ingredients, you are a *Fight Club*–themed science experiment carried out on a wing and a prayer.

This angered me enormously. And several nutrition experts I interviewed agreed. According to Associate Professor Teresa Mitchell-Paterson, a leading nutritionist who also advises Bowel Cancer Australia, trying to use ascorbic acid to stop nitrosamine formation is 'a very delicate balance, and not one that we are capable of calculating to an exact measure to create the same effect [as] what happens in natural foods'.[24]

'It's okay,' the meat industry seems to be proclaiming. 'The nitro-additives won't cause cancer because we are sending in the troops to fight!'

But to me, the inclusion of ascorbic acid feels more like a sniper sent in as backup during a battle, or to protect a president.

And sometimes snipers don't manage to stop the first bullets.

Chapter Three

SWALLOWING THE BAIT*

> The HOGGONE® product uses sodium nitrite, an approved food preservative that in low doses can kill pigs quickly in overdose. HOGGONE® is humane and kills by oxygen depletion to the brain and tissues (known as methaemoglobinaemia).[1]
>
> Centre for Invasive Species Solutions, 'HOGGONE® meSN® feral pig baits (available)', 2023

Swine kill

Kangaroo Island, 13 kilometres off the coast of South Australia, is an alluring slice of paradise.

With abundant wildlife it's one of the prime places in Australia to catch glimpses of native animals including koalas, kangaroos and seals. White sandy beaches, turquoise seas, unusual natural geological formations and interesting maritime history help make Kangaroo Island unique. There's a good reason it's known as Australia's Galapagos.

---

* This chapter contains descriptions of suicide and suicidal ideation.

Yet it has also recently played host to scientific field testing that has a deeply troubling link to the bacon, ham and pepperoni sticks in your fridge.

A three-year eradication program was launched on Kangaroo Island in 2019 to cull feral pigs because their large numbers were becoming a serious biohazard, risking spreading phytophthora, a fungal disease that's potentially lethal for native vegetation. The rare Kangaroo Island river daisies were also being directly impacted through disturbance. The cull program used thermal-imaging cameras for aerial culls, and baiting stations using a new poison.[2]

So far, I thought, so fair.

However, the new 'poison' in question, called HOGGONE®, is what made me gulp. The active compound in HOGGONE® is sodium nitrite—the same preservative added to processed meats.[3] While this bait is said to be far more humane than existing baiting systems, the processed-meat manufacturers probably don't want the general public to be aware that this same poison is in their bacon, ham and other products. It's not exactly great for the image of all those bespoke, expensive slices of salami and ham, is it?

The irony wasn't lost on me. An ingredient commonly used to preserve pork-based processed meats—and many meats—is used to kill pigs.

It's not the actual use of this new bait that is my main concern—it's fatal for the wild pigs, of course, but they are problematic in many countries, and especially in Australia. They cost Australian agriculture more than $100 million a year, and there are fears that figure will increase if African swine fever gets into Australia and into the feral pig population, which would make the disease extremely difficult to eradicate.

After the Kangaroo Island field testing went well, HOGGONE® received regulatory approval in 2021 after more than a decade in development by Animal Control Technologies Australia (ACTA). A media release by the company, written in an excitable tone, declared this was great news for 'Australian farmers, state government agencies, local councils, pest control businesses and other land managers', who could now all access the 'fast-acting, humane, targeted feral pig bait'.

'Sodium nitrite is a food preservative which is safely used in low concentrations,' ACTA managing director Dr Linton Staples was quoted as saying. 'People and most animals can tolerate modest amounts of sodium nitrite, but pigs lack the protective enzyme that is present in other species.'

The bait, which contains a whopping 100 grams of sodium nitrite per kilo, and has peanut butter in the mix to make it appetising to pigs, renders the animals 'unconscious before they die, typically within one to three hours, without suffering', Dr Staples clarified. Apparently non-targeted species like birds are not affected by eating the dead animals once they die.[4]

So how does it work? At high doses, sodium nitrite ($NaNO_2$) induces methaemoglobinaemia in mammals, a condition that restricts the transport of oxygen by the red blood cells. In severe cases, this leads to central nervous system anoxia (where the whole body doesn't get any oxygen), lethargy and death.

Obviously a product with the capacity to cull large herds of a pest species, hopefully quickly and humanely, is a good thing. But when I read how the sodium nitrite actually works in killing the pigs, it made me feel highly uneasy. This stuff is lethal—literally. It's about to dominate the feral-pig-killing market all over the world. Yes, it's used in much higher doses for killing pigs than it is in preserving meats, but it's still a killer poison. And it's in packets of kids' pepperoni sticks, and the ham in the sandwiches they eat at kindergarten.

Knowing this potentially lethal ingredient is added to most processed meats, even in much smaller quantities, just didn't sit well with me. How about you?

If the pig-bait revelation ruins thoughts of your next carbonara, I apologise . . . but don't shoot the messenger.

I soon found out that this dark link between sodium nitrites and death doesn't end with animals. I moved on to read, with unfolding horror, how sodium nitrite, in high enough doses, is a deathly poison for humans too.

One fatal dose

When young Perth man Elia Wani was last seen by his doctor on 7 May 2019, he appeared to be doing relatively well considering his difficult battle with bipolar affective disorder, which had meant several admissions to hospital as an involuntary patient.

Born in the East-African country of Uganda in 1989, Elia moved to Australia in 2006, settling in the suburb of Armadale. From the outside, it looked like he had everything to live for amid his large family, including two brothers and three sisters.

He completed a diploma in digital marketing, and worked in the security industry. Outside of work he enjoyed playing soccer and singing, and had even taken to the stage as a stand-up comedian after taking acting classes. Elia had also written a book called *Discovering Your Universal Purpose*.

It would be documented later that when he saw his doctor for the final time, he denied any 'thoughts of harming himself or anyone else' and didn't show any signs of mania, depression or psychosis. He reported he was working casual shifts as a security guard and it was recorded that he had support from his family. He would never been seen alive by that doctor again.

Tragically, Elia died on 21 May 2019 from 'acquired methaemoglobinaemia in association with sodium nitrite toxicity', according to the WA coroner. He had consumed a product containing sodium nitrite with the intention of taking his own life. He was just 29 years old.[5]

As we learned earlier, the toxic effect of nitrites in large doses lies in their ability to stop oxygen getting around the body—anoxia—with fatal consequences. Elia's death didn't make the news. Suicides often don't, for fear of copycat attempts to end lives. However, the WA coroner certainly had something to say about the way Elia died. He made two recommendations aimed to minimise the risks associated with the misuse of products containing both sodium nitrite and sodium nitrate:

- **Recommendation No. 1** The Therapeutic Goods Administration consider whether products containing sodium nitrate should be the subject of similar

restrictions as those about to [be] imposed in relation to sodium nitrite, given the similar effect on the human body of both substances.
- **Recommendation No. 2** The Therapeutic Goods Administration should consider advising suppliers of products containing sodium nitrite that these products have been widely promoted as capable of causing death in the context of euthanasia and suicide, and suggesting that suppliers take all possible steps to ensure that the sodium nitrite products they sell are intended for legitimate purposes.

In his moving final comments, coroner Michael Jenkin said Elia had been a 'much-loved son and brother' with a longstanding mental health condition. He said his death highlighted the risks associated with the misuse of this commonly available substance. Those risks had already been identified by Australia's Therapeutic Goods Administration (TGA), he said. In 2022, three years after Elia's death and also following the death of a woman in Victoria from sodium nitrite ingestion, the TGA decided to further restrict access to more concentrated forms of sodium nitrite. Elia's tragic death highlights the potentially fatal effects of nitrates in high doses. The incidence of sodium nitrite self-poisonings have sadly been increasing since 2017.[6] Studies show it could well be the result of online sellers, combined with recommendations shared on websites. It's a problem that seems to be growing, and it's attracting the attention of concerned coroners.

In 2020, British woman Linda Gillchrest died with a high level of sodium nitrite in her blood. It was found that she had bought an ebook that gave detailed instructions for self-administering a fatal dose of sodium nitrite, and had purchased on eBay a quantity of sodium nitrite—a larger quantity than the amount suggested in the book for a fatal dose—for less than £5 (about A$9). As coroner Richard Travers noted, 'Both purchases were made without any restriction being imposed by the sellers.'[7] This alarmed the coroner, who recommended action be taken by eBay and by the UK Government to 'prevent future deaths'.

A few months earlier, another Brit had suicided, and coroner Leslie Hamilton found that Jason Thompson, 49, had acquired sodium nitrite on eBay without difficulty a few days before his death. The coroner struck out hard against the platform, going as far as saying there was a future risk that more deaths would occur unless action was taken.[8] He suggested that eBay may be 'promoting a particular method of death by suicide' and therefore was breaking criminal laws.

Thankfully, eBay did the right thing and banned the sale of sodium nitrite on its platform. It also made the sensible suggestion for authorities globally to enact wider bans among other online sellers.

'As you will be aware, sodium nitrite in its pure form is still available for sale on the internet via other websites and platforms,' eBay's UK director said in a letter to the coroner.[9] 'We would therefore support stricter regulations restricting the online sale of sodium nitrite as a chemical in its pure form via the internet in order to prevent further such tragic cases in the future.'

In the US, a major court case was launched against Amazon in 2022 by parents of two US teens who had died by suicide. Both cases illustrated how easy it has been for teens to access sodium nitrite on Amazon.[10] In the first matter, regarding a teen named Kristine, the court heard she had started experiencing suicidal ideation in September 2020. She registered on an online suicide forum, on which users were linking to Amazon to encourage others to buy sodium nitrite as a method of suicide. Even though she was under eighteen, Kristine was able to create an Amazon account (the lawsuit alleged that Amazon does not verify age) and ordered the chemical from Loudwolf, an Amazon seller. The package arrived two days later; the next day, her family found her dead, with the bottle and the Amazon packaging beside her.

The other case in the lawsuit involved a teen named Ethan, who used his mother's Amazon account to place an order in January 2021. Ethan's mother assumed her account had been hacked and cancelled the order, but the package was already in the post. Ethan intercepted it and died soon after.

Over in the US, a health advisory was issued by the New York City Department of Health and Mental Hygiene in 2022, advising medical facilities in the city to make sure they had stocks of a special antidote due to a rise in attempted suicides using sodium nitrite. 'Providers should maintain a high suspicion for sodium nitrite toxicity if a patient presents with clinical signs of [methaemoglobinaemia] and/or reports ingestion of curing products or food preservatives,' it read.[11]

The health advisory described two cases of severe poisoning. One was a 30-year-old New York woman who was found in cardiac arrest with a nearby bottle of sodium nitrite. An antidote was given by emergency doctors but the woman died. The second example was a 22-year-old woman who had intentionally taken sodium nitrite in a suicide attempt. Before her death, the woman had read online instructions for taking a fatal dose. 'The patient recovered without permanent injury,' New York's Department of Health reported.

Worryingly, I also came across examples of vulnerable young teens accessing 'nitrite suicide kits' online. In a 2023 article in the *Journal of Forensic Sciences*, a group of scientists reported an 'alarming increase' in the number of cases linked to suicide using nitrites or a nitrite suicide kit. In one case, a thirteen-year-old girl had died with a glass containing sodium nitrite alongside her. 'Suicide kits are available on the web and nitrites are relatively easy to source and inexpensive,' the authors note. 'The fact that nitrites are readily available online underscores the importance of establishing effective preventive measures such as limiting the access and use of this chemical.'[12]

While these examples of nitrite use in suicides are deeply concerning, the history of nitrite is also stained with criminal behaviour. In 2020, a schoolteacher in China was sentenced to death for having attempted to poison 23 children by pouring sodium nitrite into their food. In the US, American law enforcers arrested a woman named Tina Vazquez who stole sodium nitrite from the meat-processing plant where she worked, filled two small capsules with the nitrite and gave it to a neighbour with flu symptoms who she wanted to kill, brazenly passing it off as antibiotics.[13] The dose wasn't high enough to be fatal, but Vazquez was sentenced to twenty years in prison for first-degree assault.

Along with the tragic suicides and attempted murders, there have also been large numbers of accidental poisonings all over the world, spanning decades. In 1948, *The New Yorker* ran an extended feature about 'The Case of the Eleven Blue Men'. After eleven men were admitted to hospital with severe illness and a blue tinge to their skin, a rapid investigation found that the men had sprinkled what they believed to be salt on their oats in a cafe, a common habit at the time. It was sodium nitrite. The cafe had made a devastating mix-up, it turned out. After treatment, the men all survived. Just.

However, there are far worse stories of individuals who have lost their lives due to accidental poisoning by sodium nitrite. In 2012 it was reported that the cause of a fatal food poisoning in Kulob, southern Tajikistan, was the presence of sodium nitrite in high concentration in a post-funeral meal. The incident affected 22 mourners and killed five, leaving their friends and family devastated. Yet again it was a disastrous mix-up with table salt that was the cause.[14]

Reading about these heartbreaking incidents made me increasingly concerned about the nitro-preservatives in the meat that Australians are eating every day. There wasn't any political lobbying on this matter in Australia, as far as I could tell.

But it turned out that 16,000 kilometres away, in France, there was an influential group of scientists, doctors and MPs who had been making rather loud noises about nitrites for nearly a decade. It was time to track them down to find out more about this meaty French Revolution.

Law and disorder

French mother Chantal Dupuy was just 54 years old when she passed away in 1988 from bowel cancer. Her year-long illness had been brutal. When she was diagnosed, cancer cells had already spread from her colon to several areas of her liver. It was a similar diagnosis to mine, but sadly for Chantal the treatments and surgical interventions were far less advanced and aggressive than they are today.

Making her tragic death even more devastating was that Chantal had a fifteen-year-old son. In a twist of fate, her eldest child, Florence, then aged 30, was married to a French scientist who was a well-known and respected expert in drug resistance in gut bacteria.

His name was Professor Denis Corpet, who lives in Toulouse in south-west France, close to the Pyrenees mountains. A man with one hell of a backstory. A retired scientist who in my view changed the world but, thankfully, had the time to reply to many emails from a pesky journalist working on a book in Australia.

Professor Corpet kindly shared the family's tragic story and revealed to me how grieving the loss of his mother-in-law had changed the trajectory of his entire research and career.[15] It was the first time he had spoken publicly about Chantal's passing in detail.

'Before her death I had no insight on colorectal cancer, but I started to read and think about it from that point,' Professor

Corpet told me. 'I was motivated to "save people", to stop this horrible process before it starts.' He took a sabbatical year in Toronto at the Ontario Cancer Institute to study oncology methods, which would turn out to be a significant move: Denis went on to be the team leader of a group who conducted the first research in the world establishing a link between nitrites in meat and bowel cancer.[16]

Leading the research at the University of Toulouse, the professor and his team demonstrated that while an experimental nitrite-cured ham promoted colorectal cancer in rats, the same ham cured without nitrite did not. It was gobsmacking, terrifying and groundbreaking in equal measure. Nitrites had been added to processed meats the world over for decades and sold in ever-increasing amounts to consumers.

This finding was then backed up by other scientific studies around the world which pointed to the way nitrites produce N-nitroso compounds, including nitrosamines, when they are added to processed meats, cooked and then ingested by humans. N-nitroso compounds, as we know, are carcinogenic chemicals.

Put simply, Professor Corpet and his co-author Dr Fabrice Pierre realised that adding nitrites to processed meats was at the core of the cancer risk.

Their important work built on more general scientific studies from the 1970s and '80s suggesting a general possible link between nitrites and the formation of nitrosamines in the digestive tract. They were studies which prompted aggressive pushback from the meat industry and were alarming enough for health-conscious, forward-thinking Nordic countries, including

Denmark, Finland, Norway and Sweden, to move to restrict or lower nitro-preservative levels in their own processed-meat production.[17] (Denmark in particular would eventually go head to head with the European Union in 2003 in a fierce court bid to make its own decisions on the matter.[18])

What was so influential about Corpet himself was that he would go on to become a panel member of the International Agency for Research on Cancer (IARC) that studied the health impacts of processed meats for the World Health Organization. Yes: Professor Corpet was involved in the decision by WHO to issue its now infamous warning in 2015 about the dangers of processed meats, which briefly sparked all those headlines. In fact he was co-chair of the WHO panel in question. Being able to speak directly to the professor about this significant study was essential and also a privilege.

'In our landmark 2015 IARC report, we classified consumption of processed meat as "carcinogenic to humans" (Group One) on the basis of sufficient evidence for colorectal cancer,' he wrote to me. Yet he has been dismayed at the 'unsatisfactory response' from 'those who hold the levers of power' ever since the IARC study was published and its findings reinforced by the WHO.

Frustrated, annoyed and impatient, the determined Frenchman was convinced that nitrites in meats were causing suffering and deaths all over the world. He spent time deciding his next move.

Then, in February 2019, Corpet decided to write a letter. This particular letter needed impact. It had to be forensic, yet plain in form. Most of all it needed to go to those who had direct personal power to make change. The movers and shakers. The dynamic decision makers.

He narrowed down his choices and decided to send it to two incredibly influential figures on Europe's political stage. The first was Matthew Hancock, the UK's Secretary of State for Health and Social Care at the time, and one of the closest and most trusted confidants of then UK prime minister Boris Johnson. If Hancock wanted to make any kind of change regarding nitrites in meat, he certainly had the power—and the ear of the boss. Additionally, anything the British Government did on matters of public health policy would be noted, and potentially copied, by other countries, including the ones with whom they had a special relationship. And yes, that could include the US—and Australia.

The second political giant in Corpet's sights was Dr Vytenis Andriukaitis, a former heart surgeon who was the European Commissioner for Health and Food Safety. Since 2014, the health of EU member nations—including France, Spain, Germany and Italy—had been his remit. With the looming 2020 Brexit date, the UK would soon move outside his sphere, which is why Hancock had to be in the mix.

Corpet was ready. The letter was written and sent—a week before Valentine's Day, as it turned out, but these weren't exactly words of amour.

'What did you say?' I asked him.

'I'll send it to you,' he replied, adding a smiley-face emoji, kindly sharing this significant piece of processed-meat industry history.

PROCESSED

Thursday 7 February 2019

To:
Rt Hon Matthew Hancock MP,
UK Secretary of State for Health and Social Care
Mr Vytenis Andriukaitis,
EU Commissioner for Health & Food Safety

Dear Mr Hancock and Mr Andriukaitis,

    I respectfully write to you following the intervention of senior UK parliamentarians, food scientists and medical experts in December 2018, who called for a public awareness campaign on the health risks posed by nitrites in processed meats. They rightly said, as covered by *The Observer* newspaper, 'that not enough is being done to raise awareness of nitrites in our processed meat and their health risks'.

    As a panel member of the International Agency for Research on Cancer (IARC) that studied the health impacts of processed meats for the World Health Organization, I wish to add my name to these renewed calls for urgent action from policy makers. In our landmark 2015 IARC report we classified consumption of processed meat as 'carcinogenic to humans' (Group One) on the basis of sufficient evidence for colorectal cancer. The Global Burden of Disease Project estimated that 34,000 cases of colorectal cancer are directly attributable to diets high in processed meats.

The research team I led at the University of Toulouse demonstrated that while an experimental nitrite-cured ham promotes colorectal carcinogenesis in rats, the same ham cured without nitrite does not. This and many other scientific studies points [sic] to nitrites producing N-nitroso compounds when they are added to processed meats, cooked and then ingested by humans. N-nitroso compounds, that include nitrosamines, are carcinogenic chemicals.

The addition of nitrites to foods such as ham and bacon is thus central to the cancer risk—and marks out those meats that contain these chemicals as significantly more dangerous than other processed meats, such as traditional UK sausages or Italian Parma ham, which do not.

Since the IARC study was published and enforced by the World Health Organization four years ago, there has been an unsatisfactory response from those who hold the levers of power—and that includes your administrations in the European Union and United Kingdom.

In the years since, more evidence has exposed other wide-ranging health risks posed by nitrites. For instance, a study recently carried out by Johns Hopkins University in the United States found a direct link to mental health difficulties. People who had experienced manic episodes were three-and-a-half times more likely to have consumed nitrite-cured meat. Glasgow University, who surveyed more than 260,000 women, found those who ate nitrite-cured meat increased their risk of contracting breast cancer by 21 per cent.

Yet, despite these facts, those responsible for ensuring the food consumers eat is as safe as it possibly can be have failed to act.

While a few companies can be congratulated for investing in holistic innovation that has removed the need for nitrites in their products, including Nestlé in France with their Herta brand of ham, and Finnebrogue in the UK with their Naked Bacon and Naked Ham brands, politicians have largely been found missing in action.

The failure of governments globally to engage on this public health scandal is nothing less than a dereliction of duty—both in regards to the number of cancer cases that could be avoided by ridding nitrites from processed meats—and in the potential to reduce the strain on increasingly stretched and under-funded public health services.

And while bacon has been in the headlines, I would like to draw your specific attention to cooked ham, which plays such a fundamental role in the diets of children. The vast majority of ham contains these cancer-causing chemicals—and the vast majority of parents are not aware of the risks. In a ComRes survey of 2,051 parents in the UK, 53 per cent were 'completely unaware' of links between nitrite-cured meat and cancer. It is surely the responsibility of your administrations to educate parents of the risks posed by ham in their children's lunchbox—and to facilitate the growth of safer nitrite-free ham alternatives.

I urge you to seize this golden opportunity to work with experts and the food industry across Europe to drive the nitrite-free agenda.

Yours sincerely,

Professeur émérite Denis E. CORPET
Ingénieur AgroParisTech, PhD, HDR

Despite his excellent letter, which I felt, considering Corpet's work on the issue, showed extraordinary respect and restraint, the result, at first, was a deafening silence. Professor Corpet could see the peaks of the Pyrenees from his home town, but he couldn't yet see his postie, or rather *le facteur*, coming over the horizon with a letter from Brussels—or London. I could tell he would have been happy with a letter from Verona if it had meant a nod in the right direction.

And then, at last, he got a response. The EU honcho had clearly needed a little time to gather his thoughts. It had taken an entire month.

Corpet told me how Mr Andriukaitis laid out in detail, with a somewhat defensive tone, all the measures the EU had taken over the years to ensure 'safe' levels of nitro-preservatives in meat products across member countries.

However, in the final paragraphs of the three-page letter he then conceded that a special report delivered by the European

Food Safety Authority (EFSA) in June 2017, had stated concerns over the consumption of nitrites among children. The report, the Commissioner admitted, also linked nitro-preservatives with cancer.

'Could I see the letter?' I asked.

'Of course!' Corpet replied. 'Let me look through my records.'

Eventually, he found it. And I was hugely grateful he did. It serves as a vital piece of history—showing the first move by a major powerful authority to take concerns seriously since the infamous 2015 WHO report.

He concludes the letter by writing: 'I have asked my services to work on the potential revision of the maximum levels of nitrites . . . discussions on this matter are ongoing.

'Please be also informed that the EU, represented by the Commission, has been very active on this matter at the meeting of the Codes Committee on Food Additives raising awareness as regards the controversy related to the use of nitrites and steering the discussion to find the most appropriate risk management approach at the international level. Finally, the EU also supports efforts to investigate replacement of nitrites in meat products.

'I hope you find my reply informative and that it shows how seriously the Commission takes this matter.'

As for a reply from Hancock, it could not be found in Corpet's records, but he doesn't remember it bearing as many, if any, practical promises as the EU letter.

'I may have just put it in the bin,' Corpet sighed.

Sadly, as it turned out, the two recipients of Corpet's letter soon had other distractions on their agendas anyway. Hancock became a highly controversial figure due to his mishandling of the Covid-19 pandemic in the UK, later resigning in disgrace following an extramarital affair with a colleague. He never did engage the British public on the dangers of processed meat as Corpet had requested, but after leaving politics he did take a large payment to appear on the British version of reality TV show *I'm a Celebrity . . . Get Me Out of Here!*.

A review of the show in *The Guardian* observed that Hancock had displayed qualities which made him a 'terrible politician':

> There was never any sense that he was balancing risk, or that he was able to think things through in any meaningful way. There's a fundamental lack of humanity that at times is quite chilling.[19]

As for Andriukaitis, well, he soon landed a plum new job, becoming the WHO Special Envoy for the European Region in March 2020.

I could tell that the lack of immediate action by these two leading politicians had really upset Corpet at the time. But, thankfully, others were inspired by Corpet, including fellow concerned scientists, and they began to act. Their actions eventually led to small steps of change.

French charity La Ligue contre le cancer (The French League Against Cancer) and the European non-profit Foodwatch, which campaigns for better practices in the food industry, together started a public petition banning nitro-preservatives in ham in particular. Finally, somebody in politics joined in: a motivated French MP, a former restaurant critic named Richard Ramos, set up a special parliamentary committee with many stakeholders, including Corpet and his colleague Dr Fabrice Pierre.

'There is a link between colorectal cancer and nitrates in charcuterie, so we must ban nitrates,' Ramos said. It was a hard task and the pushback was tremendous. The influential French press didn't seem won over either. It was reported that '300 small to medium-sized French companies in the sector would struggle to manufacture their products without the use of nitrites, as lack of the preservative would reduce shelf life and increase the risk of bacterial infection'.[20]

However, on a momentous day in October 2020, Professor Corpet and Dr Pierre were invited to speak at the Assemblée nationale, the French parliament, in Paris. Ramos and three other MPs then wrote a proposal for legislative change and published it on 21 December 2021.

'My role then was mostly scientific,' Corpet explained. 'To discover and publish in scientific journals, and to explain science to lay people and journalists.'

Eventually, in 2022, this background work started to pay off, sending a salami-scented shockwave across Europe. Following the publication in July of a study by France's national health agency, which concluded that nitrites in processed meats increased the risk of cancer, the French Government committed to eliminate the use of nitrites in food production where possible.

Naturally, French charcuterie producers went ballistic, characterising the move as an assault on 'national gastronomy'.

Meat-industry bodies in France meanwhile reacted by stressing the industry had already reduced its use of nitrites and was working to do more. 'Craftsmen and charcuterie companies have already voluntarily reduced, since 2016, by 40% the maximum quantities of nitrites compared to European regulations, which makes France, with Denmark, the country that uses the least in the world,' said Joël Mauvigney, president of meat-industry body CNCT.

Another trade body representative, Bernard Vallat from FICT, argued that there would be shorter expiry periods for meats if nitrites were not used to preserve them, which could increase the risk of bacterial contamination such as salmonella. 'If we caused microbial accidents because there are no more nitrites it would be even worse than the hypothetical risk mentioned,' he said.[21]

Confounding their outrage, the European Food Safety Authority published an updated draft regulation that suggested levels of nitrites in food could signal a health concern.

Amid this bacon-themed battle, a group of UK scientists, including Professor Chris Elliott of Queen's University Belfast, then started a campaign to ban the use of chemicals in processed meat. Elliott knew a thing or two about dodgy meat, you see. He had led the UK Government's independent investigation into the shocking horsemeat scandal that ignited in January 2013 and went on to embroil large parts of the UK food industry. Major British retailers, including Tesco, Asda and Aldi, as well as manufacturers such as Findus were made to withdraw millions of beef patties, ready-made meals and mince amid fears the products contained horsemeat. Companies right across Europe were caught up in the adulteration.

Thankfully, a few years after dealing with this complex inquiry, Professor Elliott somehow had the energy to be involved in a research trial at Queen's University Belfast in which mice were fed a diet of processed meat containing nitro-preservatives.[22] The result? The mice 'developed 75% more cancerous tumours in the duodenum'—the small intestine just beyond the stomach—'than the mice fed nitrite-free pork', reported *The Guardian*.

'The European Food Safety Authority and the French government are following the facts,' Elliott said. 'It's time the UK government did too.'

And what alarmed me to read about Elliott's study the most was that the team also found lab mice which were fed pork containing nitrites developed 82 per cent more tumours within the colon than the control group.

And here was a further finding that strongly added weight to previous reports. Dr Brian Green, one of the authors of the study, said eating processed meats when you actually have cancer could make it even worse. 'The results from our study clearly show that not all processed meats carry the same risk of cancer and that the consumption of nitrite-containing processed meat exacerbates the development of cancerous tumours.'[23]

I started to feel even more angry about that ham sandwich I had been presented with after my second liver surgery. Processed meat, in the form of hams, bacon and hot dogs, are served to patients in hospitals all over Australia and indeed the world.

Journalists in the UK clearly felt the same. *The Guardian*'s health policy editor Denis Campbell authored multiple reports on the nitrites issue from London, including a hard-hitting article about the inclusion of processed meats in meals in UK hospitals. In July 2023 he reported that 61 NHS trusts (out of a total of 141) in England had admitted to serving meat in their hospitals that may contain nitrates or nitrites, despite 'growing evidence internationally implicating them in the development of cancer'. Two of the 61 trusts mentioned are responsible for two of the best-known hospitals for cancer treatment in the UK: the Christie in Manchester and the Royal Marsden in London.[24]

I suddenly remembered that the Royal Marsden was the hospital where one of the most inspiring members of my stage-four bowel cancer community—Dame Deborah James, better known on her widely followed social media accounts as 'Bowelbabe'—had been treated for many years. Had she been fed processed meats while she was a patient too?

On a positive note, some British meat producers now make nitrite-free bacon options, including M&S, Waitrose and Better Naked. It's a new trend that is far more established in the UK than in Australia.

As for the final decision of the European Commission, there was a partial win in October 2023 for the campaigners, including Professor Corpet and his fellow scientists, plus the growing gang of concerned MPs and food-safety advocates. The EU didn't declare a total ban on nitro-preservatives in meat, as the campaigners would have liked, but instead introduced stricter limits on them. These limits were endorsed by EU member states—except the UK, of course, which set sail from the EU in 2020—and aimed to cover the diverse range of products and manufacturing methods across Europe. Food businesses have two years to adapt to the new rules.

Stella Kyriakides, the current European Commissioner for Health and Food Safety, said the decision formed part of Europe's Beating Cancer Plan, which was announced in 2021. 'I now call on the food industry to swiftly implement these science-based rules, and wherever possible, to reduce [nitro-preservatives] further to protect the health of citizens.'[25]

All this was incredibly inspiring and heartening. The humble, softly spoken Professor Corpet had helped spark this fightback. And, most importantly of all, Chantal Dupuy's tragic death had not been in vain. Far from it. Her passing was at the core of this entire uprising, and this movement will forever serve as her lasting legacy.

Overlooked and overruled

Amid my pleasure at discovering these campaigns and subsequent changes in Europe, I was also uncovering some distressing history. I found the precise historical moment in which the meat industry became a ruthless, bullying power-player—a player that cared little for people's health. And nitro-preservatives were at the heart of it.

In the later decades of the nineteenth century, there was a buildup of brooding disquiet in the US about what the meat-packers—the US term for the companies that slaughter, process and distribute meat—were using to preserve their products. This industry in the land of broad stripes and bright stars would later influence laws in other countries, including Australia, about the pervasive use of nitro-preservatives. Concerned groups in America formed the 'Pure Food Movement', which was spearheaded by medical doctor and chemist Dr Harvey Wiley. Wiley ran the Bureau of Chemistry at the United States Department of Agriculture and was the driving force in campaigning for US food laws that limited the use of dangerous additives.

At first, Wiley hadn't expressed much concern for the then widespread use of saltpetre, also known as potassium nitrite, which by that time had been used to preserve meat for centuries. However, after scientists in Germany began to express deep concern, US Congress asked the Department of Agriculture to 'investigate the character of food preservatives, coloring matters, and other substances added to foods, to determine their relation to digestion and to health, and to establish the principles which should guide their use'.[26]

Wiley's team at the Bureau of Chemistry was commissioned to run what was effectively a clinical trial, though one devoid of the ethics and rules that are in force today. Author Deborah Blum, in her 2018 book about Wiley called *The Poison Squad*, describes in detail how a group of 'human guinea pigs', in the form of a rotating group of young 'robust' men, were given three free meals per day and a regular amount of potentially toxic and damaging food additives—including saltpetre—to see the effects on the body. This kind of research is simply not allowed by today's standards.[27]

The brave men, many of whom fell ill during the research, thankfully recovered (bar one who died later with the link never proven) but the results of the risky tests, which led to Wiley telling a hearing of the US House of Representatives that the observations from his experiments, including sickness and headaches, made him highly concerned and converted him to believing in the possible dangers of certain food preservatives. As a result, when the new standards for meat preserving were published in 1903 and 1904, they did not permit the use of saltpetre.

Unsurprisingly, the meat-packing industry in America had a collective meltdown and demanded that its use be reinstated, fearing consumers would not buy meats without the characteristic red or pink colour that saltpetre had created. 'Some inspectors might think that the very small quantity of saltpetre we use is deleterious, and yet in the small quantity in which it is used it is all right,' a leading figure in the meat-packing industry told the House of Representatives in 1906.[28]

And so it went on. Wiley came up with more concerns from his research. The determined meat industry fought back—so much so that 70 meat-packers founded the American Meat Packers Association to protect their interests. Under intense pressure, the US Government eventually backed down and decided to publish new regulations. Which, yes, you guessed it, meant saltpetre was permitted once more.

Around seventeen years later, in 1925, the US Government then gave the industry the green light to use a new, cheap and even more active product—sodium nitrite, in the form of 'nitrited curing salt'. According to author Guillaume Coudray in his book *Who Poisoned Your Bacon Sandwich?*, health experts were appalled, saying the product should be looked upon with 'suspicion'.

'With one voice, the meatpackers and the chemists at the Bureau of Animal Industry responded that the nitrite levels in nitrite-treated products were acceptable because they were no higher than in products treated with nitrate [saltpetre],' Coudray writes. 'Consequently they couldn't be more harmful ... So why ban them?'

While some countries stood firm in banning sodium nitrites in meat—including all of Europe except Austria—its illegal use became widespread in the following decades, causing all sorts of poisonings along the way. Meat-industry figures frequently complained that US companies had an unfair competitive advantage, especially in the way the stronger sodium nitrite allowed processed meats to better withstand the journey across the Atlantic to be sold in Europe.

How does all this American backstory affect processed-meat consumption here in Australia and around the world? Well, the US was as influential then as it is today, and finally, in 1964, with the founding of the European Common Market, sodium nitrite was allowed to be used in meats processed by European member states. Other countries such as Australia and New Zealand followed suit. It was a triumph of what was known at the time as 'the chemical method' or 'the American cure'. It was also a triumph of utter absurdity; the world knew the dangers so very long ago, banned them, then unbanned them—and then everyone just seemed to forget there had ever been a problem.

As discussed earlier, FSANZ permits the addition of nitrites and nitrates to a range of food products, including processed meats and cheeses, at limited levels. At the time of writing, these levels are not under any threat of being changed. 'Australian consumers should be reassured that exposures to nitrates and nitrites in foods are not considered to represent an appreciable health and safety risk,' FSANZ's website declares.[29]

But what if Australian consumers knew in detail what I now know about these nitro-preservatives? I asked myself. What if they knew the full history of the many health concerns about their use, let alone what was unfolding in England and France? What if they hadn't seen the headlines about the new EU rules for the nitrite levels in the EU meat industry?

That's where annoying little wasps called journalists come in. We don't always get good press. But we do serve an old-fashioned and important purpose when it comes to challenging authority and holding the powerful to account. My purpose on this issue was getting more clear-cut by the day.

It had been vital speaking to Professor Corpet, a welcome new comrade, new friend and regular correspondent. He wrote in the same tone as he spoke, with a wry smile and a jolly sense of humour, and understood where my inner drive was coming from considering my ongoing arduous cancer journey.

While friends and family seemed a little bemused at why I was researching an entire book on processed meat, Professor Corpet was supportive and understanding. I appreciated it hugely. 'I understand why you are so motivated, maybe angry, to reduce the toll of this horrible cancer in your country,' he said in one exchange, encouraging me to keep moving forward. 'You really went through a kind of death, and I am happy you survived!'

He also shared a French proverb: *Petit à petit l'oiseau fait son nid*. 'Little by little, a bird builds her nest.' He knew firsthand how exhausting this sort of in-depth investigation was—and that's without cancer treatment in the mix—and he gave me the boost I needed.

I had to keep flying, even if my project was continually halted and delayed by my various cancer treatments. My heart sank every time I had to email my very patient publisher Elizabeth Weiss, informing her I would have to extend the deadline for the manuscript. Again.

She totally understood, of course, and knew I needed to keep stopping to have aggressive treatment, when needed, to survive. And so I could hopefully—eventually—be cured and still carry out my most important roles: being a wife, mother, daughter, sister and friend. But I think she also could tell I wanted to get through the treatments so I could complete this book, which seemed more and more important by the day.

I kept asking myself the same question, over and over. *How can anyone seriously know for absolute certain that even just a tiny bit of these nitro-preservative poisons in our processed meat is okay?* After all, as the British investigative food journalist Joanna Blythman states in her book *Swallow This*, 'no-one really knows how much of a carcinogen it takes to cause cancer, or how much of a toxin it takes to poison your nervous system'.[30]

I knew the wise professor was right; like a bird, I had plenty more twigs to gather. But the impressive early changes over in Europe reassured me I was definitely building my nest in the right tree.

PROCESSED

My next task soon dawned on me. It was time. The Australian public needed to know exactly how common nitro-preservatives were in the processed-meat products in our own supermarkets and popular fast-food restaurants.

I didn't have wings. In fact, I'd lost quite a lot of internal organs in my advanced bowel cancer-related operations; half my liver, my gallbladder, my entire womb, a third of my bladder and 25 centimetres of my large colon were gone. I would soon even be approved to go on a waiting list in Melbourne for a liver transplant.

But that didn't matter. I still had all that I needed: two feet and a heartbeat.

PART TWO

Chapter Four
CLUB BILLIONAIRE

> The inescapable fact is that certain people are making an awful lot of money today selling foods that are unhealthy . . . They do not want you informed, active, and passionately alive, and they are quite willing to spend billions of dollars annually to accomplish their goals.[1]
>
> John Robbins, author and food activist, 2006

For what it's worth

And so it came to pass that bemused customers of our three leading supermarket chains—Woolworths, Coles and Aldi—plus the wholesalers Costco, witnessed a blonde mother in black runners and a puffer jacket photographing various processed-meat products in the fridges and freezers. It must have been a baffling sight.

In those first few hours of snooping around the shelves, I had no idea of the trouble I'd end up causing, and the headaches I'd probably induce, for the executives at various billion-dollar meat companies and their media advisers.

Stand by, folks. This chapter gets as juicy as those slices of picnic salami sweating on the beach in the scorching Australian summer sun.

My first stop was Woolworths, affectionately known as Woolies—a supermarket giant that, according to its last published annual report, made more than $1.62 billion in profits in 2023.²

I decided to focus on some of the most popular family favourites among the processed meats in each store. In the newly styled refrigerated area of the Highett Woolworths in south-east Melbourne, I started by reaching for Woolworths' own brand of short cut bacon.

For $4.50, I could buy 200 grams of 'gluten free' bacon with 'no artificial colours or flavours', according to the package. Top marks for effort; the marketing department had managed to make bacon sound almost healthy. But I then saw what also comes inside this wrapped package of salted pork: 'Preservative (250)'. Yes, here it was—the e-number for sodium nitrite. Just like the packaging, this ingredients list was, though legally legitimate, only partly transparent about the contents.

I soon found out that this same nitro-additive was in nearly all the processed-meat family favourites at Woolies alongside the bacon, including slices of leg ham, champagne ham, mild Hungarian salami, frankfurts, smoked ham off the bone and tinned processed meats. Plus I found it in items such as quiche and pizzas that were topped with processed-meat products. In fact, preservative 250 was in nearly all the pork-based processed-meat products on the shelves. The exceptions were fresh-meat sausages, and two small ranges of 'nitrite-free' ham and bacon. One was produced by Australian meat company D'Orsogna and marketed as the 'Natural' range, which contained 'No artificial Nitrite', which I found confusing considering the rest of their huge range contains nitro-preservatives.

If they think there is a problem which could impact the health of their customers then why still use it in their other products?

Not that organic nitrates could really, truly make them risk-free anyway, for, as we know, this is where the major fault-line lurks with trying to make processed meats 'healthy'.

In the wise words of Kana Wu, a senior research scientist in the Department of Nutrition at Harvard T.H. Chan School of Public Health, 'it is best to treat those nitrite-free processed meats the same as any other processed meats'.[3]

And of course processed meats containing red meats such as pork and beef also contain heme iron, which can potentially enhance the formation of carcinogenic N-nitroso compounds in the body.

As I was carefully checking the ingredient labels on all the processed-meat products in the store, something caught my eye. Something heart-shaped, colourful and decorated with canine cartoon characters from the popular kids' cartoon show *Paw Patrol*.

I bent down to the bottom of the fridge and saw rows of some of the most hideously child-marketed snacks I've ever seen.

PROCESSED

Except these weren't designed like other lunch-style snack packages; the way they were presented by Primo Foods made it clear they were designed for toddlers, perhaps to take as morning tea to preschool or to eat during an outing.

The red-coloured package contained a couple of chunks of pale pink salami meat, a few cubes of cheese and some small chocolate-chip cookies. The label on the blue package said, 'Leg ham, tasty cheese & choc chip cookies', while the label on the yellow package said 'Chicken breast, tasty cheese and choc chip cookies'.

All the contents were the ideal size for really tiny fingers. And tiny mouths. And tiny stomachs.

And, worst of all, when I looked at the ingredients, there were those familiar, depressing words—'Preservative (250)'—on the red and blue packages, which contained the pork-based preserved products.

Not that the 'chicken breast' was actually pure chicken breast—yet another misleading trick the food industry likes to use. Do you know what goes into these little pieces of 'chicken'? The chicken 'breast' (bits of breast from a large number of chickens) is mixed into a sloppy cake-style batter of water, modified starch, acidity regulators, salt, sugar, soy protein, mineral salt, vegetable gum, natural flavours and preservative (sulphites). But do you know how Woolworths describes it in their online store? 'A delicious mix of diced chicken breast, cheese and choc chip cookies featuring your favorite *Paw Patrol* character on top.'[4]

So, let's be blunt here and state the facts as clearly and fairly as possible, based on the evidence at the time of writing this book. Australia's leading supermarket, Woolworths, which makes billions every decade in profits from hardworking parents of this nation who buy their weekly groceries from its stores, is selling manipulatively marketed, toddler-directed Primo products that contain sodium nitrite—and all sorts of other additives, stabilisers and salts.

'For fuck's sake,' I whispered as I held these heart-shaped packages in my hands, coming close to putting them all in the nearest bin.

I realised in that moment how literally *nobody* in the Australian food production and selling chain, which had led to these hideous products being on display, cared about the consumers, or their dietary habits, or their health. And in this case, the consumers were without doubt going to be toddlers or young children sitting on a mat at a local preschool during snack time.

In fact, not only did nobody care, but the meat industry was trying to get children to develop an addictive chain reaction, a lifelong love of the salty, springy sensation of their 'ham' nice and early, so as they went to primary school and high school they would hopefully ask for the other Primo lunch box offerings, such as 'Mild twiggy bites & cheddar cheese'. It was depressing and enraging all at once.

Later that day, I checked Primo's Facebook page, which has 76,000 followers, and one of the most recent posts included a competition, in conjunction with children's pay-TV channel

Nickelodeon, to win a kid's movie ticket, with 1000 of them 'up for grabs', or a family holiday to Sea World. The catch? 'Head to any Woolworths cheese aisle (or Woolworths online) and get your paws on one of these packs of Primo Mini Mix Ups.' Included in the promotion was a picture of the line-up of their *Paw Patrol* packs.[5]

But then, later, I spotted a couple of items on the Woolworths website that I hadn't seen stocked in the store I visited: two more heart-shaped packs in this jaunty range of nightmares that was literally targeting baby consumers. Yes, *babies*. Instead of *Paw Patrol*, the theme was 'Pinkfong Baby Shark', the animated children's series that originated in Korea but is now produced by Nickelodeon.

The first pack, which contained 'Reduced sodium ham, tasty cheese & sultanas', featured a large, yellow cartoon shark, seemingly to represent either a mummy shark or a daddy shark, along with a smaller pink shark leaping from the water. The second pack had the same design except the baby shark was blue.

So far, so gender stereotyped. But that aside, I started to seriously wonder how the senior executives at Primo slept at night.

On the labels of the packs of 'food' for their youngest consumer targets are words that I believe are clear and transparent manipulations of the parents or carers buying these products. It hints that the Baby Shark offerings are somehow more appropriate than the *Paw Patrol* range for very young children. More gentle. More baby-friendly. Healthier. The right choice for tiny little bambinos. *Your* bambinos. The future adults of this nation.

And just to really make sure they win the hearts and money of Australia's parents, Primo adds in bold text on the bottom part of the blue-baby-shark twiggy-sticks label: 'No artificial colours or flavours. Low in sugar.' On the pink-baby-shark ham pack, they state: 'No artificial colours & flavours. Source of protein.'

Those statements may well be true. But they are a manipulative distraction from the ultra-processed mishmash of ingredients, which includes the omnipresent nitro-preservative—which is *artificial*. It's the one simply listed as 'Preservative (250)', as is so often the case. On the ham pack, we have these ingredients:

Sultanas [Seedless Sultanas, Vegetable Oil], Cheese [Milk, Salt, Starter Cultures, Enzyme (Non-Animal Rennet), Anti-caking Agent (460), Preservative (200)], Reduced Sodium Ham [Pork, Acidity Regulators (326, 262), Water, Cure [Mineral Salts (508, 451, 450), Salt, Sugar, Antioxidant (316), **Preservative (250)**, Natural Flavour], Vegetable Gum (407)].

Thankfully, my rising anger fuelled the energy I needed to keep on wading into the deepening muddy waters of these highly questionable marketing tactics—and revealing the billion-dollar companies at the very top of this 'food' quagmire. I hadn't expected to be pushing out so far, but this challenge had my name on it.

First, I decided to read the latest annual report to be made public by Woolworths. Woolworths Supermarkets, owned by Woolworths Group, is Australia's largest supermarket chain, operating around 1000 stores across the country. Over in

New Zealand, the stores operate under the Countdown brand, with nearly 200 full-service stores. The 2023 report didn't dwell much on healthier choices or products, but it did focus on its increased sales revenues and future expansion.[6]

'In 2024, we celebrate our centenary,' CEO Brad Banducci wrote. 'As we reflect on the first 100 years, and look forward to the next chapter, we are united and galvanised by our shared purpose of building a better tomorrow.'

It would be interesting to know how much popular processed meats directed at children's lunch boxes contribute to Woolworths' annual bonanza of share dividends. It's a bonanza that you can bet your bottom dollar their stakeholders won't want any tiny fingers—or large ones—to take away.

Inspired by my new plucky comrade and friend Professor Corpet and his hard-hitting letter to European leaders, I decided to write a little letter of my own—and a strongly worded one at that. Yes, it was time to send some questions to Woolies, whose well-known slogan is, ironically, 'The Fresh Food People'.

After introducing myself and the nature of this book, and informing them that I had proof that their stores stocked many processed-meat products that contain nitrate/nitrite preservatives 250 and 251, I posed the following questions:

1. As it stands The Food Standards Code (of Food Standards Australia New Zealand) requires advisory statements/warnings on certain products. The advisory statements required by the Code currently do not include processed-meat products. However,

as a business do you feel you are operating with full integrity and with a duty of care to your customers in regard to processed meat considering the damning evidence about their health impacts?
2. Out of brand integrity and care for your customers do you have any plans to introduce or lobby for warning labels (regarding their link to cancer in particular) to be added to these products as a duty of care to your consumers?
3. Do you feel your customers should have the right to know about these harmful links with full transparency in regard to your processed-meat products?
4. Some shops and brands have started promoting and selling nitrate-free meat products. You only stock two small ranges of nitro-preservative-free ham and bacon. Do you have any plans to expand this choice?
5. Any further comments on this matter.

I waited with bated breath to a response to my bold demands. Would they address the issue? Or at least hint at a review? Would they take ownership of the products in their stores, even if they weren't the actual producers of the products? Yes, okay, I'm something of a daydreaming optimist, always hoping people, even large companies, will do the right thing.

After a notable delay, a spokeswoman came back to me, in October 2023, with a single sentence that read:

Thank you for the opportunity to contribute, however FSANZ [Food Standards Australia New Zealand] would be best placed to respond to these questions as the Australian authority on food safety.

Yes, we know the attitude of FSANZ to nitro-preservatives already from their website, thanks. They think it's all hunky-dory.

So there you have it. Our biggest and most profitable supermarket chain is passing the buck, not wishing to even engage in a discussion on the issue. It wasn't a surprise. But it was revealing. This nitrite issue was clearly a touchy subject for our supermarkets.

Anyway, it was time to move on. I had some more secret shelf-snooping to do.

Thirty-two million reasons

With a sense of foreboding, I then made my way to Coles at Southland Westfield in nearby Cheltenham. It's one of their enormous flagship stores and was completely refitted several years ago.

Founded in 1914, there are more than 800 supermarkets throughout Australia employing over 120,000 people. Its large head office site in Melbourne's inner south-east has 4000 of those employees inside. They include much sought-after British executives from leading UK supermarket giants such as Tesco, which know a thing or two about selling to the masses.

After I strolled over to the long rows of fridges at the Southland store and began reading ingredient labels, it soon became clear that nearly all the bacon, ham and salami products, as far as I could see, contained sodium nitrite. Even the large Christmas hams on sale amid the tinsel and the jolly Christmas tunes echoing through the store had the words 'Preservative (250)' on their labels. I knew that my publisher, Elizabeth, had been wondering about this, having mentioned it was one of her favourite items on her family's table every Christmas. I really didn't want to be the one to spoil her Yuletide menu plans, but there it was, clear as a bell, printed on the label.

Naturally, I was on high alert for any heart-shaped items bearing the Primo branding. And there they were, placed in an arrangement similar to the display in Woolworths. The fridge was laid out like a school complex—the jaunty *Paw Patrol* packs aimed at preschoolers at the bottom, rising up to the brightly coloured, rectangular Primo packs of various salamis and ham for primary-school-aged kids, packaged with tasty cheese and/or crackers—either Shapes or Jatz.

The top row hosted offerings for the more mature gourmet, ideal for adults of course but also any high-school kids wanting to feel more grown up, leaving the 'younger' products behind for their siblings. For them, it wasn't salami bites, tasty cheese, choc chip cookies and cartoons. Oh no. They could have Coles' own brand 'Tasty cheese with chorizo bites & pretzels'—or, wait for it, even 'Tasty cheese with salami & Lavosh crackers'. Just the word 'Lavosh' has a sophisticated, glamorous ring to it, don't you think?

This didn't just feel like a school layout in order of age. It felt like the processed-meat version of the first, second and third classes of the *Titanic*. And we all know how that ended.

PROCESSED

While Coles' own brand, and meat brand Bertocchi, were part of this lunch box horror story, offering a few versions of these products, Primo was the producer of the majority of the packs targeted at younger children, most notably the heart-shaped snacks of doom.

And it's not just my concerns around nitro-preservatives that fuel my belief that these salty, fatty foods should be in the sin bin. They may contribute to a range of health risks, including childhood obesity, which is associated with a range of health conditions. According to the WHO, 39 million children under the age of five were categorised as overweight or obese in 2020. And in 2016, more than 340 million children and adolescents aged five to nineteen were categorised as overweight or obese.[7]

As dietician and nutritionist Jemma O'Hanlon explained to me, children need to develop healthy eating habits at a young age. 'We need to move away from introducing unhealthy habits to our kids in order to shift the way we eat as a community,' she told me. 'Having salami and pepperoni sticks in lunch boxes encourages a liking for foods high in saturated fat and salt. We need to focus on getting plenty of fruit and veggies into the lunch box, and whole foods like yoghurt and cheese.'[8]

With Jemma's words echoing in my mind, I decided to investigate the ownership structure of Primo Foods—and I'm afraid this is where those smiling canine cartoon characters really got under my skin.

The Primo story ended up big but began small in a Sydney butcher shop operated by Hungarian migrant Andrew Lederer in 1957. It wasn't long until he became one of the leading sellers of continental products such as smoked hams and salamis.

Today, Primo is enormous. It owns its own abattoirs, manufacturing plants, packing facilities and distribution centres, and, according to the company website, is 'Australia's largest manufacturer of ham, bacon, salami and deli meats, supplying smallgoods to major retail groups across Australia'—except it's no longer an Australian company.

It's now part of JBS Australia, which in turn is part of Brazilian multinational JBS S.A., which owns over 500 industrial plants and commercial locations in an astonishing 24 countries.[9] Primo was acquired in 2014 for US$1.23 billion (A$1.3 billion). Commentators said at the time that the Primo acquisition appeared to be an important strategic move by JBS Australia into pork, given the strong demand in China and Vietnam and other Asian markets, with strong traditions of pork consumption.

The problem with this new association with the South American meat giant is the two infamous and wealthy brothers, Joesley and Wesley Batista, who own the entire conglomerate. They've been in a spot of bother over the years, you see. Let's call them the Billionaire Brothers.

I'd already done quite a lot of research into these meat-hungry siblings, and was starting to wonder if they had ever considered the health of their Australian consumers, when the ABC's *Four Corners* ran a report in 2022 called 'The Butchers from Brazil'. It echoed what I had read about how the brothers had bought up substantial parts of the Australian meat industry, amid allegations of substantial bribes and corruption in their home country.

The program charted the massive rise of the family empire, which had begun in the 1950s like so many of these meat companies begin: as a small butchery, in regional Brazil, overseen by businessman José Batista Sobrinho.

When Sobrinho's sons Joesley and Wesley—the Billionaire Brothers—took the reins, the business expanded throughout Brazil and South America. Then came the move that made the brothers international players: in 2007, JBS paid US$1.4 billion (A$1.8 billion) to take over US beef processor Swift. That meant that JBS now had control over Australia's biggest beef processor, Australian Meat Holdings, which was a subsidiary of Swift.

JBS then turned its attention to the meat business Down Under. 'The following year, JBS paid US$150 million [A$166 million] for Tasman Group, which owned abattoirs in Tasmania and Victoria plus a feedlot in NSW,' explained the ABC in its *Four Corners* companion article.[10]

Suddenly, JBS had sites in many locations in Australia, yet the brothers soon faced allegations of corruption and insider trading in Brazil, including allegations of payments to senior politicians.

'The supremely well-connected Joesley Batista had orchestrated the company's global acquisition spree, buying up competitors while expanding its supply chain,' the ABC reported.

Coles, Woolworths, IGA and many other Australian chains, plus service stations, all stock the company's processed-meat products—all ultimately owned by the Billionaire Brothers.

Despite the scandals in their homeland, it was announced in January 2022 that the Brazilian meat company had a deal to buy Rivalea, Australia's top pork-processing company.[11] Farmers opposed the buy-out, worried by a loss of competition, but it was still approved by the Australian Competition and Consumer Commission and the Foreign Investment Review Board.

The deal means these controversial brothers now have total control of three of the four export pork abattoirs in southern Australia. They also bought 100 per cent of Rivalea Holdings Pty Ltd which owns two subsidiaries incorporated in Australia, Rivalea (Australia) Pty Ltd and Diamond Valley Pork Pty Ltd (majority shareholding).

By 2021, the company had also bought one of the largest producers of farmed salmon, Huon Aquaculture, for A$425 million. Despite the corruption scandal faced by the brothers they were found not guilty of insider trading in October 2023 and were returned to the board of directors of JBS S.A. in April 2024.[12]

After taking all this in, I felt it was time to fire off another little note, this time to the person in charge of media at Primo Foods. And, quite suitably for a supersized meat company, I didn't mince my words.

People say that you should never write an email when you're angry ... but it was too late for that. My comrade Professor Corpet had sent a gust of motivation from France, which had set off a monster cyclone in the Southern Hemisphere.

After spelling out the scientific links between cancer and processed meats, particularly as a result of nitro-preservatives, I posed the following questions to Primo, making sure I included a mention of their bosses, JBS Australia—and the Billionaire Brothers.

PROCESSED

1. Woolworths and Coles (and others) currently stock a large number of Primo Foods products marketed towards very young children, in particular the *Paw Patrol* snacks in heart shapes and bright colours.

    The ham and salami versions both contain nitrites. Can you understand growing concerns regarding Primo Foods creating child-centric marketed products, including the stackers range, for very young Australians with this sort of highly processed package, especially considering the nitrites inside the meats? Would Primo Foods like to comment on this considering you are the largest producer of ham, bacon and smallgoods in the Southern Hemisphere with a huge influence on daily diets of Australian children?

2. Does Primo Foods—now part of JBS Australia after JBS Brazil acquired the business in 2014 for 1.23 billion US dollars—consider the future health of Australian children when creating new child-centric products, considering it is a widely accepted fact by health experts that lifetime dietary habits can be formed at a very young age?

3. Can you explain the process of the background of the development of the *Paw Patrol* products in particular to help me understand whether it came as a direction/product idea from JBS Brazil or was created and developed by Primo Foods in Australia?

4. Does your senior team at Primo Foods and JBS Australia believe that their ultimate bosses, the

> Batista owners of JBS, who own multiple meat companies in multiple countries all over the world, are fully motivated and mindful of the future health of Australian toddlers and children? Is this something they have ever discussed together and do they intend to make any changes to any processed-meat products to help keep Australian toddlers and children healthy in light of the growing concerns regarding processed meat and also nitro-preservatives?

During my career, I've often had to 'speak truth to power' and have taken on some powerful organisations and individuals in pursuit of the truth. On this matter, it seemed more important than ever. So I was pleased I'd said my piece to Primo and spoken plainly to Australia's biggest processed-meat company. That's what journalists should do. We should speak up for those without a voice, and aim to be truthful, not neutral.

Even if Primo, whose catchline is 'There's good. There's great. And then there is Primo', decided to totally ignore my questions, they would at least have to read my email. I was sure about that. I felt pleased that I might have planted a seed and pointed out what I'd learned. I could only hope that it might one day make a difference.

But something still didn't feel quite right. I also felt angered that the promotion on the Primo *Paw Patrol* and Baby Shark packs were being done in conjunction with Nickelodeon, the highly profitable American TV channel that launched in 1979.

It made history, at the time, for being the first cable channel for children. In Australia the channel is now run by Channel Ten and in New Zealand on Sky. It's ultimately owned by Paramount Global, which operates more than 170 networks and reaches approximately 700 million people in 180 countries.

It turns out Nickelodeon often joins forces with major food companies, such as McDonald's and other popular brands, for cosy little campaigns that serve their interests of target branding, increased sales and higher profits. Do you think they give a hoot that some of the products they help promote contain processed meats and nitro-preservatives? Are their executives ever aware of the precise ingredients anyway?

More pertinently, does the CEO of Paramount Global, who at the time of writing is a chap called Bob Bakish, spare much thought for just one of the promotions of just one of the company's global businesses? Does he consider the impact promotional relationships with processed-meat companies such as Primo might have on the future eating habits and health of Australian children?

In light of the fact this senior leader brings animation to the world's children, let's just call him Cartoon Bob. I may be Hampshire-born but I'm a true passport-carrying Aussie these days. I just love a nickname.

When Paramount Global announced its quarterly earning results in October 2023, Cartoon Bob included a statement focused on 'strategy' and remaining 'on the path to achieving significant total company earnings growth in 2024'. In other words, his focus is expansion and profit.

I looked up what sort of salary this top tomcat was on. It's clear things have been rather lucrative for the CEO of late. In fact, he's had a pay rise—which is better described as a humongous windfall, with as many digits as a telephone number. Cartoon Bob's 'compensation', as the business world calls it, went up to just under US$32 million in 2022, up from $20 million the year before. According to a statement by the company in March this year, that 2022 bonanza included a base salary of $3.1 million, stock awards of $15.9 million, and 'non-equity incentive plan compensation' (which is similar to a cash bonus) of $12.9 million.[13]

In the statement, the board noted that its CEO had 'improved operational efficiencies' in Paramount's businesses, 'prudently managed costs', and worked to develop 'a high-performing workforce, foster an inclusive workplace, and continue supporting the diverse communities and audiences' of Paramount's operations.[14]

So, to be fair, Cartoon Bob may not be aware of some little Primo/Nickelodeon campaign in far-off Australia that is encouraging parents to buy processed meat containing nitrites for their young children. I certainly am not suggesting he is knowingly promoting a food which has health risks. And I accept that Paramount Global is huge, as is the scope of his role. But you see my point. Everyone in the chain has a boss to impress. Everyone in the chain has to drive sales so they can keep their jobs, get their bonuses, pay their mortgages. And the powerful chap right at the top of this chain is so far removed from the detail lower down that he might not be aware of every single endorsed product or joint commercial venture.

Well, that was until I decided to write Cartoon Bob a letter.

Once again, Professor Corpet had inspired me to be brave and go straight to the top, just like he had done. And why not? I had nothing to lose and I didn't have time for minions. I like to think I was polite but to the point. And no, I didn't use his new nickname. That's just between us.

Luckily for him, the letter wasn't 32 million words long—but it could have been.

After introducing myself and this project to his representatives, I wrote the following.

> I'm writing to request a comment from the CEO of Paramount, Bob Bakish, regarding a range of Nickelodeon-backed children's snack packs being sold in major supermarkets in Australia, including Woolworths, aimed at preschool children and their parents, which I will be mentioning in my book. I will also be mentioning Mr Bakish and stating his role in the company.
>
> The products are being marketed in conjunction with Australian meat company Primo Foods, which is a brand of JBS Australia, which is in turn a subsidiary of Brazilian global meat giant JBS, wholly owned by brothers Joesley Batista and Wesley Batista.
>
> I have the following questions for Mr Bakish.
> 1. Are you aware that in 2015 the World Health Organization classed processed meats as a 'Group 1' carcinogenic? They stated that processed meats, such as ham, pepperoni, bacon, hot dogs, etc., are one of

the definite causes of bowel/colorectal cancer? With this in mind, what is your view about one of your businesses, Nickelodeon, working with processed-meat companies to promote child-targeted snacks?

2. The EU recently announced new targets for the meat industry to reduce the amount of nitro-preservatives in food. This followed a campaign by leading scientists, doctors and MPs, including Professor Chris Elliott OBE, Director of the Institute for Global Food Safety, who said in December 2022: 'The everyday consumption of nitrite-containing bacon and ham poses a very real risk to public health.' What is Paramount's view about working with processed-meat companies who use nitro-additives in their products?

3. In particular, the Nickelodeon brand is being used as a joint venture with Australian meat company Primo for their three heart-shaped processed-meat snacks, which include dogs from the popular *Paw Patrol* show aimed at preschoolers and younger.

Not only are these packs ultra-processed but the ingredients on the label of two out of three of these products include the chemical preservative 250—sodium nitrite. While the levels of this substance may well be 'safe' in the eyes of Australian food standard laws, what concerns me as a bowel cancer patient is that your company is promoting this food on a backdrop of mounting scientific evidence that they can cause cancer and other health impacts.

109

What is your response to this as the ultimate boss of the entire chain of all your global companies? I accept all the senior staff in those companies have their own roles and responsibilities regarding commercial relationships etc., but they all are ultimately answerable to your leadership. Therefore does the health of Australian children—who are also your viewers and effectively helping drive profits for your global billion-dollar business—concern you? Will you be mounting an investigation into this campaign with Primo?

4. What processes are in place at either Paramount or Nickelodeon to ensure any promotions you do jointly with food brands are in the best interests of children—your consumers/viewers—in particular?

5. I was particularly concerned that Nickelodeon was backing these products—and also a recent promotional competition campaign in Australia on social media channels—considering there are also two Primo products which are clearly aimed at children even younger than preschool age. They are based on Nickelodeon's popular Pinkfong Baby Shark cartoon series. Considering it's accepted by experts that diets in early childhood often form lifelong habits, do you feel this is an appropriate snack pack to be associated with as a global company?

6. Are you aware that the ultimate owners of Primo, the Batista brothers, who own global meat giant JBS Brazil, have in the past faced insider-trading allegations?

7. Are you personally willing to investigate establishing new guidelines at Nickelodeon Australia (and globally), a brand which as you know is highly influential in terms of its cultural reach, popularity and impact on children, to cease working with Primo/JBS/Batista Brothers and other processed-meat companies for the sake of the future health and wellbeing of children all over the world?
8. Do you agree with my opinion that if you, holding the influential position as CEO of Paramount Global, were to make it known you were making this new policy then it would raise awareness of the potential dangers of processed meats and therefore possibly help to reduce the consumption of these foods globally? Therefore potentially helping the future health of your young Nickelodeon customers/viewers, who will naturally go to Australian supermarkets with their parents and would quite likely ask them to buy the Primo snack packs, containing sodium nitrite, with their favourite characters from *Paw Patrol* and Pinkfong Baby Shark?
9. Any other comments on this matter.

Many thanks for your time.
Best wishes
Lucie Morris-Marr

When I wrote the email, it felt like I'd just reached the peak of a mountain I'd slowly been climbing since my diagnosis, when

I'd first started reading about processed meats and cancer. All the research I'd done on the science and the industry links had prepared me for this moment. All the treatment I had undergone to stay alive to send this email felt worth it. Even getting in touch with the inspiring French professor had helped me reach this height, with enough oxygen in the tank.

It felt like it was meant to be: combining the experience of my illness with my decades of journalistic experience to throw a whopping great tantrum for toddlers at the feet of a mega-rich kingpin.

I went to have a lie-down and a strong cup of tea.

Would Cartoon Bob ever respond? It was unlikely. Perhaps these powerful companies and figures feared that if they even accepted a link between their products or promotions and cancer, they would open themselves to mass litigation of the kind that tobacco and fast-food companies have faced in recent years.

Whatever Paramount's reasoning, I felt satisfied that I'd tapped on the shoulder of Cartoon Bob, one of the most powerful men in the world in terms of influence on Australian children—not only in regard to what they watch, but sometimes right down to what they eat. Interestingly, Cartoon Bob resigned from his role as this book was being edited, with Paramount then later merging with Skydance.

One expert I approached, however, suggested that these industry bosses aren't necessarily 'billionaire bad boys' as such. I wasn't feeling sympathy for the powerful Cartoon Bobs or Gilded Georges of the world at this point, but I was prepared to listen.

Dr Tanveer Ahmed, a well-known consultant psychiatrist, journalist and TV presenter based in Sydney, told me he believes there are many decision makers who are not always connected to the potential implications of their decisions. 'They are usually looking at spreadsheets and bottom lines,' Dr Ahmed told me. 'This is partly why other regulations, through government or other bodies, are often critical at making sure these types of things are done in a socially responsible way and incorporate the variety of stakeholders. It may not always be appropriate that a financier, for example, is expected to be on top of all the various implications of their decision making.'[15] The modern world is so complex that it's very difficult for a single human to be on top of all the varieties of systems and implications of their decision making, Dr Ahmed added.

Fair point. And I agree with him that this is why we need a whole range of bodies to work collaboratively. 'This is not necessarily a dark side of the human condition,' he suggested. 'We can only process so much information and generally we can only see clearly what is in front of us. Systems are so complex in the modern world, be [they] social, financial [or] political, it is rare that people act for entirely evil reasons— although self-interest can sometimes have quite harmful implications.'

I understood his point. But if I confronted powerful companies and individuals about the dangers of processed meats, at least they would be aware of the information. The growing movement regarding the concerns about processed meats and their nitro-preservatives just might now be on their radars.

PROCESSED

Trust issues

As I continued to track Australian processed-meat products through to their billion-dollar overseas umbrella companies, complete with mansion-owning executives, I felt a little disheartened and rather alone, as if nobody else was sticking up for the toddlers and their parents who can't be totally blamed for choosing processed meats at the supermarket.

They simply may not be armed with the knowledge about the health risks involved in processed meats. They may also only be able to afford those small packs—the expensive separate cheeses, meats and other items may be out of reach financially. They certainly add up.

Indeed, a pertinent tweet about the cost of such items was reported by the *Daily Mail Australia* in November 2023. 'A Melbourne woman has exposed the grim reality of the cost of living crisis after ingredients for a ham and cheese sandwich cost her an eye-watering $22.80,' read the opening line of the article. On X (formerly Twitter), 'Miss Madeleine' outlined what she had purchased: '$5.40 bread, $9 cheese (250g is $6–7 I got 500g), Don Ham $8.40. And I did get a $2 pack of mixed lettuce.'[16]

Some sympathised with the woman; others scrutinised her purchases. In my view, I agree that these are expensive items to buy individually. But in terms of these child-marketed snack packs, I believe they simply shouldn't be made in the first place.

Professor Corpet agreed, as we continued to chat regularly over email from opposite sides of the world. His support helped me feel like I wasn't the only one feeling so incensed. After all, as we saw within the words of that letter to the two senior politicians, he had made a specific point about children and processed meats. 'I would like to draw your specific attention to cooked ham, which plays such a fundamental role in the diets of children,' he had written in his letter. 'The vast majority of ham contains these cancer-causing chemicals [nitro-preservatives]—and the vast majority of parents are not aware of the risks.'

It was very helpful to remind myself of those rousing words. And it was also helpful to read an excellent book called *Gristle*, edited by US musician and committed vegan Moby and his co-editor Miyun Park. The 2010 book was aimed at the 'growing number of people—from meat eaters to vegetarians—who are thinking twice about the perils of our system of animal processing and factory farms'.[17]

'Starting children out right gives them an early lead on developing enduring, healthy eating habits,' write Sara Kubersky and Tom O'Hagan in a chapter on children's health. 'Most parents probably just don't know any better because, unfortunately, most pediatricians probably don't either.'

For girls in particular, they said, 'healthful and humane' diets are critical for so many specific biological reasons. 'Breast tissue is especially sensitive to cancer triggers in the childhood and teenage years. Earlier puberty and breast development mean more lifetime estrogen exposure, which can mean higher risk of breast cancer later in life.'

The risks of eating a diet with too much meat are clear, yet it seemed to me at the heart of this culinary disaster was a lack of awareness on how easily meats, especially processed meats, can sneak into daily meals.

Dietician Jemma O'Hanlon agreed when she spoke to me. Our eating habits are 'shaped' over the course of our lives, she noted, starting with the foods we eat in childhood. 'Parents play an important role as role models and have a strong influence on the eating patterns of our children,' she said.

It was good speaking to Jemma and it was useful reading *Gristle*. There were indeed many others out there, especially among the vegan movement, who cared deeply about the diets of our children.

I also realised I did actually have one committed comrade close by on the home front. When I was first diagnosed with bowel cancer, my daughter, Talia, was only nine, my son, Nate, eleven. I immediately made sure processed meats were no longer part of their diets. I explained the reasons why and they were generally happy, bar having the odd snag or pepperoni pizza when with other families behind my back, which I didn't admonish them for.

But I hadn't expected my daughter to go to school and loudly warn her classmates, as they nibbled on their pepperoni snack packs and salami wraps on the school oval, that the contents of their lunch boxes could eventually be fatal. 'They could kill you!' she told them. I was mortified when one of the mothers pulled me aside to let me know that my daughter had been scaring the living daylights out of some of the children with her warnings of doom.

Part of me felt like saying, 'Don't shoot the messenger,' but, naturally, I apologised. Young children don't deserve to be scared about what they're eating, especially when meal decisions are out of their control. I'd clearly touched a nerve regarding parents' choice to include processed meats in their kids' lunch boxes. Still, these were *their* food choices and *their* children. I wasn't going to argue with them.

So I had to tell my daughter that while I was proud of her noble attempt to spread the word about our family's newfound negative feelings about processed meats, she perhaps needed to tone down her messaging tactics during school hours.

'So I need to zip it, Mummy?' she asked.

'Yes, darling,' I said, 'but don't worry. I'll do my best to spread the word for us.'

Yet thanks to my sassy mini-me, another seed had been planted, this time one closer to home. And it was down to those parents to google the rest if they so wished.

After all, why *would* these parents think processed meats for their children weren't okay, especially if they just weren't aware of the growing evidence of health risks? They probably trusted the major supermarket brands, having bought them for decades. They might have also trusted that they lived in a country that protects their dietary interests, believing that special federal government bodies like FSANZ will make sure all the products that are presented to them are safe for consumption—and at the very least have warning labels, where needed, so they can make informed choices. Now my children are teens, I've totally lost trust in school canteens in Australia which sell sausage rolls, ham sandwiches and all manner of other processed meats and foods.

Trust was actually a theme in the most recently published Coles annual report in a section written by Leah Weckert, the newly installed Managing Director and Chief Executive Officer, who said, 'With a focus on what matters most to our customers, and prioritising our investment accordingly, I am confident that Coles will deliver on our vision to become the most trusted retailer in Australia.'[18]

She thanked the company's suppliers and customers but her last line went to the most important group of all: 'And finally, to our shareholders, thank you for your continued confidence in Coles.'

So what did Coles say when I sent them the same questions I had sent to Woolworths, regarding their processed meats and products containing nitro-additives like sodium nitrite, you may ask? Well, nothing, as it turned out, and their silence was also telling.

Don't forget that Coles has those all-important shareholders to think about, not to mention its 120,000 employees. They all have a lot at stake; reputation, as well as the billion-dollar profits, is everything in the food industry. It's the same modus operandi the world over.

Not-so-special buys

After checking all the processed meats on sale at my local Aldi store, I discovered a familiar, increasingly depressing, nitro-themed picture. Aldi, the privately owned German discount-supermarket chain that now has over 12,000 stores across nineteen countries, is of course growing rapidly in popularity in Australia. As I write, there are 594 Aldi stores in the country, and the company holds around 10 per cent of the grocery market in Australia.

Aldi, I discovered, offer some of the cheapest processed meats on sale in Australian supermarkets. A pack of eight cocktail frankfurts is just $2 for 500 grams, and in the middle of a cost-of-living crisis I accept that this could provide the basis of a simple meal for a family of four very cheaply. As you know, I'm not judgemental about that.

What I am against is consumers not being fully aware that these products have links to cancer, and products being made with risky ingredients in the first place. All the cured products that I photographed in the store, from the bright-red frankfurts to their Berg range of hams and salamis—a range produced by Don KRC, owned by our English friend Gilded George—contained preservative 250.

So who owns Aldi, anyway? Well, the largest shareholders are various members of the uber-rich Albrecht family. It was the Albrecht family matriarch, Anna, who opened the first store in Essen, Germany, in 1913. In the 1930s, her husband, Karl Albrecht Sr, became unwell and could no longer work, so she had to run the store to support their family.

Anna and Karl Sr's sons, Karl and Theo, took over the business in 1946 when they returned from serving in World War II. Karl's son and daughter, Karl Jr and Beate, inherited half of the Aldi fortune after their father's death—the two reportedly sit on the company's board. They have a combined net worth of an eye-watering US$36.1 billion. In short, the Aldi Albrechts are among the richest families in Europe, funded by the global sales of their products—including their cut-price processed meats.

PROCESSED

When I approached the media department of Aldi, it probably shouldn't have been a surprise that the gilded family has one of the world's most well-known, and expensive, public relations companies—Ogilvy—on their payroll. Ogilvy is an advertising and marketing agency that advises businesses, including major food companies like Aldi, for a handsome monthly retainer—and deals with any awkward questions from uppity, annoying journalists like me.

Indian-born Devika Bulchandani is the global CEO of the company, reported to earn US$2–3 million per year.[19] Let's just call her Spin Queen Devika. When I sent a letter asking for information on Aldi's processed-meat offerings and the use of nitro-preservatives, it was one of her PR account executives, working on the Aldi account from the Sydney office, who emailed a reply.

The email response said: 'Thank you for reaching out with the opportunity to be included in Lucie Morris-Marr's upcoming book. Confirming ALDI Australia does not have anything to share at this stage.' Knowing how the media and PR industries work, I can tell you that one sentence cost the Aldi Albrechts a large percentage of Ogilvy's monthly retainer. Perhaps even a few thousand US dollars per word.

For a company that prides itself on offering low-cost products, I don't think they're getting very good value for money from Ogilvy, do you? After all, I wasn't asking Aldi to 'share' at all. I was asking for their precise response to questions about products containing nitro-preservatives. Instead, a minion of Spin Queen Devika had just spun me a line straight from the public relations playbook.

Anyway, by the time I got their response I was already moving on.

I was lost and alone within the vast aisles of my local Costco store, trying to sniff out processed meats like a French pig hunting for truffles in the woods of Provence.

You may have noticed how, over the past few decades, Costco Wholesale Corporation has grown into a major warehouse-retail player in the US, and in countries like Australia, by offering low prices on large packages of brand-name products. Like Aldi, but on a far grander scale, it lures in customers with all sorts of wild and wonderful goodies, from giant packs of donuts to washing machines, coffee makers and engagement rings. It has more than 100 million members—business owners and individuals—all over the world who purchase long-term memberships to gain access to their sprawling, warehouse-style stores.

In the twelve months to February 2024, Costco generated a profit of US$30 billion.[20] To put it plainly, since its founding in 1983, Costco has become a golden success story. You can easily get lost in one of its stores for days, but that's another matter.

Ron Vachris, the company's US-based president and CEO appointed in October 2023, is certainly an interesting chap, and a hardworking one to boot, having worked all the way up from forklift driver at Costco's predecessor Price Club to the top job in the company. Let's call him Costco Ron, to make things easier.

After navigating the maze of aisles at my local Costco store in Moorabbin, Melbourne, and coming across the biggest array of processed meats I'd ever seen in one store, I had a few questions for Costco Ron. And I wasn't in the best mood, to be honest. I'd spent so many hours photographing all the processed-meat items and their labels—all of which, without exception as far as I could tell, contained nitro-preservatives—that I faced the very real risk of catching a chill.

The sheer scale of their catering-sized, multi-packs of ham, bacon, salami and sausages had also made me somewhat nauseous. It didn't help matters that on the way out, just beyond the tills, were queues of customers waiting to buy their famous hot dogs for lunch. Then there was a final display near the exit of the store that really pushed me over the edge: an actual coffin, displayed to promote a funeral package. I felt like I was experiencing a dark plot twist, like a character in the futuristic Netflix show *Black Mirror*. Was this really real?

I'm afraid so. Costco, as it turns out, writes its own, rather baffling scripts.

Anyway, what did the company have to say about its enthused commitment to processed meats containing nitro-preservatives? After a short wait, I got a brief email from a marketing manager for the Australian and New Zealand stores.

'Unfortunately, management has declined to comment on this piece. Best of luck with the book!'

It was certainly charming of them to wish me luck. But it wasn't me that needed it. They were already in the manuscript.

Chapter Five

TAKE AWAY THIS

Apparently, our Italian @mcdonalds fans loved the Crispy McBacon so much that they're getting tattoos of it . . . that's a true sign of approval![1]
Chris Kempczinski, CEO, McDonald's, 14 July 2023

Too hot to handle

Deep in the Okavango Delta in Botswana, I reached for a stick to stoke the smouldering branches on the fire as darkness drew in.

The flames went up briefly, the smoke lingering in the balmy night air. My friend and I had already cooked our supper of rice and beans in a small pan over the flames, sharing it with our magnificent local guide. The father of three was leading us on an incredible canoe safari through the annually flooded terrain of this extraordinary and unique part of Africa. It was an experience so vivid, so intense, that it has remained clear in my memory nearly twenty years later.

We had no running water, no showers and no access to cooking facilities. In fact, we didn't even see another human being in five days.

This romantic and somewhat daring adventure also had a twist of danger in its midst—our guide had to keep the fire going all through the night to ward off African wildlife, including lions and herds of elephants. I spent much of the latter part of the trip fearing for my life after an enraged hippo had lunged towards us on our canoe and nearly attacked us when we ventured too close to its offspring . . . but that's another story.

The only reason we didn't have to sleep high up in the trees with the monkeys and baboons each night was the fire. It enabled us to sleep at ground level in small canvas tents. It also gave us warmth, the ability to prepare hot food, and a sense of comfort and safety.

The first stage of human interaction with fire is a point often argued among experts but it's generally considered to have occurred as early as 1.5 million years ago in Africa. It's also likely to have been opportunistic, by all accounts.

While our closest living relatives, the chimpanzees, live on a diet of foods such as fibrous and bitter leaves, grubs, fruit, raw monkey meat and brains, humans have an almost endless list of food options.[2] We also have techniques for changing their composition through the use of heat—cooking—which have propelled us towards our modern addiction to processed meat.

When we cook food, more energy is extracted from it, so our bodies don't need to expend so much energy in digestion. In meat, heat breaks down collagen, its connective tissue, and cooking plants softens the cell walls to release their starch and fat. Cooking also kills off parasites and bacteria in our food.[3]

There were certainly other advantages to cooking over an open flame: it starts the process of breaking down protein and makes nutrients more readily available, after all, the expanding hominin brain needed all the help it could get.

By releasing the potential in meat by roasting it, early hominins were able to feed their growing brains—the body part that uses up to 20 per cent of our calories.[4]

Fire would also have been useful for light, for warmth at night, and for frightening off predatory animals—just as I had experienced firsthand in Botswana. Early humans could then sleep safely on the ground. Smoke, too, proved to be useful, keeping insects away, just as it does in campsites across Australia today as families try to combat mosquitoes.

As geologist Andrew C. Scott wrote in *Time* magazine, 'This ability to "stretch" fire was a novel feat, only developed by humans.'[5]

Evidence shows that food then started to be cooked on hot stones in this early phase, according to Guy Crosby, an adjunct professor of nutrition, in his book *Cook, Taste, Learn*.[6]

Around 30,000 years ago 'earth ovens' were then developed in Central Europe, Crosby says, to cook a wide array of beasts including large mammoths.

'This was clearly an improvement over rapidly roasting meat by fire, as slow cooking gives time for the collagen in tough connective tissue to break down to gelatin', which 'makes the meat easier to chew and digest', the author wrote.

Indeed, it's clear fire didn't just make meat more digestible; it also brought people together to eat, laying the foundations of human society. And cooking meat over a flame has been bonding us ever since, from elaborate feasts to Sunday roasts and casual barbecues. In short, we discovered the flame and there was no turning back.

Thanks to the chemical process known as the Maillard reaction, our meat went from raw and chewy to crispy, tender, and far easier to eat and digest. It's a reaction that produces an utterly addictive result, argues Marta Zaraska in her book *Meathooked*. She says it's the marriage between 'carbohydrates and amino acids in a slightly moist, hot environment (between 300 and 500 degrees Fahrenheit), which produces aromas so delightful they make us go weak at the knees'.[7]

But here's the problem with heat, flames and meat: the combination can in certain circumstances cause cancerous end products which are linked to cancer, as it turns out. For example, you might not be aware that fried bacon contains more of the carcinogenic substances called heterocyclic amines (HCAs) than any other cooked meat. It also contains high levels of advanced glycation end products (AGEs), another group of substances linked to cancer.

Both HCAs and AGEs are produced by the Maillard reaction. The reaction causes browning, so cooking methods that involve little browning also usually result in fewer HCAs and AGEs. 'So your cancer risk could depend on how you cook your bacon,' writes nutritionist and lecturer Richard Hoffman—and how you cook other processed meats such as sausages. Lightly cooked and 'lightly browned bacon has only one-tenth the HCAs of well-cooked bacon'. Grilling under a naked flame may also be a bad idea, as the drying effect and the high temperature also increase HCA formation.[8]

These are the sort of vibe-killing facts that would send those bacon addicts on Facebook into a full-scale frenzy. Especially when it's likely that the dreaded microwaved bacon has far lower levels of AGEs than fried bacon.

Sadly, bacon—the meat capable of turning vegans into meat-eaters from its aroma alone—is just not coming out of this well, is it?

Australia's Cancer Council gives a clear warning to the public about charred meats in particular. 'Heating meats at high temperatures may result in the formation of mutagenic chemicals, thus consumption increases the risk of cancer. Cancer Council recommends as a precaution avoiding charring food while cooking.' Eating grilled or barbecued meat and fish has also been associated with a possible increased risk of stomach cancer.[9]

While I applaud major charities giving out this advice, the Australian Government and the meat industry have been well aware for some time that the public may be causing themselves harm, due to the way they cook items after purchasing them.

Buried in that explosive 2020 CSIRO report, the one jointly funded by Meat & Livestock Australia and the government, which suggested ideas to replace nitro-preservatives in processed meats, they also note there could be ways of cooking which could reduce cancer risks.

'... studies have shown that boiling (lower heat) or microwave (indirect heat) produces fewer n-nitroso-compounds than direct heat application by deep-frying and pan-frying of dry cured raw sausages,' the report states.[10]

This came out nearly half a decade ago now, so where are the advisory or warning labels? Has more research and development taken place? Don't worry, they'll be getting a deep-fried missive from me soon enough.

But it's not just high temperatures and charring that increase the risk. There is a particular new trend that is also causing alarm.

Smoke signals

Look, I get it. I do. There's nothing like the smell of smoked meats. Barbecue smokers are currently a huge and growing backyard trend all over the world, a common Father's Day gift for the man who has everything. At Bunnings stores they range from as low as $50 for a simple version to $1400 for one of the most elaborate types: the Oklahoma Joe's® Longhorn Combo Charcoal/Gas Smoker and Grill.

'Equipped with both a charcoal and gas grill chamber and an attached offset firebox, this multi-purpose smoker and grill allows you to barbecue your way,' says the description on the Bunnings website. 'Built with durability in mind, porcelain-coated cast-iron grates and heavy-gauge steel construction ensure easy cooks and delicious food every time.'[11]

The reason these contraptions are so popular is that meat can be preserved by 'smoking'. If the smoke is hot enough to slow-cook the meat, this will also keep it tender.

Of course smoking helps seal the outer layer of the meat making it more difficult for bacteria to enter and can be done in combination with other preserving methods such as salting.

There are multiple smoking styles including cold smoking, hot smoking and smoke roasting (pit barbecuing). But put down that pork belly: there are some serious health concerns you should know about before planning your next smoky feast. Smoking meats also renders them 'processed'—and, yes, that means there are health risks too.

In a rather confronting article published in 2022, dietician Gillian Culbertson states the case against smoked meats in rather blunt terms.[12] Culbertson works at Cleveland Clinic, a well-respected medical and academic centre with branches around the US and globally.

Smoked meat, the article begins, is 'contaminated meat'. 'The smoke itself is a source of contaminants that can be harmful,' Culbertson explains, forming HCAs—which we know from the Maillard reaction—and polycyclic aromatic hydrocarbons (PAHs). Both are harmful by putting you at risk of cancer, forming when meat is cooked at high temperatures.

Though grilled and pan-fried meats can also lead to the formation of PAHs and HCAs, during the smoking process, the smoke creates both these substances, carrying them onto the surface of the meat. Certain wood types, such as beech, acacia and eucalyptus, may be less risky but it also depends on temperatures and moisture content as to whether PAHs are formed.

'High exposure to these compounds can lead to increased risk of cancer of the intestinal tract, notably colon and stomach cancer,' Culbertson says. 'Some recent research also suggests that red and processed meats, including smoked meats, may increase your risk of breast and prostate cancer.'

As an interesting side note, it's not just smoking meat which has got experts concerned; fears also extend to smoked cheeses and smoked fish too, which is a blow personally as smoked salmon has been my bacon replacement at brunch now for a few years.

A 2022 review by fisheries researchers at Ege University, Turkey, reported that during the process of smoking fish, carcinogenic PAH compounds can be formed. 'Reducing the temperature in the smoking oven and using a special filter system . . . also reduces the formation of these components,' the authors wrote.[13]

I'm afraid the news isn't any better for those who enjoy the distinct flavour profile of smoked meats of any kind; in April 2024 eight types of smoke flavourings were banned for use in the EU, following scientific assessments by the European Food Safety Authority.[14] They had 'genotoxicity' (the risk of a chemical agent to change DNA and lead to cancer) concerns over the flavourings, which can be added to a wide range of foods including smoked cheeses and smoky bacon flavoured chips but also processed meats such as hugely popular smoked sausages.

The smoked meats industry in the EU now faces a very precarious balancing act of meeting consumer demand, while also making sure ingredients are safe and adhere to the safety of its ingredients in line with the new rules. Businesses will have to seek safe, more natural alternatives, yet whether this ruling will influence Australian or New Zealand food processing methods is yet to be seen. That revealing 2020 CSIRO report admits

PAH content is 'not something that appears on a retail label', because the amount, 'if any', depends on several factors.

Some readers may well be aware however of news reports on the risks of smoked products, nitro-additives and cooking at high temperatures. But based on the many conversations I've had with friends and contacts, there seems to be a gigantic gap in awareness around most meat-related health risks.

And one thing is certain: if there's one market constantly expanding in Australia, and all over the world, that is heavily influencing our consumption of processed meats, it's the fast-food industry. It's something which, as the mother of two teenagers, I have come to know well.

Digging under the Subway

Whenever my forever-famished teens sneak to Subway for a 'foot-long sub' sandwich for lunch, they know the question that's coming their way.

'Did you have the pepperoni in it too?' I always ask them.

'No, Mum,' they say, rolling their eyes.

They've seen my suffering firsthand and they know that I don't wish to take even a tiny risk with their eating patterns and future health, so they are simply not allowed processed meats at home except some very occasional nitrite-free bacon.

We have managed to eliminate them since I first realised the full extent of the risks following my diagnosis. Thankfully, they don't eat them now, except occasionally, behind my back, when ham wraps are on offer on a school camp or they just can't resist a pepperoni pizza at a party. I understand that, in Western countries avoiding it altogether is impossible. Sometimes there isn't even an alternative choice.

The reason I have a particular dislike for Subway pepperoni slices, among all the processed meats in the take-away market, is that, in my view, you can see, with your own eyes, how low its quality is just by the look of the fatty, cheap-looking meaty circles.

Subway outlets are franchises, which operate in the same way as other major take-away outlets. They have to pay fees and a portion of profits to the franchisor (Subway), plus rent, staff wages, and other overheads such as water and electricity bills. Franchisees are always desperately trying to eke out a profit.

Of course, Subway restaurants don't display posters that list all the ingredients and fillings in their sandwiches. You have to work harder than that. I found a document listing their Australian ingredients and—surprise, surprise—it was full of bad news.[15] Let's look at its oh-so-popular pepperoni:

> PEPPERONI: Pork and Beef (92%), Salt, Soy Protein, Dextrose (Tapioca, Maize), Spices and Spice Extracts, Maltodextrin (Maize), Lactose (Milk), Natural Colour (160c), Antioxidants (316, 307b, 392), Dehydrated Vegetables (Garlic, Onion), Mustard Flour, Starter Cultures, **Preservative (250 [Sodium Nitrite])**, Fermented Red Rice, Mineral Salts (450, 451, 452), Rice Flour, Yeast Extract, Sugar, Flavour, Acidity Regulator (262), Herb Extract, Hydrolysed Vegetable Protein (Maize, Soy), Vegetable Oil, Maize Starch, Wood Smoked.

Yes, there was my old foe, sodium nitrite, right there in this stomach-churning swamp. And if that doesn't put you off, think about the hormones, antibiotics and so on that may have been used to rear the pigs and the cows, which aren't even listed. Neither is the origin of the meat.

Ordering pepperoni at Subway is akin to agreeing to eat something wholly mysterious. It's highly processed—to an extreme degree. And Subway's other processed-meat ingredients, including salami and bacon, make for grim reading too:

SALAMI: Pork and Beef (95%), Salt, Spices, Lactose (Milk), Maltodextrin (Maize), Dextrose (Maize), Mineral Salts (450, 451), Antioxidant (316), Dried Vegetables (Garlic, Onion), Sugar, **Preservative (250 [Sodium Nitrite])**, Starter Culture, Natural Wood Smoke.

BACON: Cured with: Water, Salt, Sugar, Smoke Flavoring, Sodium Phosphate, Sodium Erythorbate, **Preservative (250 [Sodium Nitrite])**.

If I had my way, Subway would at least use nitrite-free or organic nitrate processed meats—or even offer a wider range of healthier protein alternatives.

They have proven they are capable of change. After all, in the past they have adapted. In accordance with Hindu beliefs, Subway restaurants in India do not serve beef products, and the country's huge number of vegetarians led the chain to offer more vegetarian options.

PROCESSED

In the meantime, in the UK and Ireland, Subway claim to have reduced salt content across its entire range by 33 per cent and has vowed to make further cutbacks to adhere to government targets. This company is clearly capable of change.

So, armed with this 'evidence' about the contents of the pepperoni, salami and bacon in the Australian stores in particular, I wanted to find someone who was in charge of this culinary mess of sandwich fillings.

It certainly wasn't anything to do with the original owners. Famously, Peter Buck gave college student Fred DeLuca the idea to open a 'submarine sandwich shop' to help pay his university fees. Buck provided an initial US$1000, and their first restaurant opened in Bridgeport, Connecticut, in 1965. The popularity of their brand, and their freshly made sandwiches, continued to grow over the decades.

It's no surprise that the owners of the entire global franchise chain today are a hemisphere away from our Subway restaurants in Australia—in Atlanta, Georgia, to be precise. The hugely successful Roark Capital Group is a private equity firm that manages about US$37 billion in assets, including Subway, which it acquired in August 2023. The company's founder and managing partner is an American chap by the name of Neal K. Aronson. He'll be Subway Neal to us.

Just how much did Roark Capital pay for this global franchise, you may wonder? Well, *The Wall Street Journal* reported the purchase price was around US$9.6 billion, which was apparently slightly below the chain's $10 billion asking price.[16]

And yes, you guessed it, I did drop Subway Neal a little French-inspired letter about my concerns about the nitro-preservatives in the processed meats in Roark's newly purchased chain of franchised Subway stores. I mentioned that I was more than a little concerned that his new acquisition could potentially harm Australian teenagers in particular, including mine, who once loved to order foot-long subs filled with pepperoni before their annoying mother put her foot down.

I'm not suggesting Subway Neal is knowingly doing anything which could have a negative impact on health. However, I'd thought that as the founder of Roark, managing so many brands including food chains The Cheesecake Factory and Cinnabon, he would be quite good at answering important emails. But so far, so quiet. But hey, maybe he's in a tunnel somewhere on the 'subway' and there's no wi-fi? In any case, I had to disembark for my next stop on this fast-food express line.

World domination

I remember once, as a young child, pointing to an ambulance parked outside a McDonald's restaurant in central Windsor, England. My late grandmother mused sagely that maybe 'someone had suffered a heart attack'.

'Why, Grandma?' I asked her.

'From trying to suck a super-thick shake through a straw!' she replied, chuckling and looking up at the ancient stone walls of Windsor Castle over the road. 'I really hope it wasn't the Queen. It takes a lot of effort to drink that stuff!'

That was about the extent of our health concerns about fast food in the early 1980s. McDonald's, the world's largest fast-food chain, was always such a treat; our whole family loved the soft, juicy cheeseburgers with their little pickle, along with the thin, salty, crunchy fries. There was nothing I didn't love about it—just like millions and millions of others all over the world who still enjoy McDonald's today. It was only much later, when we began to understand the causes of heart disease, diabetes and cancers, that major brands such as McDonald's started getting questioned by health experts and the media.

Who could forget the 2004 smash-hit US documentary *Super Size Me*? The film documented a 30-day period in 2003 during which late director and star Morgan Spurlock only ate McDonald's food for breakfast, lunch and dinner. The result? Some drastic effects on his physical and mental health and well-being; Spurlock tragically then went on to have a premature death twenty years later, from cancer, aged 53 in May 2024.[17] The film also examined the fast-food industry's influence, including how it encourages bad nutrition for its own profit. It sparked something of an anti-fast-food revolution in terms of awareness, but it did not stop the growth of these brands.

Some brands, such as McDonald's, have reacted to the pushback over the past two decades by adding healthier items to their menus. When I was growing up, there simply weren't any salads, wraps, slices of apple or smoothies to choose from. But now the choices are, to be fair, extensive.

In Australia alone there are more than 1000 McDonald's restaurants over 85 per cent of which are operated by franchisees, according to the company. As such a dominant force in the lives of millions of Australian customers, surely McDonald's wouldn't offer foods containing that dreaded sodium nitrite?

Surely they had done a really good job of cleaning up their act after so much bad publicity in the past? But it's yet more bad news, I'm afraid. If you order anything that includes bacon, such as the BBQ Bacon Angus or the Bacon & Egg McMuffin®, you will be eating the following ingredients, according to McDonald's own website:[18]

BACON: Pork, Water, Salt, Sugar, Emulsifiers (451, 450), Dextrose (Maize, Tapioca), Antioxidant (316), Acidity Regulator (330), **Sodium Nitrite (250)**, Rosemary Extract. Smoked.

Sadly, even some of the so-called 'healthier options', such as a crispy Chicken Caesar McWrap® and a Caesar Chicken Salad, contain bacon—which contains the controversial preservative. The list of other ingredients in what is actually a highly processed 'salad' is also concerning. But it was seeking out the nitro-preservative in the mix, like spearfishing for a snapper, that was my focus.

So who is the top boss in charge of all this, you may ask? His name is Chris Kempczinski, the chain's relatively new chief executive, who was appointed in 2020. Staff call him 'Chris K', but let's call him McChris, because as you can tell I enjoy committing to a theme.

To be fair, McChris has a mind-boggling role; McDonald's has 1.7 million employees globally and serves nearly 68 million hungry customers on average every day from its 33,000 restaurants in 119 countries.[19] The company's annual spend on marketing per year is said to be in the region of US$4 billion, ensuring the world and the younger generations are just as hooked as the older ones. Business-wise things couldn't be in better shape for McChris; in 2023 the company's profit was just over US$14.5 billion.[20]

Like Subway, McDonald's has adapted to local market needs and religions and, where necessary, they have deviated from the usual global menu. Restaurants in Asia in particular serve soup; a product called McRice is served in Indonesia; the Ebi (prawn) burger is on sale in Singapore and Japan; and McDonald's restaurants in China include items such as fried buns and soy milk on their breakfast menus.

In an interview with Canada's *Financial Post* when he was first made CEO, McChris proudly told the interviewer he eats McDonald's twice a day, in their stores all over the world.[21] During the chat, in a McDonald's restaurant in the US, he asks for 'a Filet-O-Fish, medium fries, a more modestly proportioned Diet Coke and a plain vanilla sundae to be delivered later'. Earlier he'd ordered 'Egg McMuffins with no bacon' for breakfast, the journalist reports.

No daily bacon for McChris? Interesting. Why? He certainly seems okay about running off the calories as part of his exercise regime. What's his beef with McDonald's bacon, then?

Was it for religious reasons? I couldn't confirm his religion online, but I then spotted an Instagram post from July 2023 showing the CEO trying out new products at a McDonald's restaurant in Italy—including a burger called the 'Crispy McBacon'.

'Apparently, our Italian @mcdonalds fans loved the Crispy McBacon so much that they're getting tattoos of it . . . that's a true sign of approval!' he wrote in the caption. I watch the video as he takes a bite of the burger and declares, 'Mmm . . . the bacon adds something extra. Love that!' before quickly putting it down and moving on to a range of mini pizza pockets. I could be wrong, of course, but I sensed this bite of a bacon burger wasn't taken by someone who avoids bacon for religious reasons.

So I was left to wonder: is the CEO of McDonald's purposely avoiding eating the company's very own bacon on a regular basis? And where does all the bacon for the global chain come from? Does the company have any plans to reduce or ban preservative 250 from its bacon? And is McChris concerned about the growing evidence regarding links between processed meats and cancer?

I knew McChris would be a hard chap to pin down, especially zooming around the world on the company jet. And so far he hasn't answered my letter with a McFlurry of answers. Maybe he's on a mid-morning McRun, running off his breakfast McMuffin—with no bacon. Or maybe he does chow down on a rasher now and then. Who knows?

It probably won't be a surprise for you to know that another take-away giant, pizza company Domino's, has also remained completely silent in response to my questions about its processed-meat ingredients. Founded in 1960, Domino's Pizza, Inc. is led by CEO Russell Weiner who is based at its HQ near Ann Arbor, Michigan, in the US. As of 2022, Domino's had almost 20,000 stores worldwide, bringing in a total revenue of around US$4.5 billion.[22] Here in Australia, Queenslander Don Meij, who worked part-time in a pizza business as a teenager, is the group CEO and managing director of Domino's Pizza Enterprises Ltd (DPE). Let's call this fella Domino Don—it's got the perfect 'Door Dash' ring to it, don't you think?

Anyway, under his leadership, DPE has grown into a large international enterprise of its own, with more than 3800 outlets in Australia, New Zealand, Belgium, France, The Netherlands, Japan, Germany, Luxembourg, Taiwan, Malaysia, Singapore and Cambodia. According to his online biography, Domino Don, a former high-school teacher, has turned his hefty franchise slice into 'the biggest Domino's business in the world outside the United States—with seven pizzas sold every second and a net profit of more than $150 million' (in the 2021 financial year).[23]

The now extensive Domino's menu on offer doesn't just contain pizzas, of course. They are hooking into meat trends and fads and incorporating them into baked wraps (called 'Meltzz'), fries and pasta. Pepperoni Meltzz, BBQ Meatlovers Loaded Fries and Smokehouse Pork Belly Pasta are just some of the options.

It soon became apparent, however, as I researched the nutritional information for the main Domino's pizza toppings like pepperoni and ham, that the company does not make public the precise ingredients in its products. Not in Australia, anyway. I found this very odd, and surprising—McDonald's and Subway are at least transparent about every single ingredient of every component used to make their final products.

Instead, Domino's only provides the nutritional tables—calories, protein, fats and so on—and lists any potential allergens within the dishes, as required by Australian food laws, such as dairy, soy and nuts.

But where were the missing ingredients that went into the popular processed-meat toppings such as salami, ham and pepperoni, all of which we know contain multiple additives, preservatives and the rest? The list would be long.

I tried to have a word with Domino Don about all this. I contacted his company, via its Australian media department, to ask about whether their meat toppings contained nitro-preservatives like sodium nitrite, but there was only silence. I sent a follow-up email. Nada. Zip.

I wasn't going to give up that easily. It's just not in my nature, as you may have gathered. Considering my teens are regular customers, and in an ideal world would love pepperoni again on their pizzas, I thought it was only fair to lodge a little comment on their feedback form online. These weren't undercover journalistic tactics; I was a mother of actual Domino's customers and this point was also in the public interest. So I wrote the following;

Hi there,

I just wanted to know the precise ingredients of your pepperoni toppings. On your nutritional information area online it does not state what it's made from, unlike the menus for Subway. The ingredients only state that it is gluten free. Please can you send me the ingredients of the pepperoni you use in your Cheltenham store in Victoria? My local store? I need to know if the ingredients include preservative 250 (sodium nitrite) which my family don't eat due to the link to bowel cancer.

Please respond asap. Many thanks.

Again, no reply. How strange. Although I did have to put my real name and email on the form, so there's that. Maybe they'd heard on the grapevine about a bothersome journo on a meaty mission.

Or maybe, just maybe, Domino Don and his executive team worry that including a list of precise ingredients may affect share prices, something in which the CEO personally has a key interest. In the 2017 financial year, he was the top-earning CEO in Australia, ending up that year with nearly $37 million from his salary, his bonus and cashing in some shares. Yes, he may not have earned that sum in the more financially precarious years since, but that sort of windfall can buy a hell of a lot of pizzas. Or fast cars. Or holiday homes. Or luxury yachts.

I can't be certain, of course, and I'm only speculating, but maybe Domino Don just doesn't have much of an appetite for the company revealing the full extent of its ingredients. Or it slipped their mind when they designed their website. I'm in no way suggesting Domino Don is purposely allowing a product to be sold which could harm customers. If only he would just check his emails, or even just send a delivery moped over, with his answers warm and safe in a cardboard box. I'll happily take them via a carrier pigeon, along with a two-for-one meal deal, at this rate.

For now, the only appetite that is increasing is that of Domino's customers, largely teenagers like my own children, thanks to their aggressive marketing and cheap deals, which often come with soft drink, garlic bread and desserts.

By the way, it's not just the preservatives I worry about in the food of Domino's and the other take-away giants that are dominating the Australian food landscape. It's also the overall unhealthy and addictive nature of the products.

'It's worth noting that big food companies put considerable effort into identifying the combinations of ingredients that make their food particularly moreish, which drives overconsumption,' Kim Pearson, a nutritionist and the founder of Intelligent Weight Loss, told *The Guardian* in May 2023. 'It's much easier to overeat a highly processed pizza containing refined carbs, fat and salt, compared with a plate of vegetables or salad. In the case of meat, it's highly unlikely that your takeaway provider is using free-range, organic meat. They are far more likely to be using poor-quality, factory-farmed meat.'

As journalist Joel Snape noted, 'A single slice of takeaway pizza might be 250 to 350 calories, which doesn't sound too bad until you accidentally eat four (or was it five?) of them.'[24]

Whether it's the bacon in the McDonald's burger, or the pepperoni in the Subway sandwich, or the 'ham' on the Domino's pizza, this demand is part of the ongoing surge in Australia's production of processed meat. I'm also concerned about how the Australian take-away industry gives discounts to their poorly paid teenage employees, ensuring the eating habits of a new generation.

I felt it was time to go backstage. Now was the moment to pull aside the heavy, burgundy-velvet curtains to investigate what industrial-scale meat production really entails for the animals involved in this sorry mix—and its impact on our environment.

Dust to dust

I'll never forget witnessing thousands of cattle as they were herded onto a gargantuan ship in Broome, Western Australia, destined for the dinner plates of meat-eaters in Indonesia.

I was on a guided kayaking tour with my family, paddling underneath the pier on which the animals were heading on the way to their long, hot, cramped voyage and a final, brutal destiny inside a foreign abattoir.

One young cow, a beautiful fawn-brown colour with wide, expressive eyes, paused and seemed to look straight at me, just metres below. *Look where I'm going. Does anyone care?*

I've never forgotten that haunting moment, connecting directly with that doomed, gentle animal, because it was a reality I'm usually so far removed from. We all are.

When we see the packs of minced meat or beef sausages in the supermarket, the reality of how they are produced often seems so abstract, so distant—if we even pause to think about it at all. It suits our mental wellbeing, our inner peace. And that suits the meat industry just fine.

It's often too hard to think about. With the exception perhaps of those who are vegan and vegetarian, most of us push it aside. I know I have in the past. We all know suffering happens. How can it not, even with the most noble of intentions?

Animals, even the happy, free-range, grass-fed beasts from the Yarra Valley to the Hunter Valley, eventually have to be killed for the meat we eat. The meat industry glosses over this moment of finality, when animals are slaughtered, with several gentler-sounding words including 'processed' and 'euthanised'. But the truth is that every minute and every hour, animals in Australian abattoirs are stunned, gassed and cut in various ways—some more effective and quick than others, depending on the conditions, skills and practices.

And because our appetite for processed meats is largely dominated by pork products, I decided to turn my attention to the pig-farming industry. I didn't want to have to. I had to take a deep breath and compose myself.

It was time to get real because while pork is also sourced from overseas there are roughly 2.4 million pigs in the Australian industrial pork rearing system at any given time.[25] It was only fair that I gave them some thought. And it soon became clear why the industry is not keen for you to know about some of the more murky and distressing aspects of the nation's daily ham-sandwich fest.

In April 2023, a group of animal-rights protesters broke into a slaughterhouse in Benalla, in the north of Victoria. Fifteen were charged with trespass.[26] The cause of their upset? The protest was sparked by footage released by animal-protection group Farm Transparency Project, which showed pigs suffering terribly inside carbon dioxide gas chambers at the three largest pig abattoirs in Victoria. The founder of Farm Transparency Project, Chris Delforce was arrested and charged at the protest, along with six others, with eight more charged seven months later.

'While we're aware that we broke the law by entering Benalla slaughterhouse and locking ourselves to the gas chamber used to painfully suffocate pigs, we felt that this was the only option we could take,' Delforce said afterwards. The group claimed they had only decided to stage the protest because Australian Pork Limited and the federal agriculture department had refused to meet them and listen to their concerns directly. 'Ultimately, we know that revealing the reality of what happens inside Australian slaughterhouses is in the best interests of the public. We don't plan to stop any time soon.'

In Australia, it's common practice on some of the country's 4300 production sites to move pigs into steel cages called 'gondolas', then lower them into chambers that have a high concentration of carbon dioxide. In around 20–30 seconds, the pigs lose consciousness.[27]

Delforce strongly believes the pork industry has failed to be honest with consumers about the reality of the process. 'The industry is saying these pigs . . . [are] going into the chamber, they're coming out asleep. And that it's perfectly humane,' he told the ABC.

What's important to mention is the sheer scale of some of the pig farms in Australia. One of Australia's biggest pig-farming operations, Rivalea—bought out by the Billionaire Brothers, who we learned about earlier—has about 45,000 sows.[28] Free-range pork only represents about 5 per cent of the Australian pig industry. Pasture-raised pork is an even smaller fraction of the total and, in truth, it's estimated that more than 70 per cent of the pork we eat in Australia comes from overseas, where conditions are even worse than here and to some extent unknown.[29]

As Jonathan Safran Foer writes in his book *Eating Animals*, suffering is guaranteed for farm animals, no matter how well they are reared. 'For nearly all farmed animals, regardless of the conditions they are given to live in—"free-range," "free-roaming," "organic"—their design destines them for pain.'[30]

In Australia at least, thanks to past campaigns by animal-rights activists, you will notice that some pork product labels in Australia contain the words 'sow stall free' on the labels. But what does this mean for pigs?

Sow stalls are individual pens that pregnant sows are kept in on many pig farms. Each one is barely bigger than a sow, meaning that the animals cannot turn around or leave their stalls. According to the RSPCA, the Australian pig industry is phasing these out and moving all female breeding pigs (sows) to indoor group housing.[31] So the term 'sow stall free' is used to label pork products from pigs that have been born to sows in group housing.

The move from sow stalls to group housing is a very important first step, but animal-welfare groups point out other issues, like the use of farrowing crates that may be used to confine sows for up to five weeks around the time piglets are born. There are also concerns about the painful procedures piglets often go through without pain relief, such as ear tagging or notching, teeth clipping and tail docking.

As for the male pigs, the boars, there is great concern for their welfare too in Australia. Like sow stalls, boar stalls often only allow enough room for the boar to stand and lie down—not walk around. Boars, who can become chronically stressed like confined cows, are only needed to be led out of these stalls for mating (either semen collection or natural mating) or twice a week for exercise. As it stands, the RSPCA points out that the Australian pig industry has made no promises to phase out the use of boar stalls in pig farming.

Matthew Evans, a former food critic and chef, has witnessed the inner workings of large-scale pig farms up close. Now a farmer and restaurateur, he raises pigs on a small farm in Tasmania. I've been a big fan of his writing ever since I edited his food columns for the Sydney-based weekly magazine *Grazia* in 2008.

In his book *On Eating Meat*, Evans—who confesses that he adores the pigs on his farm—gives the reader an intimate understanding of the thorny issues involved in producing and consuming animals.[32] In particular, he explores another shocking aspect of pig farming I'd never heard about, and maybe you haven't either: 'Minimal Disease' (MD) pigs.

In theory, the reasoning behind the concept seems understandable: pig farmers generally want their piglets to start life free of any contact with bacteria or pathogens that could lead to disease, which could then potentially spread around the entire piggery.

So how do farms ensure their piglets are pathogen-free? Well, there are several processes, all of them harrowing but some more distressing than others. One is 'snatch farrowing', or removing the piglets as soon as they are born. Another is 'medicated early weaning'—removing suckling piglets five days after birth and subjecting them to a course of antibiotics. The third form, however, is the MD one Evans describes as a 'very grim tale'. And I have to agree.

In order for the 'low-disease' piglets to have zero contact with the mother pig, the sow is killed before the piglets are born, and the piglets are surgically removed from the sow's body. Evans is blunt in his appraisal of this practice, calling it 'a questionable if not downright condemnable practice'. He states that if the Australian public knew the full story about this, it wouldn't pass what he calls 'the supermarket test'.

As Evans found during his own research, I realised that gaining access to information on how exactly the sows are killed during this process is difficult, if not impossible. The Queensland Government website does admit that MD pigs are separated from their mothers as piglets and reared in total isolation from other non-MD pigs. 'Piglets that are reared in total isolation from their sow and all other non-MD pigs will not become infected with certain disease-causing organisms (pathogens) that are normally present in pigs,' the website says. It goes on to state that MD pigs are expected to be free of 'enzootic pneumonia, pleuropneumonia, swine dysentery, external parasites [and] internal parasites'.

It's true that the pork industry is dealing with pressing concerns about African swine fever, which has wiped out half the global pig population. If the disease came into Australia, it could cost more than $2 billion to the economy.[33] I read many documents describing how pig farmers and piggeries can try to reduce their risks.[34]

I also read a great deal about the antibiotics and other drugs often administered to pigs in the rearing process. What I discovered is that the main industry body for Australian pork admitted to a Senate inquiry in 2009 just how many drugs the industry uses to rear pigs. 'It is a reality that modern agriculture utilises a range of chemicals,' the submission from Australian Pork Limited said in its submission to the inquiry. 'Chemical use is not limited to intensive animal production systems, nor is it limited to animal production.'[35]

Some of the main drugs listed as used in the rearing of pigs are antibiotics, which the industry claims are not for growth purposes but for prevention of disease or treating a disease; 'growth promotants' called Oliquindox and Kitasamycin; and hormones—porcine somatotropin ('to enhance lean muscle deposition in finishing pigs'), Improvac (for boar castration) and Paylean ('fed to pigs in the last four weeks before marketing to increase feed efficiency and muscle growth, and reduce fat deposition').

The key question, you may well ask, is: do any of these drugs end up in the tissues of the pigs and therefore find their way into human digestive systems?

Australian Pork Limited argues that 'residues' are regularly tested for in pork, including 'agricultural chemicals (e.g. pesticides and antibiotics), environmental contaminants (e.g. heavy metals), and other chemicals that have trade concern (e.g. Dioxin)'.

But it certainly made me wonder—is this system foolproof?

If any of this meat did contain any of these drug residues, then went on to be processed, with all the various nitro-preservatives and additives chucked in, to be made into ham, salami and other cured meats, it sounds like one hell of a risky snack. And 'risk' is a word I don't like when it comes to food. When it comes to imported processed-meat products the government conducts inspections, but according to the Department of Agriculture, Fisheries and Forestry the main tests centre around checking for listeria or salmonella.[36]

As for the beef industry, which also provides key ingredients for processed meats such as biltong, salami, jerky and sausages, the allegations of cruel practices have stalked farmers and meat giants for decades.

Animal-welfare campaigners such as PETA Australia are particularly concerned about the daily lives of beef cattle on cramped, sprawling feedlots (farming facilities where cattle are fattened up) where they can face extreme temperatures and painful diseases such as footrot and botulism.[37] They too are concerned with the heavy use of antibiotics and growth hormones in the beef industry and the potential of these substances reaching human stomachs. There is also concern over the way cattle are placed on trucks, sometimes without food or water, and taken to an abattoir where they are usually stunned in the head with a bolt-gun. They are then hung up by one leg before having their throats cut, while hopefully unconscious, and then skinned and gutted.

'They don't always die at once. They usually die piece by piece,' one former Australian abattoir worker from Queensland told me. He had left the industry pretty quickly and turned to crop farming, after being appalled by the common practices he witnessed.

'The cattle are supposed to be unconscious before their throats are cut, but they are often still mooing and staggering,' he revealed. 'They feel it and if anyone had to see it for themselves they'd never eat beef again. I didn't.'[38]

What the industry is always trying to avoid is stressed animals, but that's not necessarily with their welfare in mind; it's because stress can make the meat tough and affect the taste. Stunning the cattle before cutting their throats is generally the form of slaughter used for halal and kosher meats in Australia. Then there are the cattle destined to be crammed onto those huge ships as part of the highly controversial live export industry.

The controversy regarding the production of meat doesn't end there, of course. In recent years there has been growing public awareness that consuming dairy and meat, including processed meat, isn't good for the environment because of the way production methods affect the climate—and the way intensive farming can also pollute soil and water systems.

Raising livestock contributes to 14.5 per cent of global greenhouse gas emissions.[39] In Australia, the beef industry alone is driving significant deforestation, including destroying the habitats of threatened species. One analysis identified 13,500 hectares of deforestation across 57 beef cattle properties in Queensland in just three years—between 2018 and 2021.[40]

The analysis suggests that, despite Queensland passing laws in 2018 to curb deforestation, loopholes have allowed landowners to continue to clear their properties, even in places that may be important to threatened species.

Meat giant JBS Australia, owned by those Billionaire Brothers in Brazil, has significant operations in Queensland, including two major feedlots. But when the analysis was revealed, JBS was unable to say if it supplies meat from any of the properties identified. According to Greenpeace and other media reports, the firm would only say it is 'committed to deforestation-free supply chains'.

It's not only the beef industry that has come under fire for its impact on the environment. More pertinently to my processed-meat research, piggeries wanting to expand their stock often face tough pushback from local communities across Australia. For good reason.

Residents erupted in anger when they heard about a plan for an outdoor pig farm for up to 5000 swine near wetlands in north-central Victoria.[41] They argued it would have a damaging impact on local tourism and the natural environment.

Western Plains Pork was trying to get approval to develop 440 hectares of land at a site near Koondrook, which borders a vital waterway called Gunbower Creek and is known for its canoe trails and wildlife. What potentially could enter the air and water systems around piggeries makes for grim reading. It's not only the obvious faeces and waste. 'Poor carcass management practices' may contaminate groundwater and surface water, cause odours, spread infectious diseases and attract pests. After all, there is a lot of death in pig production—not only those distressed sows and boars whose services are no longer required, or those animals who die of disease, but stillborn piglets and the afterbirth.

What it all adds up to is that processed meats—and other red meats—are some of the most environmentally damaging foods we can eat, in a multitude of ways.

The meat-industry giants of the world have contributed to this en masse, after gobbling up the smaller farms and meat producers in Australia and all over the globe. They include JBS Brazil, JBS USA, JBS Australia, NH Foods Ltd, Smithfield Foods, Cargill Incorporated, Conagra Foods Inc., National Beef Packing Company LLC, Tyson Foods Inc., Cherkizovo Group PJSC and OSI Group.

Author and environmentalist Tim Flannery is dismayed by the impact of all this industrial-scale farming on the environment. In particular, he finds the reliance on the same type of meat sources confusing. In his 1994 book *The Future Eaters*, he wrote, 'I find it remarkable that despite a shift in continents and the space of 200 years, with some minor exceptions, Australians have not added a single new source of meat to their limited diet.'

A typical grazing property in New South Wales, he pointed out, would generally support large populations of three or four species of kangaroos, sheep, goats, cattle, feral pigs, rabbits, dogs, horses and emus. 'All of these species are highly edible, and all are esteemed by one or more cultural groups somewhere in the world. Yet the traditional Australian attitude to them is strange and highly wasteful.'[42]

Wasteful, perhaps, but there is another troubling aspect to intensive farming that is often completely overlooked. The human cost. The impact on the daily lives and health of the thousands of meat-processing and abattoir workers—also known as the great unseen.

Notes from a factory

I've enjoyed poetry since I was a child. I love how it can impart a clear understanding of a range of emotions and subject matters. Yet I've never read anything as powerful as the prose-poem book *On the Line*, by French author Joseph Ponthus and translated by Stephanie Smee. I was gripped. And the critics felt the same when it was released in 2019. '*On the Line* is not just an extraordinary debut novel, it is also a hard-hitting work that is, dare I say it, essential,' enthused a review in *L'Express* newspaper.

Over its 250 pages, line by raw line, in one long poem, it evokes the daily nightmare of the life of the author when he worked in processing plants and abattoirs in Brittany in northwest France. Ponthus had been unable to find work in his field of social work and teaching, and signed up to a temp agency in dire need of an income to support his family. The result? One of the world's most searing and evocative accounts ever written on life as a meat worker, which reveals exactly just how huge the toll, mentally and physically, can be for those working long, bloodstained shifts, day after day. The injuries. The pain. The depression. The nightmares.

Ponthus writes many times within the pages about the immense personal risks he and his fellow workers took each shift:

PROCESSED

'It's the most bloody annoying thing trying to find a
Fingertip on the floor'
Jean-Paul's busy telling me
'With the blood and all the meat scraps that are
Constantly lying around
A fingertip for god's sake
You can easily miss it
But he was strong Brendan was
He didn't even pass out
Cock-up with the automatic lift-arm
Got his finger jammed
Cut off at the first knuckle'
A kid of twenty-two who works here like so many others
Waiting for something better
Namely an electrician's apprenticeship that the
Government agency's refusing to pay for
A chopped off finger
The graft didn't take
That's today's news
Today I almost buggered my finger on a meat hook
My femur on a chute
Made me stop and think about my workmate Brendan
Freshly amputated at the age of twenty-two
As a result of failing to touch wood
I'm touching bone
Those of my own carcass
Those of the cows[43]

Closer to home, another young abattoir worker by the name of Ronny Lewis found himself part of a groundbreaking photographic exhibition and book called *Working Men*, commissioned by New Zealand's National Art Gallery in 1982. In a photograph of Lewis, in white boots and overalls, there is part of a dead pig dangling at the top of the frame, while the walls and floors are almost entirely covered in blood. It was quite a rare sight in an era where such images weren't often seen by the public—unlike today, when the internet is filled with horrifying videos from inside abattoirs made by animal-rights groups and whistleblowers.

'I like animals and I feel sorry for them when I kill them,' Lewis was quoted as saying in the accompanying essay in the book. 'I only done it really because it was a job I had to do . . . some of these jobs are real hard, and I think a lot of people would get a hell of a shock if they came and had a try at it.'

Paul McCartney famously said that if slaughterhouses had glass walls, everyone would be a vegetarian. The modern-day problem in Australia and New Zealand is that local applicants for these highly risky and difficult abattoir and processing roles are few and far between, which isn't surprising considering the nature of the work.

As a result there is now a reliance on foreign workers who are motivated to work in the meat industry as a means to try to gain permanent-residency visas. In yet another dark layer of this murky meat story, it's clear these employees risk their mental and physical wellbeing for our plates and take-aways in the hope of a better life.

But there are often allegations that their vulnerability is taken advantage of. Many are fleeced before they even arrive, paying as much as $70,000 to overseas 'recruitment syndicates', which demand obscene prices to secure their jobs in Australia. In 2021, *The Age* and the *Sydney Morning Herald* newspapers reported how the senior leader of a large Victorian abattoir threatened the visa status of dozens of his Chinese workers in a bid to punish them after an altercation between an overseas worker and a local manager.[44]

While there is great sympathy for those who are working in this often ruthless end of the meat industry, there have also been some horrendous allegations of cruelty and violence by workers. Over the years they've been caught on secret footage hitting and kicking animals, and worse. While groups such as PETA Australia don't take kindly to such behaviour, and will expose it and call it out, they also acknowledge the long-term mental health impacts on those who do this work.

'When we witness cruelty to animals on factory farms or in slaughterhouses, it's easy to lay blame on the workers,' says the PETA Australia website. 'However, we need to consider that the meat and animal-skin industries don't protect human rights, either. Within these systems of human oppression, cruelty to animals flourishes. "Perpetration-induced traumatic stress" is the term used to refer to symptoms of post-traumatic stress disorder experienced by abattoir workers, which include depression and suicidal thoughts.'[45]

There is certainly research that has found that aggressive behaviour has been so high that they were 'similar to some reported for incarcerated populations', says PETA. It's a sensitive issue but it makes sense that potentially some of those who spend their working days killing animals, may become desensitised to violence, making them more likely to be violent outside work too. Flinders University sociologist Dr Nik Taylor said research showed if someone is cruel to animals they are more likely to be violent to humans. 'They're a pretty angry bunch and that anger shows,' she told one Australian media outlet.[46]

Other studies have also shown that in communities where abattoirs are a source of employment, rates of domestic violence, rape and child abuse are also sometimes high.

As for the abattoir worker-turned-author Ponthus, I hoped to contact him to ask him for an interview. But I was very saddened to read that in an inconceivably tragic turn, he died of cancer in 2021, at the young age of 42. I felt very thankful that he had at least lived to see his unflinching and original work recognised in France. *À la ligne*, as it was known in French, was awarded several prestigious literary prizes.

While the human cost of processing meat is clearly highly complex and troubling—though far better understood thanks to Joseph Ponthus—it was time to turn my attention to the other human aspect I was keen to explore in more depth: the health impacts linked to eating processed meats.

I knew this part wasn't going to be easy and wasn't going to improve my mood, especially as my first stop was digging deeper into the link with bowel cancer. But I went for a refreshing swim in Port Phillip's magical Half Moon Bay, gathered my thoughts and got ready to dive in to the next stage of my investigation.

Yes, it was time to get personal.

Chapter Six

GUT INSTINCT

> The human gut is a delicate ecosystem. Processed meats, laden with saturated fats and chemical additives, disrupt this balance, creating a favourable milieu for cancer cells to thrive.[1]
>
> Professor David A. Johnson,
> Professor of Medicine (Gastroenterology),
> Eastern Virginia Medical School, 2015

In the bag

'I'm afraid I've only ordered margheritas, boys,' I say, as I drive my son, Nate, and his friend Zac to the local pizza shop one Friday night. 'I hope you understand, but we don't eat processed meats in our family and so I also feel uncomfortable buying them for others. Don't worry, though, I'm sure the pizzas will still be delicious.'

I could see Zac's face in the rear-view mirror. He looked aghast. 'But . . . um . . . pepperoni is my favourite!'

No one likes to let down children, least of all the friends of our own children, so I tried to gently explain further.

'The thing is, Zac, I'm reading a lot about the link between processed meats like pepperoni and cancer, so I just don't want to give it to children.'

Zac, bless him, was still in shock. He'd had pepperoni pizza every Friday since he could remember. At fourteen, he also had a bold, 'cheeky' side and wasn't afraid of speaking back to teachers—or parents, as it turned out.

'Well, I don't care if I get cancer!' he blurted out, red-faced, his fury growing.

'Oh, I think you would, Zac. I think you would,' I replied calmly.

I wasn't offended by Zac's outburst and I understood it. For most fourteen-year-olds—or even older, for that matter—the idea of any kind of disease or bad health can seem so abstract and distant. You feel invincible as you race around, driven by a youthful metabolism and glowing with health, inside and out. You're living for the moment, without a care in the world and, hopefully, with little knowledge of what suffering from a brutal health condition involves. Being older and possibly sick is such an alien concept it doesn't even compute.

In some ways, though, the same could also be said about many adults too, those who are fortunate enough not to have been touched by a cancer diagnosis, either their own or a loved one's. For many, cancer seems like something that happens to other people. 'Anyway, *everything* supposedly gives you cancer' is a phrase I often hear if I mention that I don't eat processed meats anymore.

I will never know for certain if consuming processed meat was the cause of my own early-onset bowel cancer, but as my research deepened I became more and more suspicious. By the time I'd written half of my manuscript, there it was: firmly in the frame as a prime suspect.

I knew it was time. Time to reveal the little-talked-about complexities that life battling bowel cancer can involve, much of which is not spoken about plainly or openly because it's so confronting, so personal. But I felt this moment would be vital in the book. I needed to highlight what the 'risk' of getting a serious bowel cancer diagnosis really entails. And why some of us might not want to dismiss those risks out of hand.

I wanted to make it clear that cancer doesn't just affect you physically—the mental impact can sometimes be almost just as debilitating and overwhelming. You have to find a spark in the dark, somehow, in a way you may never have needed to before.

In my case, late at night, in those few days after the surgeon handed down my stage-four diagnosis in late 2019, I wept and violently shook as I instructed my ashen-faced husband to choose a new wife from a list I had made of single and divorced school mums we knew.

'I want to know the kids will have a mum,' I uttered, my teeth chattering, during the first of several severe night-time panic attacks, the likes of which I'd never experienced before.

He refused. 'You're going to make it, I promise. It's going to be a lot of treatment but you're going to make it. You will,' he said, with the air of confidence I needed with all my being.

We had tried to speak in whispers, behind closed doors, in a bid to protect the children from the full horror of the unfolding emotions, including the fears. They had been told I had a 'small little lump' in my belly and all would be fine. *It will be sorted in no time*, we said.

They were too young, we felt, to handle the full diagnosis and yet old enough to find out the life-expectancy statistics on Google. It was a potential upset we felt we were under-resourced for.

Our attempt to shield them from reality failed, of course; children have famously strong instincts. My son slowly opened the bedroom door late one evening and admitted he had been listening to one of our conversations.

'I know it's serious, Mum,' he said as he broke down in tears. That shattering of his innocence and sense of safety at just eleven years old was devastating. As I held him in my arms I vowed from then to be more open about the treatment plan, while also still trying to keep him feeling safe.

I also decided in that moment to not look too far ahead but, where possible, focus on the day I was in. Mindfully, living in the moment. Meditation apps and books helped. I vowed to be as positive and happy as I could, if I could. I wasn't always cheerful on the scale of, say, Mary Poppins, but I stopped having panic attacks at least. 'Why spoil today with fears about the future?' became my daily motto. I would turn to multiple books, inspiring figures and authors for strength and inspiration. 'If you're going through hell, keep going,' Winston Churchill famously said. I was and I did. That's not to say the start of the actual treatment wasn't still traumatic. The first stage of the treatment was a small operation to insert a porta-cath in my chest; it would be the main way to administer the forthcoming chemotherapy. 'This is where the journey begins,' I remember my husband saying as he held my hand in the pre-operative waiting area.

The next morning, the waves of nausea started almost instantly when the chemotherapy began infusing, drip by drip, through the IV line. When my eyelids started twitching I knew this was a frightening, uncharted life experience for me that would take all my focus, and resolve, to endure.

After the initial dose in hospital, I was sent home with a portable pump, and the chemo carried on infusing into my body for 48 long and horrific hours, drip by arduous drip.

I can't sugarcoat those hours at home during that first round. They were hell—sheer debilitating hell. Others fare differently, of course, but I had to take so many anti-nausea medications to try to cope with the side effects that I was in a semi-conscious state at times. I felt like the woman who swallowed the bird who swallowed the fly; I had so much medication rolling around inside me I must have rattled.

I declared to the nurses when I saw them next that administering a dose of chemotherapy would do the trick in a torture scenario; I would have told anyone anything they wanted if they could have made it stop.

I couldn't eat or talk. I just lay in bed for days, motionless and miserable, just trying to survive. I honestly felt at times that it would be easier to die than to endure the treatment, such was the effect on my mental state. But I knew I had to keep going for the children, to see them grow up. To be their mum. Life was suddenly condensed into that single ambition.

By the end of the treatments, as I mentioned earlier, I'd lost many body parts in a total of four major open surgeries between 2020 and 2022. Piece by piece, my body became like a reverse jigsaw puzzle. After my first operation, where half my liver was removed, along with my gallbladder, I suffered an infection and had to be readmitted to hospital.

Then, two weeks after that operation, I suffered a bowel perforation near the primary tumour. A dangerous infection developed that could have claimed my life within days due to septic shock. As a result I had a 25-centimetre section of my sigmoid colon removed, a hysterectomy and a bladder resection.

As Covid-19 gripped the country, I spent weeks in hospital without seeing my children due to health restrictions. My husband was only allowed through the doors for one hour per day. I was so lonely I would drag my trolley of drips along the long corridors, which were devoid of visitors and the usual bustle, and take the lift down to the cold, empty chapel. I wasn't religious as such but I found strength in looking at the pretty stained-glass window and praying to the force of the universe that I would survive.

In the meantime my hair fell out on the chapel pews, strand by strand.

When I was finally allowed home there were some close calls; at least twice I had to trust my instinct to go back to hospital because I knew something wasn't right. It was so tempting to lie down and sleep, but each time the decision to get up and get help saved my life. I had septic post-surgery infections.

'I wish it was me suffering, not you,' my son said, tears welling in his eyes, as I struggled to finish my round of postoperative chemotherapy during Melbourne's strict stage-four lockdown in the wretched winter of 2020.

Stage-four cancer mixed with stage-four lockdown meant we were at home and completely cut off from our friends, our support network and the world around us. The entire nightmarish situation was repeated again in the winter of 2021, when I had to have more chemotherapy in yet another lockdown. It was the cancer-themed version of *Groundhog Day*.

Like other families, though, who had their own challenges during the pandemic, we turned to mindful pursuits to get through the difficult days together. We adopted a rescue cat and transformed the grassy council strip outside our house into an enchanted garden. We made scented candles and baked. I gained great comfort from us all being together in the family nest, knowing I was simply lucky to be alive.

As I grew stronger, we would take walks in the park and on the beach. Where we could we made the children feel safe by any measure possible. Familiar routines—and tastes—helped when the narrative of their childhood had become the tales of the unexpected. On Sundays we made the exact same meal; a roast chicken dinner with Yorkshire puddings. Later, we would keep returning to the small, riverside campsite in Victoria's Yarra Valley where they had been staying on holiday since they were toddlers. A place where the cockatoos still squawked at dawn and they could buy eggs from the little farm next door; time stood still, unmarked by disaster.

While I would later agree to be interviewed about my diagnosis in the media, in an effort to raise awareness of early-onset bowel cancer with Bowel Cancer Australia, there was one detail I didn't share. I had also been left with a stoma and colostomy bag from the emergency surgery when my colon burst in April 2020.

It was such a shock to wake up from the operation to find this out, and it took me a long time to come to terms with it and to learn how to live with it. I felt embarrassed to tell people and would try to hide it under baggy clothes. When I came home after the operation, I screamed the first time I changed the bag because a loose stool continued coming out of the opening of the stoma, like a fast-moving snake, and started heading for the carpet. I had to catch it with wet wipes before it fell. It felt like not long before I'd been a happy, healthy suburban mum doing the school run, but now, suddenly, I was starring in my own horror movie.

As time went on, I got used to managing the bag, of course; I camped, swam and cycled, and was determined not to let it stop me living life to the full. Naturally, though, it was difficult. I'd be out shopping or walking and realise the bag was quickly filling up. Or I'd have to change it in a public toilet that wasn't exactly sweet-smelling or clean.

Probably one of the lowest moments came when I had to change the bag in the bathrooms of a campsite where we were staying in Bright, in the alpine region of Victoria, and a lady brought her large dog into the block on a lead. I was in a cubicle cleaning the stoma, basically an open hole of my large intestine poking outside my stomach, as I heard the dog pacing around outside the door. In that moment I regretted trying to stubbornly still live a normal active family life, I felt so vulnerable to infections.

Thankfully, I would later have my stoma reversed in an operation in 2021 and now my bowels operate completely normally, but millions of brave bowel cancer patients are left with permanent stomas, dealing with changing the bags up to five or six times a day for the rest of their lives. Some people with rectal cancer often end up with bags too, when their anus has to be permanently sewn shut or removed. Yes, these are the cancer details you might not hear about, because many feel shame and embarrassment, which is obviously heartbreaking.

When you are impacted so suddenly and brutally, it's easy to lose yourself and your confidence. You have to somehow find your new lane. The new you.

A biopsy early on in my diagnosis had revealed my type of bowel cancer was a 'KRAS wild-type', meaning that it didn't involve a mutation, and it wasn't an inherited condition that I knew of.[2] So my disease probably wasn't down to nature. It was nurture—nurture gone very wrong at some point in my past, or perhaps over a lengthy period of time in my past, building up to a sickening crescendo. Could it have been processed meats?

When I was diagnosed, I was told that my primary tumour, in my colon, could have started growing from a tiny polyp anywhere from ten to fifteen years before. Therefore I may have even been pregnant when the cancer was starting the journey towards its destructive destiny.

Only 5 per cent of people who develop bowel cancer have inherited mutations that can lead to them getting the disease.

In the US, the highest rates of colorectal cancer are among American Indian and Alaska Native people. African American people also have elevated risks compared to other groups in the US. Worldwide, Ashkenazi Jews (that is, Jewish people of Eastern European descent) face some of the highest risks for colorectal cancer of any group.[3] Researchers believe that 6 per cent of Ashkenazi Jews carry a particular gene mutation that increases their risk of bowel cancers.[4] The other high-risk groups are those prone to bowel polyps and those with a condition called Lynch syndrome.

Out of all the adverse health conditions that have been associated with eating processed meats, via respected scientific studies, bowel cancer has the clearest link.

As we know, the WHO declared in 2015 that eating processed meat definitively increases the risk of bowel cancer. For every 50 grams of processed meat eaten per day, the IARC said, there is an 18 per cent increased risk of bowel cancer. That's just a couple of slices of ham or bacon.

If you eat more—say, a bacon roll for breakfast, a salami salad wrap for lunch, and sausages and mash for dinner—the risk of colorectal cancer has been shown to increase by 35 per cent with every 100 additional grams of processed meat, and by 12 per cent for every additional 100 grams of unprocessed red meat. Colorectal cancer is the third-most common cancer worldwide.[5]

It is estimated that more than 15,300 people in Australia were diagnosed with bowel cancer in 2023. The average age at diagnosis is 69 years old, but the number of people diagnosed with early-onset bowel cancer when they are under 50, like I was, is rising year by year. Rates in the 25–49 age bracket have increased by a disturbing 52 per cent in the UK since the 1990s, according to Cancer Research UK.[6] Bowel cancer is the fourth-most commonly diagnosed cancer in Australia, and it is estimated that one in twenty people will be diagnosed by the time they are 85.[7] The hunt is on among experts for the causes, including processed meats, ultra-processed foods, antibiotics and pollutant exposure.

Like other patients who have been prepared to go public I've tried, where I can, to raise awareness. In late 2020 I helped launch a campaign with the excellent charity Bowel Cancer Australia to call on the government to lower the age of the National Bowel Cancer Screening Program, where free test kits are sent in the post every two years, from the time people turn 50. 'Aren't we lucky there is this test so let's use it . . . give it out to younger people and it will save lives, save agony for families,' I said in an interview with Channel Nine.[8]

In truth, I explained, I would rather the charity had demanded kits were sent out from the age of 30 instead of suggesting 45, but I understood their position that they had to call for an achievable outcome. Nearly four years later, in 2024, a compromise was announced that Australians aged 45–49 will be allowed to request a screening test—but they have to opt in rather than a free one automatically being delivered to their homes.[9] It wasn't ideal, but it was a move in the right direction. What's so concerning, given when caught in the early stages bowel cancer is highly treatable and curable, is that when Australians are getting their free tests through the door the majority aren't actually using them.

'It's a simple test, but only 40 per cent of Australians do it,' researcher Dr Joachim Worthington told the ABC in April 2024. 'There's definitely scope for a lot more people to get into screening or return to screening if . . . they've lost that habit over the pandemic.'

Despite this depressing statistic campaigners, including many stage-four bowel cancer friends, keep working hard to raise awareness. In recent years, every June, a large group of young-onset bowel cancer patients and carers, organised by Bowel Cancer Australia, have travelled to Parliament for a special 'Call on Canberra' visit, where they meet MPs and ministers to lobby them on a number of issues around prevention, testing and treatment. It's vital work.

On a personal level signs to be aware of include abdominal pain, blood in stools, changes in bowel movements, weight loss and tiredness. However, in my view, it makes sense to try to stop the problem happening before it needs to be solved, because solving it comes at great cost in terms of suffering and pain. For me, prevention is key and if I'm able to help even just one person avoid my hellish, near-fatal collision with bowel cancer by sharing all the intimate and personal details, it will be the best gift I will ever receive.

I didn't mind being vulnerable in print and sharing my story. I felt I had to be completely honest for the Zacs of the world, and for anyone else who may not have been fully aware of what a serious cancer diagnosis involves. While those cheese and ham toastie snacks for years on end might do you and your children no harm at all, with all that is at stake with a serious cancer diagnosis, is it really worth taking the chance?

Because, as we know, preservative 250 is listed on the ingredient labels of the majority of processed meats on sale in Australia, therefore that 'chance' is lurking on each slice, glistening in plain sight.

Fallen stars

Bowel cancer certainly doesn't discriminate. It affects individuals regardless of their fame or fortune, and many well-known faces have been taken prematurely due to the disease. Some may have inherited the genes that meant bowel cancer was their destiny; for others, like me, they would have had a wild type of bowel cancer, meaning it may have been down to something in their lifestyles.

Reading through the stories of famous people who got the disease left me with the troubling question we will never know the answer to: did processed meats perhaps, just perhaps, play a role in causing their disease?

Of course, I accept there are other factors that could play a role too, many of which remain unclear to the scientific community: the complexity of gut health, weight, genetics, activity levels and so on. But still the question lingers.

One of the most sudden losses the entertainment industry has faced in recent years was the passing of actor Chadwick Boseman at the age of just 43 in 2020. Known for his groundbreaking role as Black Panther in several Marvel films, Boseman battled bowel cancer privately while continuing to work on film projects. His strength, talent and resilience inspired millions, making his death a significant blow to the industry.

In addition to playing Black Panther, Boseman is also known for his portrayals of historical figures, including baseball star Jackie Robinson; Justice Thurgood Marshall, the first African American judge in the US Supreme Court; and singer James Brown.

Back in 2018, Boseman spoke about the impact of Black Panther, and became emotional when discussing his relationship with two young fans who had died of cancer before the movie was released.

'Throughout our filming, I was communicating with them, knowing they were both terminal. What they and their parents said to me was, they were trying to hold on 'til this movie comes. To a certain degree it's a humbling experience because you're like, this can't mean that much to them,' he said. 'Thinking back now to when I was a kid, waiting for Christmas to come, waiting for my birthday to come . . . I did live life waiting for those moments. It put me back in the mind of being a kid and feeling those two boys' anticipation of this movie.'[10]

Boseman's death emphasised the importance of regular screenings and early detection, as colon cancer often shows no symptoms until it reaches an advanced stage. Many were tested as a result, and many may have been saved from aggressive treatment or losing their lives. Or both.

And who can forget the effervescent actress Farrah Fawcett, known for her iconic role in the TV series *Charlie's Angels* in the 1970s and '80s, who fought a brave battle against rectal cancer before her death in 2009. Fawcett's journey was documented in a widely watched television special, raising awareness about the disease, and shedding light on the importance of early detection and treatment options.

There are also celebrities who have survived, in part due to early diagnosis. Sharon Osbourne, well-known television personality and wife of rock legend Ozzy Osbourne, battled stage-two colon cancer with surgery and chemotherapy in 2002 after a small tumour was found. Thankfully she has remained cancer-free ever since.

Reading about the loss of famous personalities with bowel cancer reminded me of the indiscriminate nature of this disease. There have also been some individuals who, with incredible courage, have purposely become famous during the course of their illness to help raise awareness.

Most famously was 'Bowelbabe', Dame Deborah James, in the UK, one of my personal heroes. I took great delight in witnessing her on social media dancing through her chemo sessions and living life to the full. I mentioned her earlier in this book and she was an inspiration as I began my own bowel cancer journey.

Deborah's story began when she was diagnosed with stage-four bowel cancer at the age of 35. Faced with this devastating news, she refused to succumb to despair. In fact, where she could, she dressed up and danced before and after every chemo session.

James was a deputy principal in a high school when she was diagnosed, but stepped away from her career and began blogging about her diagnosis under the name 'Bowelbabe' in 2017. She went on to become a newspaper columnist, publish a book called *F*** You Cancer*, and co-present the popular BBC podcast *You, Me and the Big C* from 2018.

I was heartbroken when she passed away in June 2022. A statement posted by her family on Instagram said: 'Deborah shared her experience with the world to raise awareness, break down barriers, challenge taboos and change the conversation around cancer. Even in her most challenging moments, her determination to raise money and awareness was inspiring.'[11]

James candidly detailed her treatments, progress and diagnosis to her large Instagram following, which rose from 300,000 to 500,000 towards the end of her life.

In a post shortly before her passing, she said she had never expected to reach her fortieth birthday, or see her children grow up. On the last appearance on her podcast, she thanked listeners and strongly urged them to watch for signs of bowel cancer, said in her own humorous and unique way.

'Thank you guys for everything, for being our partners in crime in the club that you never wanted to be part of. I suppose that's it from me. It's a very sad thing to say, but I'm pleased that I have got to the point where I can say it and we'll see each other again somewhere, somehow, dancing. Oh, and also: check your poo. I can't leave on any other words.'

Here in Australia, I was lucky enough to meet one of Deborah's friends, patient advocate Nicole Cooper, who also had stage-four bowel cancer. We met on social media but would often chat in hospital together while we were both undergoing chemotherapy.

She told me once, smiling widely, how when she met Deborah in London for the first time they decided to share a chilled bottle of French champagne to celebrate the fact they had survived and because 'life is short'. I watched in awe as Nicole, a beautiful young mother in her thirties, worked tirelessly to help other patients. Armed with her own story and a determination to spare others the pain her family had endured, Cooper became a prominent figure in the Australian healthcare landscape.

Like all her friends and those who admired her, I was devastated when Nicole passed away in January 2023. She had undergone multiple operations on her liver, lungs and bowel in her five years of bravely fighting the disease, not to mention thousands of hours of chemotherapy.

She fought with dignity until her last breath. In the end, it was simply a common cold that took her life; it turned into pneumonia and, despite all efforts—including two weeks in intensive care—her damaged lungs could not recover. In the hours before her death, she bravely said goodbye to her young son, Josh, her husband, Tim, and the family and friends who were at her bedside.

In her final, beautifully written words to her 10,000 Instagram followers Nicole, who was granted an OAM honour after she died, displayed her trademark intelligence and extraordinary ability to connect with people to raise awareness.

'It's the fragility of this, the incomparable everythingness, the preparedness to take every risk for this group, to truly declare that living in my most sacred and vulnerable and weak and wonderful [way] was worth it all,' she said.

As I worked on the manuscript for this book, another dear friend was at the end stage of his bowel cancer journey, having fought so valiantly and hard for more than three years. Kieren Gaul, a former Sydney financier, ski racer and snow entrepreneur, had become a welcome new friend and cancer mentor. We had visited each other's homes and families, and spoken on the phone a few times a week for more than two years.

With his trademark energy and optimism, Kieren—with his incredible and devoted wife, Paula—travelled the world from Germany to the Gold Coast in search of different and new treatments. As I was working on this chapter, he uploaded a heartbreaking final post and selfie on Facebook. He bravely shared how he was doing his best to live two more weeks so the youngest of his three strong, beautiful daughters could finish her Year 12 exams before he died, near their home in Pambula, New South Wales.

'Cancer is eating me alive,' he wrote, alongside a picture of his incredibly thin frame. 'Almost no muscles. Distended belly. All the fluid is draining into my feet. Hard to walk. Need twice the amount of pain killers as last week. Dying fast . . . I have had so much love and support. Sometimes just all the care and love people have provided make me emotional and cry . . . Whatever it is living is awesome. Make the most of your short stay on this planet.'

In his final sentence, he added: 'Leave a little more love than you take.'

Kieren, to whom this book is dedicated, passed away early in the morning on 17 November 2023, surrounded by his family and beloved dog, Kiko. In a beautiful memoir called *Growth Truth Adventure Love*, he wrote about his extraordinary life full of travel, risk and positive determination. He also suggested his own wild-type bowel cancer may have been caused by the severe stress he faced after an avalanche injured many of his ski guests at his Big Red Cats business in the Canadian mountains. For years he had lived in terror of being sued and losing everything.

However, he was always very interested in my research into processed meats and said that, like me, while he'd always been a healthy eater, red and processed meats were there occasionally in his diet.

Shortly before his death, knowing I was working hard on the manuscript for this book, he sent me a message: 'Processed meats are classified as a class 1 carcinogenic by the World Health Organization. Adding nitrates to meat should be banned.'

Through tears of sadness, I reflected on Kieren's and Nicole's tragic, unfair stories, and on those of other high-profile bowel cancer sufferers. I hope this gives a further glimpse into how devastating this disease can be.

The truth needs to be seen, no matter how raw and confronting. So the narrative of this whole book isn't centred on abstract statistics, which creates distance from those actually living with a disease that might, just might, have been caused by consuming processed meats.

On the website of Bowel Cancer Australia it is made clear that there has been a proven link with the disease.[12] 'Eat very little, if any, processed meats,' the advice reads. Other experts are now also raising the alarm, flagging the link between gut microbiome and bowel cancer. Commonly used emulsifiers, including maltodextrin which is often used in salami and other processed meats, can possibly dramatically change the microbial system.[13] I accept there are other risk factors, and also a lot of unknowns with more research needed, but we do know bowel cancer is life-threatening for the patients, and life-changing for their loved ones. Reminding myself of these tragic stories further fuelled me to continue to investigate how processed meats are impacting health, and possibly causing tragedies such as these. As I was researching these links, I was also being carefully monitored, with blood tests and scans, in case of any reoccurrences.

But I didn't want to stop my work. I accepted that life as a stage-four cancer patient meant regularly fighting hard to stay alive when you had to, but also to keep doing what made your heart sing—and in my case, this meant working on this book. Though grieving the loss of Kieren, my motivation was as strong as ever to get the project to the finish line. My brave, bold friend would have wanted nothing less.

Let's take a journey

You're sitting in the shade on a warm afternoon at a park with a tasty charcuterie board laid out for your picnic. There's nothing more civilised. Perhaps you have some bubbles in a plastic cup, a rug, and a few hours to lie back and read a book.

Before you relax you pick up a slice of salami. Like me, perhaps you've never thought much about exactly what your body does to digest that little piece of meat. Like me, you have probably spent most of your life not really even thinking about your colon, twisted deep within your belly, just quietly going about its business.

Before I was diagnosed with bowel cancer, the science of my digestive system was to me, quite frankly, the great unknown. So, taking inspiration from German author Giulia Enders, who wrote a charming and funny book called *Gut*, I've decided to find out about the journey a piece of salami takes through the human body.

Our bodies, as I've learned the hard way, are incredibly fragile and precious. We don't always appreciate them, or treat them properly or thoughtfully. After all, as Enders says in her book, 'the gut, in most people's eyes, is good for little more than going to the toilet. Apart from that, people think, it just hangs around inside our bellies, letting off a little "steam" every now and then.'[14]

In her book, Enders charted the journey of a piece of cake through the alimentary canal, the series of organs that begins at the mouth and ends at the anus. So I decided to track a piece of salami instead.

First, you put the salami in your mouth. The body's most powerful muscle is the jaw muscle and the most flexible muscle is the tongue. They work together as 'incredible crunchers', as Enders describes it, but also 'nimble manipulators'. You also need the incredible power of your tooth enamel to pound that salami into little swallowable pieces, especially if you've placed the entire slice into your mouth in one go. (I know you have; we all have.)

As you then swallow, the salami pieces are pushed into the oesophagus, which widens to let the food pass, with help from the salivary system. The oesophagus is sealed at the bottom end by a ring-shaped sphincter muscle, which relaxes briefly, allowing the salami to drop into the stomach. When the stomach starts its job the digestive tract wakes up, which is why we often feel the need to go to the toilet after a large meal; the gut makes room for the next arrivals.

A piece of meat like salami can take a few hours to be churned up by stomach acid, producing mushy digested food called chyme. It then reaches the small intestine, where digestive juices from your pancreas and liver break down the fats and proteins in the salami while bile from your gallbladder helps to dissolve the fat.[15]

Minerals, vitamins, other nutrients and water then begin to move through the walls of your small intestine and go into your bloodstream. So too do those pesky nitro-additives. The undigested part of the salami that is left then moves into your large intestine—or colon, as it's also called—which is considered to have a number of functions. It absorbs electrolytes, vitamins and water from the undigested waste, forms your faeces and then eliminates it from your body.[16]

What surprised me further was learning that while food spends around four to six hours in the stomach and six to eight hours in the small intestine, it potentially can spend up to a whopping three days in the large intestine. When I considered this, I realised that I really don't want nasty preservatives and chemicals in my food if they are spending that long lingering in the lining of my digestive system.

In the large intestine, billions and billions of bacteria 'pick over' what the small intestine hasn't been able to manage.[17] Bacteria and other microbes are essential for digestion and so many other bodily functions.

'Countless species of multicellular organisms are so dependent on microbes to break down food, release nutrients, fight invaders, guide development and control reproduction that they could not survive without them,' writes Mike McRae in his book *Unwell*.[18] McRae believes that our affair with the microscopic world is all too casual.

There are many other ways to further explain the workings of the gut, but I found the brilliant author Bill Bryson explained it succinctly in his bestselling book *The Body*. In the chapter 'Guts', he states at the start: 'Inside, you are enormous. Your alimentary canal is about forty-five feet [13.7 metres] long if you are an average sized man, a bit less if you are a woman. The surface area of all that tubing is half an acre. The average journey time from mouth to anus is fifty-five hours. For a woman, typically, it is more like seventy-two. Food lingers inside a woman for nearly a full day longer, with what consequences, if any, we do not know.'

I found this mention of possible consequences interesting. In theory, any chemicals in processed meats could have been marinating far longer in my digestive system than in that of a man.

Overall, though, more men than women get bowel cancer globally. Could these differences between genders be down to different timings of our digestive systems and the synthetic preservatives in processed meats, or are they down to many other factors such as screening, lifestyle and hormonal influences? It could take years of future studies to find out the answer—if we ever do—but it's an interesting question.

As for that piece of salami we are following through the digestive system, we left it being oh-so-slowly digested in your large intestine, where it eventually becomes solid waste or stool. Sorry if this is too much unedifying detail, but as I now often say to my friends, family and social media followers, 'there's no taboo in poo'.

Anyway, your rectum stores stool until you're ready to have a bowel movement. In all, that piece of salami has been in contact with multiple organs and the extent of your digestive tract for possibly a couple of days—its elements are now in your bloodstream.

So how do you feel now, knowing that most major salami (and the rest) manufacturers use nitro-additives as preservatives, and knowing how long that salami takes to be digested?

Unfortunately experts can't definitively say which type of processed meat is worse than another because of the way research is currently conducted. So we can't know if that slice of salami means a greater risk for your body than the same amount of, say, Christmas ham. 'Most studies focus on highly consumed processed meats—hot dogs, bacon, sausages,' Dr Frank Hu, a professor of nutrition and epidemiology at the Harvard T.H. Chan School of Public Health, told *The New York Times* in June 2022. So, because all types of processed meats are grouped together in most studies, 'it's difficult to make a conclusive statement regarding which processed meats are better or worse than others'.[19]

That said, we know nitro-preservatives, which can kill wild pigs and humans at the right doses, go into your bloodstream and rub against the lining of the many metres of your digestive tract. None of it made me feel any better.

What's eating the Slovaks?
There's a beloved national dish in Slovakia, a small landlocked country in Central Europe, that its citizens simply adore. Its name is bryndzové halušky, and it's a dish of potato dumplings covered with sheep's cheese—similar to soft feta—and often topped with a good dose of bacon and bacon fat. To be honest, even though I don't eat bacon anymore it sounds comforting, warm and filling, especially in a country that gets its fair share of freezing winters.

The country and its 5.4 million citizens have an intense love affair with processed meats. Slovak processed-meat sales are apparently set to reach €1.06 billion (A$1.7 billion) by 2026, up from €954 million (A$1.5 billion) in 2021.[20] Put it this way: their appetite for processed meats is growing all the time.

This popularity of preserved pork in particular began back when the country was part of Hungary. (Slovakia gained independence from Hungary in 1939.) In the 1800s, tribes in Hungary had 'droves of swine' forming a great portion of the wealth of the people, 'who chiefly live on a coarse bread and wind-dried bacon'.[21] China, the United States and Japan have the top three overall rates of incidences of colorectal cancer, according to statistics ranked by the World Cancer Research Fund, which isn't surpising considering their large populations.

However, I decided to shine a light on this European country when I realised it ranked number one in the world in deaths from colorectal cancer, based on the number of deaths from the disease per 100,000 people in 2020.[22]

Scientists from the European Commission say excess cancer mortality, especially from lung cancer and bowel cancer, can

Rank	Country	Number	Age-standardised rate per 100,000 people
	World	935,173	9.0
1	Slovakia	2,584	21.0
2	Hungary	4,880	20.2
3	Croatia	2,320	19.6
4	Moldova	1,187	17.6
5	Serbia	3,356	16.7
6	Singapore	1,808	16.2
7	Poland	15,088	16.1
8	Barbados	101	16.1
9	Romania	6,903	14.8
10	Bulgaria	2,768	14.7

be partly explained by the fact that until recently, Slovakia did not have a comprehensive national cancer screening program. It is also a country in which healthcare is lagging in quality overall, plus 21 per cent of those over fifteen years old smoke.[23] So I accept there are some variables in the mix.

I also checked the estimated population numbers for those who are Jewish in the country, aware that the bowel cancer risk is higher for a small percentage of Jews of Eastern European descent. But estimates suggest there are fewer than 10,000 Jewish people in the country.[24] So the link between an increased bowel cancer risk and Jewish heritage didn't seem to be playing a large role in the cancer statistics in Slovakia.

However, here's what shocked me: I then compared the bowel cancer mortality rankings per 100,000 people to the world rankings of processed-meat consumption by country. And when it comes to eating processed meats, Slovakia is ranked number one. Yes, each Slovakian, on average, purchases a whopping 35.8 kilograms of processed meat per year to consume at home—and that doesn't even include the meat eaten in street food, cafes or restaurants. That's one hell of a lot of smoked sausages and ham.

Sitting alone in my office late at night, I felt like a winner and a loser at the same time. This wasn't something I wanted to find out. It made me feel slightly nauseous. For processed-meat consumption in 2022, by average per person the top three countries were:
1. Slovakia
2. Latvia
3. Portugal[25]

For the record, Australia was ranked twenty-fifth in the world for processed-meat consumption, with an average annual consumption of just under 17 kilograms per person.

When I tried to seek a scientific explanation of why Slovaks have such high death rates of bowel cancer per 100,000 people, I was reminded how cancer incidences in Eastern Europe increased after the tragic Chernobyl nuclear plant explosion in 1986. Depending on their distance from Chernobyl and the direction that the nuclear cloud moved, countries received varying amounts of contamination. So were Slovakia's cancer rates affected? According to major studies, while Belarus, Latvia and Estonia all saw higher rates of cancer, Slovakia's cancer rates were unaffected by the disaster.[26]

Some reports I read in fact suggested that the high bowel cancer death rates in Slovakia may be linked to the high incidence of obesity in the country.[27] Yes, you are probably guessing what I turned to next: the global obesity rankings, issued by the WHO in 2024.

And here's the interesting thing, Slovakia was placed fifty-sixth out of 200 countries so it is nowhere near the number one spot for rates of obesity (Australia was forty-fifth) ... but it *is* the number one country in the world for both bowel cancer deaths per 100,000 people and for processed-meat consumption. Are you thinking what I'm thinking?

As I would soon fully understand through my in-depth research, it isn't just bowel cancer that is strongly associated with the consumption of processed meats. I soon became dismayed by the number of other cancers that processed meats have been linked to in many well-respected yet under-publicised reports. Bowel cancer may have made more headlines over the years but, according to studies, several other cancers—like breast cancer, prostate cancer and pancreatic cancer—could be linked to red-meat and processed-meat favourites.

I learned in particular that when nitrates and nitrites in processed meats react with amino acids and form nitrosamines in the stomach, these can then be absorbed into the bloodstream and travel to other organs in the body, potentially increasing the risk of cancer in those areas as well. These other related cancers were briefly mentioned when the WHO made its infamous report in 2015, but have been barely touched upon in the media since.

There was more to uncover—more details that would worry the living daylights out of me.

PART THREE

Chapter Seven
MEAT ME IN THE CELLS

> Nitrites are found in many foods and can be perfectly harmless. But when they are used to cure bacon and that bacon is then cooked and ingested, they produce carcinogenic nitrosamines in the stomach.[1]
> Professor Chris Elliott OBE, Director, Institute for Global Food Safety, Queen's University Belfast, July 2022

Staying abreast of the bad news

As a mother in my forties, I'm beginning to see social media posts by female friends of a similar age to me, or older, who are starting a breast cancer fight. I feel crestfallen every time.

Within weeks of starting chemotherapy, their hair often falls out, including eyelashes and eyebrows, for the main drugs used target any fast-growing cells, not just tumours. Breast cancer patients often have to endure a particularly brutal drug regime, then surgery and sometimes a breast reconstruction. Altogether the treatment process can take years—that's if the cancer isn't fatal.

Breast cancer, of course, is a global health concern, and extensive research has been conducted to understand its complex biology. In Australia, breast cancer is the most diagnosed cancer among women. According to the Cancer Council it is estimated that more than 20,600 people were diagnosed with breast cancer in 2023. It is the second most commonly diagnosed cancer in Australia, and it is estimated that one in eight females will be diagnosed with breast cancer before the age of 85.[2]

Meanwhile, according to the Breast Cancer Foundation NZ, around 3300 women are diagnosed with breast cancer every year in New Zealand. It is estimated that one in nine women in the country will be diagnosed with breast cancer in their lifetime. Māori and Pacific Islander women in New Zealand have a higher incidence of breast cancer diagnoses compared to other groups.[3]

In September 2018, a major review was published in the *International Journal of Cancer*. It examined previous studies that had reported an association between breast cancers and the consumption of red meat and processed meat.[4] The researchers discovered that higher processed-meat consumption was associated with a 9 per cent higher risk of breast cancer, which they concluded 'might' be due to 'high amounts of nitrate and nitrite'.

Researchers did not find a strong link between breast cancer and red-meat consumption in general, but did conclude that 'the high content of saturated fat, cholesterol and heme iron found in red meat may also underlie the association with breast cancer'.

Yet public awareness about a possible link with processed meat was, as far as I could see, close to zero. And there is nothing more motivating to a journalist than to come across a 'gap in public awareness', especially on an issue as important as health.

How many women are eating processed meats, unaware that there are links to an increased risk to breast cancer? I certainly didn't find any warnings on the official breast cancer websites such as Breast Cancer Network Australia, which simply advised women to eat a 'healthy, well-balanced diet' to reduce their risk of getting the disease.[5]

Naturally, it's important to point out that there are many factors associated with the risk of breast cancer in women, including late natural menopause (after the age of 55); not bearing children; having had a first pregnancy after the age of 30; ionising radiation exposure from medical treatment such as X-rays, particularly during puberty; and hormone therapy. There is also strong evidence that regular alcohol consumption and obesity also increase the risk of breast cancer.

It's also important to stress that breast cancer has horrendous statistics globally. In 2020, there were 2.3 million women diagnosed with breast cancer and 685,000 deaths.[6] At the end of 2020, there were 7.8 million women alive who had been diagnosed with breast cancer in the previous five years. It is 'the world's most prevalent cancer', according to the WHO.

And, just like my own experience of bowel cancer treatment, a breast cancer journey is arduous and often barbaric. I would not wish it on anyone.

Fertile destruction

On the subject of women's health it's thanks to a few thousand female Australians that scientists examining meat and fish intake made a startling find. Their results, published in *The American*

Journal of Clinical Nutrition in 2010, suggested that 'low consumption of processed meat and higher consumption of poultry and fish may reduce the risk of ovarian cancer'.[7]

The analysis, which looked at two Australian studies from the 1990s and early 2000s, found that women with the highest intake of processed meat had a significantly increased risk of ovarian cancer. It did not find an association between total or red meat intake and ovarian cancer risk.

It's important to note ovarian cancer is the eighth-most diagnosed cancer in Australian women but has the highest death rate of all gynaecological cancers. More than 1000 Australian women per year will tragically die of the disease. Around 1800 Australian women are diagnosed each year, and around 250,000 worldwide.[8]

What's so devastating about ovarian cancer is that it's often difficult to diagnose. Common tests and scans can often only show abnormalities. Currently, the main way to confirm a diagnosis is by taking a biopsy during surgery and looking at the cells, with many women only diagnosed when their cancer has reached an advanced stage.

Reading further, I noted that the 2010 research that linked ovarian cancer rates with processed meats was partly funded by the Australian Government's National Health and Medical Research Council (NHMRC). Yet the NHMRC's national dietary guidelines, published three years later in 2013, do not mention any links between processed meats and ovarian cancer.

In these Australian Dietary Guidelines, processed meats are included on a pie chart—the same chart I've seen displayed in cancer hospitals in Australia—as 'sometimes' foods. I found this surprising, especially considering the explanations inside their detailed booklet.

'Processed and cured meats can be high in added salt and saturated fat and are not recommended as substitutes for unprocessed meat. These foods fit in the "discretionary foods" category,' the booklet states. 'As with other areas of diet and disease risk, an individual's dietary pattern may be more relevant than a direct effect from a single component.'

Yet a few pages later, the booklet warns that 'Smoked, salted and chemically preserved foods have properties that may be responsible for increased health risks.' It felt like I'd come across another example of mixed messaging from health bodies that did not make the situation fully clear to the public. It wouldn't be the last time.

Calling all men

I was a teen growing up in semi-rural Hampshire when I first witnessed humanity's primal love for meat. Each year, my family started to take part in an annual bonfire party with neighbours and locals. My brother and his friend, a meat-loving chef, would offer to help out with a spit roast—complete with piglet—and lay out fluffy white rolls and apple sauce. The pig's skin would be crisp and crackling, and the guests would be salivating. At first, they would be polite and walk away with their roll wrapped in a serviette, and enjoy watching the fireworks across the fields.

But I can still picture those early November scenes. As the sky turned black early in the evening and the spit was left standing in the dark, the men, in particular, would come out of the shadows and pick at the remains in greedy, contented silence.

It was primal and bonding, I could see that; they simply couldn't resist. Even at my young age I sensed the need to leave them alone, realising that coming between grown men and a juicy carcass wouldn't be a good idea. I didn't need to be told. I just knew. They may not have been lions on the plains of Africa around a kill, but it turns out that grown Englishmen in Barbour jackets and gumboots act in a very similar fashion.

As my research went on, it became clear that men can actually also feel pressured to eat more meat than they really want to. Dietician Jemma O'Hanlon agrees. 'Culturally men tend to have a higher intake of meat and may feel pressured to fit in with social "norms" around meat consumption,' she told me. Within families men are often keen to influence the daily meals with meat, I know that's not always the case but it's certainly the state of culinary play in my household. While my six-foot-three, fit and active husband does enjoy the occasional veggie curry or pumpkin soup for dinner his preference is meat, poultry or fish. While he's thankfully dropped 'plastic ham' white rolls, habitually consumed during his upbringing in Wales, if I very occasionally buy marinated pork ribs his smile lights up the room and his mood is ridiculously joyous.

Even in the pages of some of the books I'd collected, I could see how Australian men's role was often front and centre when it came to processed meat.

King of the Grill: The Bumper Book of No Nonsense Barbecuing by Ross Dobson is one big, blokey affair. Size is everything, it seems, when it comes to the number of pages, the portions of meat and the equipment to cook it on.

'I am lucky enough to have a front verandah with room to spare for my barbecue and me,' Dobson writes proudly in the introduction. 'It is one of those old world oversized verandahs with no logical explanation as to exactly why it need be so big. But who's complaining?' The dozens of recipes within the pages include 'Chicken with bacon and witlof' and 'Christmas barbecued glazed ham'.[9]

I felt it was important to explore this link between meat and men, not least because processed meat may be implicated in a devastating cancer that affects so many men: prostate cancer. In my own family, my beloved father-in-law battled this hideous disease for nearly twenty years, and my brother-in-law in the UK is now embarking on a journey of treatment.

Prostate cancer stands as one of the most common cancers affecting men globally. Amid the ongoing research to identify potential risk factors, the role of diet has come under intense scrutiny. And this cancer, too, has been potentially linked to a diet that includes processed-meat consumption. And this is certainly not a fact that is widely known.

A 2023 study published in the medical journal *BJU International* revealed that a standard Western diet, which includes high-fat dairy products and processed meat, could increase the risk of developing aggressive prostate cancer.[10]

The study examined the diets of 15,296 men recruited in Spain from 1992 to 1996 and used information from the Spanish cohort of the European Prospective Investigation into Cancer and Nutrition, or EPIC. Among these men, 609 prostate cancer cases were identified during a median follow-up of seventeen years. Their diets were categorised as Western (high-fat dairy and processed meats), Prudent (high in vegetables, fruit and whole grains), or Mediterranean (high in fish, olives and legumes).

Perhaps unsurprisingly the study found no effect on prostate cancer risk for the Prudent and Mediterranean diets but a 'detrimental effect' was observed with those who ate a Western diet. 'Our results indicate that avoiding unhealthy dietary habits could be the best nutritional strategy to prevent aggressive prostate cancer,' lead author Adela Castelló-Pastor, PhD, of the Carlos III Institute of Health and CIBERESP in Spain, said in a statement at the time.

Meanwhile, a major French study published in 2022 in the *International Journal of Epidemiology* concluded that nitrates and nitrites as food additives were positively associated with breast and prostate cancer risks. For breast cancer risk, the researchers pointed to potassium nitrate (preservative 252) in particular. For prostate cancer, the study found an association with sodium nitrite, or preservative 250.[11]

The study has tracked the diets of more than 100,000 French adults since 2009 and will continue to do so. 'Although these results need confirmation in other large-scale prospective studies,' the authors concluded, 'they provide new insights in a context of lively debate around the ban of these additives from the food industry.'

I'm not exactly comfortable with the phrase 'lively debate' on a matter so gravely serious, but we get the point—and the food industry should take note. It's clear more studies are needed into prostate cancer and processed meats, and I certainly call for them to happen.

After all, the statistics around this disease are haunting. Prostate cancer is the second-most common cause of cancer-related deaths in Australian men after lung cancer. By 2040, it is predicted there will be 372,000 men living with or having survived prostate cancer in Australia, representing the greatest number of men or women diagnosed with any single cancer.[12]

Nutritional advice in a special booklet on the website for the Prostate Cancer Foundation for Australia does include a note to 'limit processed meats' but it worried me that, at the time of writing, that advice wasn't made clearer on the main home pages of the platform.[13]

If there is indeed a link with processed meats, then the men of this country and beyond deserve to be told.

Grandpa's breakfast

Sitting alone in my garden office one Saturday, working on the main first draft of this book, it was a sudden realisation that made me gasp and my eyes well up with tears. It was a childhood memory that, despite the years I'd spent researching this book, I hadn't yet linked to cancer and processed meats.

My gentle, loving English grandfather, George Rolfe, was a father figure to me growing up. I often spent school holidays enjoying my grandparents' company in Burnham, Berkshire, just outside London, and Grandpa delighted in cooking meals for me and my brother.

PROCESSED

He was a World War II navy veteran, so processed meats such as bacon and sausages were very much part of his daily diet; as with so many of his generation, not a day went by when he didn't go off to work—post-war, as a salesman for EMI—without having eaten a plate of bacon and eggs to fuel his day.

That's just how it was then. Muesli, blueberries, coconut yoghurt and nuts weren't exactly health trends in the 1960s and '70s. Fry-ups, cornflakes, full-fat milk and marmalade on toast were generally the norm on breakfast tables in many countries including England, Australia and New Zealand. I knew that the traditional fried English breakfast was his daily morning meal because he used to cook me a version of his famous 'Grandpa's breakfast' when I was young.

It was, in essence, his own fry-up chopped into small pieces to be child-friendly, complete with the smoky, salty bacon bits running through it. It was sublime—comforting and delicious, like a hug on a plate. It was the familiarity of the meal that, as a child, made me feel like I was in a bubble of security and love. I still remember the joy of managing to get a tiny piece of fried egg and toast on my fork along with a sliver of crispy, salty bacon.

Then our world caved in. In 1987, when I was twelve, a tumour was found in my grandpa's oesophagus. After a brave and traumatic few months fighting the cancer, he passed away. 'I've had a good life' were the heartbreaking words he said to my uncle as he was taken to hospital, where his life ended on a Sunday, in a quiet ward, due to a post-surgical infection.

I never got to say goodbye. My last memory of him was from one of his earlier hospital admissions: him waving from the hospital window and bravely smiling after we visited.

He was just 65 and had worked hard his whole life in order to enjoy his retirement in comfort—a retirement he never got to enjoy. When I was twelve, the age of 65 seemed like old age, but now I find myself understanding fully that it was a relatively young life cruelly cut short.

It was this sudden childhood memory that was sparked as I began reading about studies linking processed-meat consumption and upper gastrointestinal cancers. 'Upper GI cancers' is the term for the group of cancers that affect the upper digestive system. They include cancers of the pancreas, liver, stomach, bile ducts and oesophagus.

Despite collectively representing a significant cause of cancer deaths, upper GI cancers have attracted less government funding for research and treatment than other kinds of cancers. Public awareness is low, sadly in part because patients who are diagnosed are usually faced with a short life expectancy. Their chances of surviving beyond five years after their diagnosis are low. Around 8 per cent of people diagnosed with cancer in Australia have an upper GI cancer.[14]

On its website, Cancer Research UK discusses the role red and processed meat might play: 'There is some evidence that eating processed and red meat increases the risk of stomach and pancreatic cancers. But we need more research to know for sure.'[15]

A similar conclusion was reached by various studies and reports I uncovered during my research. Many found evidence of an increased risk, but due to so many varying factors when carrying out these sort of studies nearly all of the scientists called for further reports.

For example, a 2013 analysis by Chinese researchers found that an intake of red meat and/or processed meat is associated with a higher risk of stomach cancer. 'Processed meat or the processing method itself may play a greater role in this contribution than red meat,' the authors concluded. 'However, the findings from our study need to be confirmed in future research.'[16]

In Australia, stomach cancer alone remains a substantial health challenge. According to government statistics 2576 new cases of stomach cancer were diagnosed in 2023.[17] While this number is lower than in many other countries, it still highlights the importance of understanding risk factors, especially in the context of dietary habits. A key 2016 report by the World Cancer Research Fund declared that foods preserved by salting 'probably' causes stomach cancer, and that eating processed meat may increase the risk of this cancer.[18]

Worryingly, I also found a 2002 study that linked pancreatic cancer in particular with grilled and barbecued meats.[19] With the barbecue culture in Australia being particularly strong, this made me sit up and take notice.

Pancreatic cancer occurs when malignant cells develop in the pancreas, which sits just behind the stomach. The pancreas is vital for producing enzymes for digestion, and for making the hormone insulin that regulates our blood sugar levels. Cancer of the pancreas has very few symptoms in its early stages, spreads quickly and is often detected late with fatal consequences.

It is estimated that in 2023, more than 4500 people in Australia were diagnosed with pancreatic cancer, with an average age at diagnosis of 72 years old.[20]

In the 2002 study, just under 1000 people provided information on their usual meat intake and how it was cooked (fried, grilled, barbecued and so on). The scientists found that 'reported consumption of grilled/barbecued red meat intake was associated with pancreatic cancer'.

As we saw earlier in the book, numerous potential carcinogens are formed in meat cooked at high temperatures: remember those awful heterocyclic amines (HCAs) and polycyclic aromatic hydrocarbons (PAHs)? How meat is cooked, the temperature at which it is cooked, and its degree of 'doneness' (rare, charred and so on) are important factors in forming these carcinogens. Well-done barbecued and pan-fried meats typically contain high levels.

The study of course was unable to pinpoint the exact meats consumed, but we all know the sort of foods, in general, that appear on the average barbecue. And processed meats, such as sausages, are usually there front and centre, which I find incredibly perturbing, especially as pancreatic cancer is often rapidly fatal. As the study authors themselves pointed out, there are very few treatments that can cure the disease, so prevention is 'a potential means to reduce mortality from this cancer'.

The more I read on specific cancers related to higher consumption of processed meats the more worried I got. A 2021 Danish study cited the risk of cancer of the oral cavity and oropharynx was a huge 91 per cent higher among the cases that ate more processed meat compared to controls. The report also revealed that for head and neck cancers the risk was 46 per cent higher among those who had processed meats in their daily diets compared to those who avoided it altogether.[21]

The researchers did conclude that there can be potential variable factors in the mix when it comes to making scientific conclusions about processed meats and health impacts, including age, sex, family history, weight, calorie intake, alcohol consumption and smoking habits. That's the problem when you can't carry out clinical trials with people eating processed meat in real time and instead largely have to rely on food diaries. Limitations aside, that doesn't mean the results can be dismissed, there's just too much at stake.

When it comes to the specific cancer that killed my grandfather researchers have found a link between consuming processed meat and an increased risk of a type of oesophageal cancer called oesophageal adenocarcinoma. The UK has the highest incidence in the world of this type of oesophageal cancer.[22] In 2022, oesophageal cancer was the tenth-most common cause of cancer death in Australia.[23]

Oesophageal cancer starts when abnormal cells develop in the innermost layer (mucosa) of the oesophagus. Oesophageal cancer can spread to nearby lymph nodes or to other parts of the body, most often the liver and lungs, if it's not caught early.[24] It's a nasty, destructive cancer that can also potentially grow through the oesophageal wall. The oesophagus is also an incredibly awkward and risky place to try to surgically remove a tumour, as my grandfather found out to his cost.

The main pre-cancerous state for oesophageal adenocarcinoma is a condition called Barrett's oesophagus, in which the cells in the lower oesophagus change to become more like those in the stomach. Only about 10 per cent of people with this condition know they have it. There is troubling evidence suggesting that inflammation is what causes Barrett's oesophagus to turn into cancer. And remember the advanced glycation end products (AGEs) that are found in cooked bacon? These baddies are potent inflammatory molecules that are linked to increased cancer risk.

Scientists don't yet know if the AGEs in fried bacon make it more of a cancer risk than other processed meat. But, as nutritionist and lecturer Richard Hoffman warns in an article for *The Conversation*, 'The majority of people with undetected Barrett's oesophagus will have developed it as a result of chronic acid reflux. So bacon lovers who are prone to acid reflux may want to avoid bacon while they seek out treatment.'[25]

On the Australian Government's Cancer Australia website it's stated that risk factors for oesophageal cancer include 'frequent and long term consumption of processed, smoked, salted or pickled food'.[26] But are Australians really aware of this?

In my view, it's vital that more research is conducted into the risk factors for oesophageal cancer and all upper GI cancers, just as studies in the past decade have explored the link between processed meats and bowel cancer.

If processed meats, and more specifically nitro-preservatives, are playing a role, then future generations need to know about it. It might be too late for my grandpa—but perhaps it isn't too late for our children.

Chapter Eight

SALTY SORROW

> Excessive sodium intake is the top risk factor for an unhealthy diet, and it is responsible for 1.8 million deaths [worldwide] each year.[1]
>
> Dr Francesco Branca, Director,
> Department of Nutrition for Health and Development,
> World Health Organization, 2023

Sydney the kidney

I once knew an exuberant British journalist called Frank Thorne, who sadly passed away in England in 2021 after complications following a kidney transplant, aged 72. He'd spent years on a dialysis regime.

With his trademark humour he had named his new organ 'Sydney the kidney', after the Australian city where he had based himself as a freelance journalist for the British tabloids for more than twenty colourful years.

He had spent years covering the mysterious disappearance of British backpacker Peter Falconio after Falconio's girlfriend, Joanne Lees, managed to escape from an attacker in the outback.

Sadly, he had to cut short his journalism career and head back to the UK to be with his family after he was diagnosed with kidney cancer.

Frank's jolly, smiling face came to mind when I came across research about the health impacts of excessive salt in our diets, which can raise our risk of heart disease and strokes by increasing blood pressure. While salt (sodium chloride) is an essential nutrient, about 40 per cent of the salt we use is made up of sodium, and it is sodium that puts pressure on our blood vessels, stiffening them over time.[2]

But what about its role in chronic kidney disease—and a possible link with processed meats? Kidney Health Australia estimates that two million Australians are living with chronic kidney disease, but only 10 per cent of them are aware of their condition.[3] As we learned earlier there are also additives often used in processed meats which experts believe could potentially raise kidney issues.

While the charity advises people to limit 'ultra-processed foods' they don't go so far as to name processed meats on their website. They do however include a lot of information about the dangers of a high-salt diet. I knew, of course, that processed meats usually contain large quantities of added salt. Just think of how salty they taste—a slice of pepperoni, say, or the chorizo that you might add to a paella. To many these are important daily pleasures, yet it's also important our precious kidneys work properly. They filter our blood and remove excess water, and require a balance of sodium and potassium to do it effectively. But a high-salt diet will alter this sodium balance, reducing kidney function and causing them to remove less water, putting strain on the kidneys and resulting in higher blood pressure.

A high salt intake can increase the amount of protein in the urine, a major risk factor for a decline in kidney function, and may make existing kidney disease even worse.[4]

Thankfully there are groups of experts who care strongly about this issue. In 2020, a survey by UK campaign group Action on Salt revealed the 'astonishing' levels of salt in bacon. The survey revealed that almost all UK bacon products (86 per cent) had a salt concentration equal to or greater than seawater. Second, it found a lot of variation in salt levels among bacon products; some contained four times the amount of salt of others. Action on Salt pointed to 'the dismal lack of progress made by the food industry in meeting voluntary salt reduction targets'.[5] One bacon sandwich, made with bread and sauce, could easily outstrip the recommended intake of salt for an entire day.[6]

It wasn't only this UK action group making a noise. In early 2023, a WHO report on salt made international headlines. 'We have a huge salt problem. Millions will die without action, WHO warns', shouted the headline in *The Washington Post*.[7] 'Excessive sodium intake is the top risk factor for an unhealthy diet, and it is responsible for 1.8 million deaths each year,' Dr Francesco Branca, director of the WHO's Department of Nutrition for Health and Development, was quoted as saying by the newspaper.

The WHO estimated that seven million lives could be saved if governments across the world included stricter sodium targets for food, labelled salt content more clearly on products and made sure people are encouraged via media campaigns to reduce their sodium intake.[8]

The problem is that many of us are addicted to the saltiness in processed meats, especially bacon. I will explore some alternatives and how to 'reset' our tastebuds later. But for now, I'm not done with health risks. I just can't leave any stones (or risks) unturned.

A mouthful of heartbreak

If you're already heartbroken about the cancer risks surrounding your favourite salami or bacon sandwich then you need to know that these very foods could also break your heart. Literally.

It reminded me of a famous quote of Homer Simpson, of *The Simpsons*: 'You know that feeling you get when a thousand knives of fire are stabbing you in the heart? I got that right now,' he says, clutching his chest and staggering around. Then he spies a plate of crispy bacon and immediately perks up as he begins to eat it: 'Ooh, bacon!'

It's probably obvious to point out that processed meats are packed not only with high amounts of salt but with saturated fats too, but it's worth a reminder. Consuming too much fat, especially saturated fat, can raise cholesterol, which can lead to heart disease and stroke.[9] So we're dealing with a double whammy here: too much salt can also raise blood pressure and raise the risk of heart disease, kidney disease and strokes. In all, these factors are a mixed tape of potential disaster.

For example, on average 100 grams of bacon contains around 14 grams of saturated fat. Pepperoni contains even more, at an average of 15 grams per 100 grams. When you compare this to lean chicken (less than 1 gram of saturated fat per 100 grams) or salmon fillet (3 grams per 100 grams), you can see how eating processed meats regularly could potentially push up your blood cholesterol.

So keeping an eye on fat intake—including hugely fatty processed meats—can help to lower your cholesterol levels and your risk of serious illness. In recent years there has been polarising debate on whether saturated fats, especially in the form of 'cave-men' diets, are in fact good for our health.

However, heart disease in particular, of course, remains a leading cause of death globally, prompting extensive research to identify its risk factors and establish preventive measures. In Australia alone, says the Heart Foundation charity, 2.4 per cent of people report they're living with heart disease, which is well over half a million people.[10] Importantly, heart disease causes more deaths than any other disease globally and is responsible for more than one in ten deaths. And cardiovascular diseases—an umbrella term that includes heart, stroke and blood-vessel diseases—account for one in four of all deaths.

I was heartened (pun intended) to see that the Heart Foundation at least advises people to stay away from processed meats (and limit red meat) in their diets, saying it 'can increase your risk of heart disease and should be avoided'. However, like many other dietary advice sections on health charity pages I discovered this important information was only found when pressing on a link for further information rather on the main lists of recommendations.[11]

Hopefully this will change in time. After all, the link between red meat and heart disease has been known for years, but there was very little research about how processed meats affect heart health until 2021. This was when a decade-long global study, impressive in its scope, was published in *The American Journal of Clinical Nutrition*, and it showed that processed meat has a more significant impact on the risk of heart disease than unprocessed red meat or poultry (chicken, turkey, duck and so on).[12]

In fact the study found that eating 150 grams or more of processed meat a week increased the risk of heart disease by 46 per cent, and the risk of death by a whopping 50 per cent, when compared to eating no processed meat. Just so it's clear: 150 grams of processed meat is only equivalent to around five rashers of bacon, two to three hot dog frankfurts, or five slices of deli meat cut a few millimetres thick. There are likely to be adult meat-eaters in Australia who could easily knock this much back on an average Saturday for breakfast, lunch or during a football game—let alone a week.

'Processed meat appears to be worse for coronary heart disease,' said study co-author Anika Knüppel of the University of Oxford. And as we know, processed meats often undergo cooking processes at high temperatures, leading to the formation of harmful compounds like HCAs and PAHs, which are also implicated in heart disease.

None of it is good news, I'm afraid. You're probably getting the sense that there isn't much good to say about that salami in your fridge you were planning to eat at a picnic or add to a school sandwich. I honestly would love to tell you otherwise.

Stroke by stroke

It wouldn't end there. I had seen some headline-making stories that specifically linked the risk of stroke to processed meats, particularly ischaemic (clot) strokes, and I wanted to know more. Ischaemic strokes, which are the most common type of stroke, occur when an artery carrying blood to part of the brain is blocked, meaning the blood cannot carry glucose and oxygen through to the brain. If this blood supply is blocked, even for just a few minutes, that part of the brain can cease working effectively and the brain tissue can begin to die.[13]

While the Stroke Foundation advises people on their website to choose 'lean meats' (as well as poultry, fish, eggs, tofu etc.) and to limit foods high in salt and saturated fats, they don't specifically mention concerns over processed meats.[14]

In late 2015, a wide-ranging study revealed that the more red meat a person indulges in, the more likely they are to suffer a life-threatening stroke.[15] Its authors found that the protein in the meat increases the chance a person will experience a blockage in the blood vessels that supply the brain. Past studies had raised questions over links between a high-protein diet and strokes, but this study was able to prove not only that a high intake of red meat increased the risk of stroke by 41 per cent, but also that 'the highest intake of processed meats like bacon, sausage and jerky was linked to a 24 per cent higher risk of strokes'.[16]

This wasn't the only research to find the link. A few years later another key study, published in the *European Heart Journal* in 2020, found that eating just 50 grams of red or processed meat on a daily basis was linked to a higher risk of an ischaemic stroke. The risks involved in consuming even just small amounts of these popular everyday meats was becoming a very familiar theme.

Does Domino Don think about all this, do you think? What about McChris? I also wanted to know, but I was still waiting for their replies.

Chapter Nine

PAINFUL REALITY

> If the reader is wise he will always abstain
> from eating sausages, unless he knows of
> their manufacture.[1]
> Edward Abbott, *The English and Australian
> Cookery Book*, 1864

Joint concerns

When it came to writing this book, I did what most authors have to do when they're pitching a project to their publisher or agent—a chapter plan. But a surprising thing happened: my planned single chapter on the possible health impacts of processed meats evolved into four.

The reason? The more I delved into the subject, the more health risks I found were associated with processed meats. I'd find myself researching one health risk and stumbling upon another in a seemingly never-ending salty daisy chain. It has stunned and surprised me. This is a 'food scare' that is even more complex and far-reaching than I ever imagined.

I didn't want to minimise these differing health impacts without giving them their own moment in the spotlight; I felt a duty to those sufferers or potential sufferers of certain conditions, because they deserved to know what I had uncovered.

The link between arthritis and processed meats is a case in point; it's something which I just hadn't planned for. But there it was. And here we are.

Incredibly, 3.6 million Australians have arthritis, of which osteoarthritis, rheumatoid arthritis and gout are the forms from which people suffer the most. That's a very concerning one in seven people, and the older we get, the more likely we are to have it. What I wasn't aware of is that, as Arthritis Australia tells us, arthritis is the 'leading cause of chronic pain and the second most common cause of disability and early retirement due to ill health in Australia'.[2]

The old saying 'You are what you eat' rings especially true for people with arthritis. Certain foods can cause inflammation or increase pain, while others can reduce inflammation and provide relief. And according to a medically reviewed article by a nutritionist in *Medical News Today*, joint pain and other symptoms of rheumatoid arthritis may be worsened by foods such as processed meats due to their inflammatory effects.[3] The expert even noted 'fried bacon' and 'deli meats' as items to avoid. All this is certainly alarming. Scientists say further research is needed to test the effectiveness of plant-based diets for arthritis symptoms.[4] If avoiding processed meats is part of reducing pain for millions of sufferers then the time is now.

PROCESSED

Mind games

Please don't shoot the messenger but there's something I can't forget to share (pun totally intended). There's also building evidence of a link between processed meat and dementia.

It's important to address this condition mainly because of its sheer scale; dementia is the second-leading cause of death of all Australians, and may soon be the leading cause of death. Troublingly, without a medical breakthrough, the number of people in Australia with dementia is expected to increase to more than 800,000 by 2058.[5]

Dementia refers to a group of illnesses (including Alzheimer's disease, frontotemporal dementia, vascular dementia and Lewy body disease) that cause a progressive decline in a person's functioning, in areas like 'memory, intellect, rationality, social skills and physical functioning', according to Dementia Australia. These illnesses are also tough for loved ones, many of whom find themselves caring for a friend or relative with dementia.

In March 2021, a study was published by researchers from the University of Leeds, England, who used data from the UK Biobank, a database containing detailed genetic and health information from nearly half a million people aged 40 to 69. As Richard Hoffman summarises in an article for *The Conversation*, the researchers calculated that 'eating 25g of processed meat per day—the equivalent of one rasher of bacon—was associated with a 44% increased risk of dementia'.[6] In medical terms, or any terms, that's a significant increase.

Strangely, by contrast, they found that consuming 50 grams a day of *unprocessed* red meat, such as beef, pork or veal, was protective, and may reduce the risk of dementia when compared to people eating meat once a week or less. 'To find opposite health effects for processed meat and unprocessed meat is unusual, especially given that many studies show that both processed meat and red meat increase cancer risk,' Hoffman writes.

However, looking at the detail, the Leeds study used a broad definition of processed meats. It not only included ham, bacon and sausages, but also pies, burgers and chicken nuggets.

Of course it's likely that people eating processed-meat products will probably have a taste for other highly processed foods, such as biscuits or lollies, which are part of the typical Western diet, increasing the dementia risk. Either way, it's clearly a risk.

Other research shows Western diets, which include processed meat, are linked to a bigger risk of Alzheimer's in particular. It's believed that the adverse effects of a poor diet on the trillions of gut bacteria are linked with serious brain disorders, including dementia but also mental health conditions.

For instance, a 2018 study carried out by Johns Hopkins University in the United States found a direct link to mania—defined as 'a state of elevated mood, arousal and energy that lasts weeks to months', which is often part of bipolar disorder but can occur with other mental health conditions. People who had experienced manic episodes were three-and-a-half times more likely to have consumed nitro-preservative cured meats. The researchers said that their study adds to evidence that 'certain diets and potentially the amounts and types of bacteria in the gut may contribute to mania and other disorders that affect the brain'.[7]

Five years after this link to mania was proposed, a sobering study in Melbourne, released in 2023, reported that ultra processed foods in general may be linked to anxiety and depression.[8] In describing their findings, the authors called for further research, which is vital in my view in regard to these debilitating conditions.

In an earlier chapter, I discussed how cooking meat at high temperatures is already being seen by some experts as a health risk. Browning on meat is an indicator that toxic compounds like AGEs have formed on the surface, and a 'high concentration of AGEs' may be linked to worsening of Alzheimer's symptoms, researchers have found.[9]

I find this wholly mind-blowing. After all, think of all those sausage sizzles and dinners that involve the browning of the skin or flesh of meat. Considering dementia is among the major causes of death and disability in ageing populations, and there are no effective treatments to reverse it, this is something that urgently needs exploring further.[10] Disturbingly, considering how many processed meat products come vacuum packed in plastic, studies have detected tiny bits and specks of microplastics in human organs and brains, in particular. Researchers at the University of New Mexico found the highest amount of microplastics were found in those who died from dementia.[11]

In her book *The XX Brain*, Dr Lisa Mosconi explores in depth just how much what we choose to eat affects our brains. 'A slew of new research, including my own, shows an important correlation between a healthy diet and a healthy brain,' she writes. 'When consumed in the right amounts and from the right sources, food has marked and measurable beneficial effects on brain health and function. The right diet does ensure that our brain remains stronger, and shows more resilience and activity, regardless of age.'

In addition, Dr Mosconi points out, a healthy diet can be a powerful force in nearly every aspect of our wellbeing.

'In boosting our energy levels, supporting heart health and hormonal harmony, and warding off the wide range of common ailments that affect the majority of adult women in particular, from slow metabolism to insomnia and anxiety.

'Further, what we eat is a powerful epigenetic lever for switching hundreds of thousands of genes on and off, which can help minimize the genetic risk of developing a mind-destroying disease like Alzheimer's.'[12]

But here's the kicker once more that makes all these studies about the risks of processed meats on health in a trial setting so difficult.

Unlike in those wild nineteenth-century experiments on humans in the US involving food additives, today's ethical standards generally do not allow researchers to ask people to eat something potentially harmful in the hope they may see a condition (like dementia) develop. So the only other option is to rely on study participants to keep detailed food diaries over a number of months or years, then try to measure outcomes that way. These studies are possibly good indicators and their results can't be dismissed, but it does make studies more complex and challenging. In a further plot twist, a Harvard study released in August 2024, which involved more than 130,000 US adults, showed those who ate two servings of processed red meat per week had a 14 per cent greater chance of developing dementia.[13]

However we look at it, the link between processed-meat consumption and diseases such as dementia—as well as mental health conditions—is a critical issue that demands attention.

Surprise me, sugar

If there was one thing I certainly didn't expect eating processed meat to be linked to at all, it was diabetes. I'd always associated type 2 diabetes with a diet too high in sugar and carbohydrates. I was wrong.

Diabetes is a life-changing and serious condition in which insulin—a key hormone that controls how glucose is stored and used for energy in our cells—is unable to work as it should. Depending on the type of diabetes a person has, the body may no longer produce insulin, may not produce enough of it, or may not use it as well as it could.[14] When people with diabetes eat foods that contain carbohydrates, the glucose cannot enter the body's cells but stays in the blood. In the long term, these high levels of blood glucose can damage blood vessels and nerves, damaging the heart, brain, kidneys, eyes and feet.

Shockingly, in January 2023, a French study revealed that nitro-preservatives could be causing meat-eaters to develop type 2 diabetes.[15] After analysing data collected from more than 100,000 people in France aged fifteen and older, who had been tracked since 2009, the study team was blunt in its conclusions.

'These results provide a new piece of evidence in the context of current discussions regarding the need for a reduction of nitrite additives' use in processed meats by the food industry,' the authors said. They also pointed out that the results 'could support the need for better regulation of soil contamination by fertilizers' that contain nitrates.

This French study hasn't been the only one to link processed meats with diabetes. Just nine months later, headlines were made with news of a study coming out of the US. 'Just TWO bacon sandwiches a week "raises your risk of type 2 diabetes" as scientists advise new limit on how much red meat you should eat,' screamed a *Daily Mail* headline in October 2023.[16]

Researchers from Harvard University reported this significant result: 'People who eat just two servings of [processed and unprocessed] red meat per week may have an increased risk of developing type 2 diabetes compared to people who eat fewer servings, and the risk increases with greater consumption.'[17] These increased risks are substantial: for every additional daily serving of processed red meat a person ate, there was a 46 per cent greater risk of developing type 2 diabetes. For unprocessed red meat, the increased risk of diabetes with each additional daily serving was 24 per cent.

That's not to say there aren't other factors at play, but nutrition researcher and co-author Xiao Gu summed it up. 'Our findings strongly support dietary guidelines that recommend limiting the consumption of red meat, and this applies to both processed and unprocessed red meat,' he said. The team also pointed out that swapping one daily serving of red meat for another type of protein, like nuts or legumes, reduces the risk of developing type 2 diabetes by 30 per cent.

In his book *Proteinaholic*, author Dr Garth Davis explores this link between animal protein and diabetes in depth. In his view, evidence is mounting that the typical high-protein meat diet is to blame. 'If we avoided animal protein and instead increased consumption of fruits and veggies, we could substantially prevent and treat most of the type-2 diabetes that we encounter,' he writes. 'This may be in part due to the high fiber in the plants, or the phytonutrients in the plants, but it is also due to the reduction in inflammation by avoiding animal protein and fat.'[18]

The author certainly gives us food for thought. Literally. But it doesn't end there.

Supersized

Humans the world over (almost) are getting fatter. The past several decades have seen a shift in the way we eat, drink and move, and it has clashed with our biology to create shifts in our body composition and our health risks. The number of people classified as clinically 'obese' has nearly tripled since the year I was born—1975.[19]

Put simply, excess energy from food and drink is stored in the body as fat in adipose tissue. The size and location of these fat stores vary considerably between populations, between people and over the course of a person's life. Excess body fat is associated with a number of chronic diseases and a reduced life expectancy. The WHO notes that weight issues, which were once associated with high-income countries, 'are now on the rise in low- and middle-income countries, particularly in urban settings'.

PAINFUL REALITY

There is firm evidence that, across the world, particularly in Western countries, there has been an increased intake of energy-dense foods that are high in fats and sugars. Even though additional calories are not the only reason a person might gain weight—there's a range of factors in play, including the quality of the food we eat, according to scientists—I was fascinated to discover that processed meats vary enormously in how many calories they contain. The following table identifies the approximate highest-calorie culprits in your local deli or supermarket.[20]

Calories may vary depending on different brands of course but these tables are important to review. As you can see, all the

Food	Calories per 100 grams
Beef salami	380 cal
Black pudding	244 cal
Chorizo	344 cal
Frankfurter	249 cal
Ham	87 cal
Honey ham	122 cal
Hot sausage	202 cal
Italian salami	348 cal
Italian sausage	293 cal
Parma ham	307 cal
Pastrami	147 cal
Pork salami	902 cal
Salami	380 cal
Serrano ham	232 cal
Smoked ham	122 cal
Turkey ham	83 cal

223

forms of salami came out on top as having the highest calorie count per 100 grams, with Parma ham and sausages a close second and third. Turkey ham is a lower-calorie processed meat, but what a table like this fails to mention, of course, is the preservatives and high level of sodium lurking within.

To help put these rankings in perspective, here is a table with some unprocessed poultry meats, which also have the benefit of not having added nitrates and salt.[21]

Food	Calories per 100 grams
Baked chicken	117 cal
Chicken breast, cooked	99 cal
Ground turkey, cooked	46 cal
Oven-roasted turkey breast	140 cal
Quail	110 cal
Rotisserie chicken	188 cal

At the same time as the Western consumption of high-energy foods has increased, there has been a decrease in our overall physical activity, due to the increasingly sedentary nature of many forms of work, changing modes of transportation and increasing urbanisation.

Obesity is associated with increased risks of multiple health conditions and diseases, including some that have been linked to processed meats: oesophageal, stomach, pancreatic, gall-bladder, liver, colorectal, breast, ovarian, endometrial, prostate and kidney cancers. Processed meats sit within this complex labyrinth of health risks—and it's time to count the cost.

Money, money, money

If anyone had recorded the sound of me writing the main draft of this book, the microphone would have frequently picked up me saying 'Oh, no', followed by a sad sigh. Reading a report on the money spent on treating cancer 'and other neoplasms' in Australia that are estimated to have been caused by dietary factors is a case in point.

It came from a graph I found late one night, buried deep within a government report on health-system expenditure on cancer for both public and private hospitals. The total expenditure on cancer in 2015–16 in Australia was a staggering $10.1 billion, including at least $2.7 billion attributable to health risk factors such as tobacco use, sun exposure, obesity and so on.[22]

And what about those cancers that, as we've seen, may be linked to diets high in processed meats? They are costing the Australian taxpayer an absolute fortune:

- breast cancer ($1.056 billion, including $269 million on screening)
- bowel cancer ($876 million, including $56 million on screening)
- prostate cancer ($684 million)
- kidney cancer ($198 million).

When I drilled down into the detail, I saw that in terms of my own type of cancer—bowel cancer, the cancer that is most closely associated with eating processed meats—the researchers at the Australian Institute of Health and Welfare (AIHW) were actually able to work out the estimated cost to the health system in terms of 'dietary risks'. And that total was estimated to be $134.2 million of the health spending for bowel cancer.

It does not narrow down which type of foods are involved—that's almost impossible, perhaps—but I was impressed and surprised that they were at least able to estimate those costs. Of course, in reality, the figures could well be higher or lower, but at least this indicates the Australian Government is fully aware of the potential impact of diet in cancer—and the cost to the nation.

In the meantime, it wasn't too surprising to find out that more than 9 per cent of total allocated expenditure in the Australian health system ($14.3 billion) in 2020–21 was attributed to cardiovascular disease (CVD).[23] As the AIHW notes, 'The high expenditure on CVD reflects its position as a leading cause of death and a major contributor to the overall burden of disease in Australia.'

The most expensive cardiovascular condition in 2020–21 was coronary heart disease, which cost the Australian healthcare system $2.5 billion, while strokes cost $983 million. As we have seen, these conditions too have been linked by researchers to the consumption of processed meat, among other factors. More important than cost of course, is the suffering and the deaths. I would soon be touched by the story of a little girl from South Australia which highlighted that along with all these long-term health impacts we have explored—many of which can take years to take effect—it's important not to forget the health issues that can strike people down, almost immediately, when the production or storing of processed meat goes terribly wrong, sometimes with fatal consequences.

Remembering Nikki

It was 1995 and the news coming out of Adelaide was about to shock the nation. In front of a gathered group of TV cameras, reporters and photographers, the then South Australian health minister, Dr Michael Armitage, was expressing his deep regrets about the death of Nikki Robinson, a four-year-old girl. She had passed away from 'haemolytic uraemic syndrome' in the Women's and Children's Hospital, he announced, in what turned out to be one of Australia's worst-ever processed-meat food poisoning cases.[24]

The news stunned the country. Armitage confirmed that 24 people had become severely ill from eating a type of salami called mettwurst, made by Adelaide company Garibaldi Smallgoods. The fermented product, it turned out, was contaminated with a strain of bacteria called E. coli 0111. This gut bacterium is found in the intestines of livestock, and it produces a powerful toxin that can contaminate meat during the slaughtering process. Humans can become infected when they eat contaminated meat or dairy products that haven't been cooked or processed properly.

E. coli causes vomiting and diarrhoea, but when it is absorbed into the bloodstream it can also attack the kidneys and blood vessels, resulting in the haemolytic uraemic syndrome that tragically killed little Nikki. 'This is an extremely tragic result of a situation that appears to be almost unique in the world. I extend my condolences to the family of the young child,' Dr Armitage said to the media. For more than fifteen years the incident would drag through the courts as the victims sought compensation. Some suffered so badly they needed organ transplants.

At the original inquest, Garibaldi director Philip Marchi maintained that contaminated meat and not his company's processes was behind the epidemic. 'My personal opinion from having reviewed the test result is that our meat source is the cause of the situation which forced our company into liquidation,' he said. In addition to the 24 severe cases, the coroner noted that 150 others had also fallen ill. Unsurprisingly the victims sued. The final claims against the smallgoods company were eventually settled in 2011,[25] bringing a welcome end to one of South Australia's most lengthy legal cases.

Whatever caused the poisoning, one thing is certain: history has taught the processed-meat industry some harsh, traumatic and expensive lessons about the need for food safety.

There are several other nasty types of poisoning the meat industry has to be extremely careful not to cause. The possibility of botulism poisoning from eating processed meats such as ham and sausage (as well as low-acid preserved vegetables and tinned fish) also comes with terrifying risks; its horrendous symptoms can range from double vision and difficulty in swallowing, to paralysis and death.[26] The spores of the *Clostridium botulinum* bacteria lurk in many foods, but sausages are said to be 'the classic example of the type of food that can be affected, and the word "botulism" in fact derives from the Latin "botulus," meaning sausage'.[27]

In the meantime, processed deli meats, along with other foods such as cheeses, rockmelon and soft-serve ice-cream, also carry a risk of listeria infection (listeriosis), caused by a nasty bacteria that can lead to serious illness and death. In Australia each year, around 150 people are hospitalised with listeriosis and about fifteen people die.[28]

People who are particularly vulnerable to it include pregnant women, unborn and newborn babies, elderly people, and anyone with a weakened immune system due to illness or medications. The problem with managing listeria is that it's tolerant to low temperatures, so it can grow in food that is stored in the fridge.

In the US, there are between 1044 and 2089 cases per year, with a fatality rate of 15.6%. An overwhelming majority of those infections are from deli meat—more than 90 per cent of cases in the US, according to findings from a 2022 study.[29]

These ever-present risks just add to my determination to answer my many remaining questions: how did millions, possibly billions, of people all over the world become so addicted to mass-produced processed meats, meats that we've seen are a danger to health and contain high sodium levels, saturated fats and nasty preservatives? Meats that, if not produced or managed properly, can lead to a swift and agonising death?

I already suspected one reason. That at the centre of this complex dietary maze is food's ability to connect us to our past—to our families, and to comfort. All of which I know is very hard to resist.

PART FOUR

Chapter Ten
MEMORY ADDICTS

> Bacon is like human catnip. If you love bacon like we do, *The Sizzle* podcast is for you . . . Now let's talk about this bacon craze while we're at it. Call it bacon mania, whatever you want. Bacon is here to stay. Bacon's not going anywhere . . . The humongous market interest and unstoppable demand guarantees that bacon is here forever. It's getting bigger. Everything tastes better with bacon wrapped around it.[1]
>
> Phillip Sellers, *The Sizzle* (podcast), episode 1, 2021

The pig in the blanket

It's 3 p.m. on Christmas Eve and I'm busy preparing the feast.

The food prep is nearly complete: two colourful salads and a pavlova, plus cheeses and bubbles chilling in the fridge.

We've been invited to Christmas lunch by Australian friends—my dear friend Debs and her husband, Matt—at their house in Bayside, Melbourne. Starters of seafood and bubbles at their house, followed by salads and more of everything on the beach. It's been nearly fifteen years since I emigrated from

London and it's my first proper Australian Christmas. This is it. It's more picnic than dinner but hey, it's time.

No more slaving over a hot oven trying to recreate the traditional turkey lunch, with all the endless trimmings, of bygone days in Blighty, followed by a stomach-ache, a food coma and passing out on a sun lounger. We can do better; we can join in. After all, we've got the citizenship certificates. We've got the passports. It's time to be true Australians.

I'm looking forward to being freed from the ritual of the hot, ridiculously heavy meal for a carefree 'arvo' on the beach. It feels like it matches who we are now as an Australian family. I'm no longer a pale, newly arrived London girl with her heartbeat made in Hampshire. And here are my two children, with their Aussie-larrikin accents, their skin tanned from a warm start to the summer, their days spent splashing in the sea and messing about on kayaks and boogie boards.

Yes. This is the year. This is the year we do Christmas Aussie style. I've been looking forward to it. It's time to go native and get a flipping grip. It's goodbye roast parsnip, farewell sage-and-onion stuffing.

I glance down to check my phone for the weather forecast for Christmas Day. A south-easterly wind is unexpectedly due to break Melbourne's run of sunny December days. There could even be a shower or two.

I pause. My stomach tightens. My breathing gets faster. Something doesn't feel right—something deep within.

This doesn't seem like it will be a hot balmy Christmas Day in Port Phillip after all. Could it even be—whisper it—*cold*?

Could this actually be close to what Christmas Day feels like back in my homeland: overcast, chilly, cloudy, English? I feel the familiarity, deep within my soul.

It's not going to be a salad kind of Christmas, I think. *It needs a roast. A big one.*

I feel a sense of longing as my mind flashes back to childhood Christmas dinners with my grandparents, when we were all together in their cosy home in Berkshire, outside London. It wasn't always snowing but was often raining and cold, and I felt safe and warm within. The smell of the ridiculously large turkey filled the house before we had even woken up.

Some of the beloved characters in my family picture have long since passed away; the home has been sold. As a child, I felt like it would last forever. Then, when you become an adult, you become painfully aware that everything is transient. Fleeting. Yet isn't it fortunate we can repeat the food, the aromas, the *tradition*. We can bring back the memories and even the people we shared them with through the sensory experience of food. We can go back there, briefly, and pretend that nothing has changed.

I can almost smell that perfect harmony between the mild white flesh of the turkey slices, with the brussels sprouts, the lemon-butter carrots, the stuffing and the cranberry sauce.

And, snuggled in between the crunchy roast potatoes and parsnips, is my favourite gem on the whole heaving plate: the cute little pig in the blanket. The salted, smoked streaky bacon wrapped around a juicy, succulent chipolata. Not a posh sausage—a basic pork sausage that's probably made from the scraps from parts of a pig we all try not to think about. The saltiness cutting through the blander flavours, all surrounded by gravy and bread sauce.

If the dinner had been served up on *MasterChef*, judges would surely declare the pigs in blankets to be 'the hero of the plate'.

I could hardly bear it. I was 12,000 miles below home. I hadn't been to England for more than two years. I'd even been diagnosed with bowel cancer but I still yearned with all my homesick heart for even just a bite of a pig in a nitrite-free blanket as my Christmas Day gift.

I didn't just *want* one. It was a *need*, a yearning. It felt primal.

If I didn't get that pig in a blanket, I feared I might just fall down into a well of despair. Without that taste, that memory, how could it even be Christmas Day? What other tangible thing remained from my happy Christmas dinners of the past?

'Debs, I can't do it. I'm going to rustle up a few hot dishes too,' I said, underplaying the true depths of my roasted Yuletide need as I started the car and raced to the supermarket.

'Sure, darls, we can eat it before we go down the beach,' Debs replied breezily, not realising the tsunami of British Christmas food that was about to smash into her front door.

And so it came to pass that we arrived with a boot packed with a full English roast outside the home of a bemused Australian family. A family that, to this day, may still be slightly offended that we weren't going to be satisfied with their incredibly generous offering of smoked-salmon canapés, champagne oysters and lobster thermidor.

Of course we never did make it to the beach that Christmas in 2020. And we never got to taste the lobster. We were all so stuffed with the carbs, the seven different hot vegetables, and those precious pigs in their divine little blankets. The pigs that tasted of home and made me feel like I was back at my grandparents' table. The taste of that steaming-hot lunch I had eaten on every single Christmas Day for 45 years, including every one of my fifteen years living Down Under as the temperatures nudged 40 degrees and bushfires raged in the countryside.

Looking back now, the idea that I wouldn't get to taste that little pig in a blanket—the Yuletide treat that had been hardwired, powerfully, into my psyche during my childhood—was holding my mental health hostage.

Yes, dear reader, I singlehandedly placed that innocent, kind and slightly bemused Australian family into a Christmas Day food coma because of my yearning for processed meat. And I bet you've been there too. Food, whether it's processed meats or another favourite, connect you to family and to memories. Above all, food makes you feel at home, as if you are sitting at the table of your own mothership or docked in your home port, no matter how far away you are.

You may have no intention of giving up processed meat, or, like me, you may have your own pig in a blanket—those particular 'Achilles heel' moments that you just can't resist.

There is a deep connection between processed meats, history and culture. It's something Rebecca Taylor, Head of Policy and Public Affairs at the World Cancer Research Fund, pointed out in a powerful blog in February 2023. 'Dishes containing processed meat often form part of a country's culinary heritage and can have a special place in people's hearts,' she wrote. 'There are many cultural and social traditions that involve food and this is one of the beautiful things about food—it brings people together.' She goes on to point out that the link between processed meats and colorectal cancer is not well known by the public.[2]

Psychiatrist and author Dr Tanveer Ahmed said he totally understood when I told him about my sudden yearning for pigs in blankets, which are part of my own heritage and culture.

'The smells and rituals associated with food evoke very powerful memories,' he said. 'Smell, for example, is one of the most primitive and powerful senses, especially in its links to memory. Things like the pig-in-the-blanket tradition hold so much meaning, that link you to past ancestry and a whole set of English traditions, including with your grandparents.'

While food has the practical job of nourishing us, he explained, it is arguably one of the most critical components in rituals, collective bonding and sustaining traditions. 'It brings us together,' he noted. 'It also underlines key events such as weddings, funerals or other sacred rituals. It enforces identity. For example, Catholics ate fish, and banned [eating] meat, as a way of marking their difference from Protestants—likewise the ban on pork for Muslims and Jews. What is eaten or not eaten often marks the sacred.'

It's true that meats often play key roles in traditions that link us to our past, particularly to our ancestors. 'This is especially true of rituals around Christmas,' Dr Ahmed said. 'Maybe how the turkey is roasted or what side dishes get served. It is also why specific dishes are only cooked at special occasions like Easter,

Christmas, the end of Ramadan for Muslims, or weddings and funerals.' Another expert agreed. Samantha Harskamp, a youth and adult psychologist in Melbourne, said studies have shown individuals can have heightened recall of autobiographical memories associated with food. 'The richness of sensory detail strengthens the memory,' she told me.[3]

If we look at traditional collective cultures, it's clear to see how food is often the key marker of status, rituals and connectedness.

'Nothing—not a conversation, not a handshake or even a hug—establishes friendships so forcefully as eating together,' writes Jonathan Safran Foer in his book *Eating Animals*. 'Maybe it's cultural. Maybe it's an echo from the communal feasts of our ancestors.'[4]

It was good having my feelings echoed by those who understand that foods can be a bridge to a past, especially for migrants like me and millions of others, who have left their homes to start a new life down under. And it was good to know that experts understand that what we eat is often about a lost connection to a loved one.

I noticed a post from one of my followers on X that said, whimsically, 'Once in a while I buy a tin of corned beef & make a meat & potato pie like my Mum did.'[5]

Tinned meat. Now that got me thinking.

You don't say ham, you say SPAM!

'Open it,' I urge my teen son, Nate. 'This isn't just food—it's a piece of food history. I'm going to write about it in my book.'

PROCESSED

I hand him a classic 340-gram tin of Spam I've just bought from among a wide range of varieties at Coles for just over $6.

'Eww,' he recoils, as the odour of the world's most infamous processed-meat brand wafts across the kitchen.

To be fair, smells are powerful forces, as Dr Ahmed had pointed out. When you smell something, to process the smell, your brain uses the same areas that it would use to process emotions and memories. And the fact is when you smell an odour, you're actually breathing in tiny molecules which stimulate nerve cells high inside the nose.

With a few million of these cells inside your nose mine were certainly activated when I smelled the tin of salty Spam.

Suddenly, I was at a different table in a different decade—a small, foldable plastic table inside a cosy static caravan in Cornwall, England, with my brother, Matthew, my cousin Sophie, and our late grandparents George and Jean. It was another long-forgotten scene I hadn't thought about for years.

As the deeply familiar smell of Spam activated something deep in my brain, I remembered our happy, carefree annual holidays there together during the 1980s, before Grandpa George had got sick from oesophageal cancer. I remembered how, after we'd spent a day splashing in the waves at the beach, my grandparents would serve up cold slices of Spam or corned beef with bread, butter lettuce, tomatoes and cucumber, topped off with a dollop of salad cream. I suddenly felt nostalgic again for my lost grandparents, my home country and my innocent childhood days—just as I had done when I bit down on a pig in a blanket.

Yes, despite my sheer hatred for processed meats by this point, the smell of that tin of Spam was making me feel nostalgic, emotional and—rather bizarrely—*happy*.

It also took me back to standing in line for hot school dinners at the canteen in my little local primary school in Hampshire. Spam fritters were a favourite. The crunch of the deep-fried batter. The soft, meaty centre.

Thankfully, my experience with bowel cancer ensured that I wouldn't start eating tinned Spam again. I didn't even want to taste it. Neither did my son. I had read about how it is made and—surprise, surprise—it starts out as a sloppy mix, just like many 'manufactured' hams. The mixture is poured into the tin and cooked, so that it can either be eaten as soon as the lid is peeled off or cooked further.

I was thankful for my son's reluctance to try the meat himself because the ingredient list, which largely hasn't changed (aside from adding a thickener in 2009[6]) since Spam was invented in 1937, reads as follows:

Pork (92%), Water, Salt, Thickener (1442), Sugar, Preservative (250), Colour (160b), Humectant (1520)

Sigh. Yes, there it was. Preservative 250—sodium nitrite. The classic tin of Spam also contained the omnipresent preservative that I was still gunning for with all my might. Our two cats and our cavoodle dog, however, didn't give a hoot about the ingredients, circling us with pure excitement.

But it got me thinking. By 1959, a billion cans of the product had been sold, and to date it has produced more than nine billion cans.[7] Therefore, quite a large part of the world's population has eaten Spam since 1937. And that means billions of people have been eating the sodium nitrite inside Spam too. And we know all about the many risks of that bad-boy preservative now, don't we? Let alone all the salt and saturated fat that also comes in every tin of Spam.

So are you thinking what I'm thinking? Could Spam, considering its global popularity since the 1930s, have played a role in possibly millions of people all over the world being diagnosed with bowel cancer and other health issues? The thought made me shudder.

Health experts have recently been raising their concerns about possible impacts. US-based dietician Rachael Ajmera believes that, as a highly processed meat containing sodium nitrite, Spam may be 'associated with a higher risk of certain types of cancer and type 1 diabetes'. Spam, she writes, is also high in sodium—which, as we know, may be an issue for 'people with a sensitivity to salt and for those with high blood pressure'. 'High sodium intake may also be linked to a higher risk of stomach cancer,' Ajmera notes.[8] The other ingredient in Spam that caused me to feel alarmed is the one listed as 'humectant'. It's actually a description for a number of troubling additive substances we've met earlier, which can add moisture, or help retain it, but presents health risks including kidney issues.

Right from its conception, Spam—initially presented as a 'spiced ham luncheon meat'—was incredibly popular as a cheap, long-life protein that could feed a whole family for dinner if it was served with potatoes, rice or bread. It could be eaten cold but also baked or fried, as millions discovered as they began to emerge from the Great Depression. It was when it was served in World War II, when more than 45 million kilograms of Spam were consumed by Allied soldiers, that the brand became a global household name.

Famously, a 1970 episode of the comedy series *Monty Python's Flying Circus* used the word 'Spam' more than 130 times in three and a half minutes. The skit setting was a British cafe in which every breakfast option seemed to contain Spam, much to the exasperation of a customer.

Such is the popularity of the brand the company even opened a museum in 1991 dedicated to the product at its headquarters in Austin, Minnesota.

Today, the United States consumes the most Spam, followed by South Korea. It's actually also hugely popular in areas of the Pacific where American soldiers introduced tins of Spam to the locals; today the average Hawaiian, for example, eats at least five tins of Spam a year. In the meantime, on the island of Guam in the western Pacific, each person eats, on average, a massive sixteen cans per year.

As for its popularity in Australia, a lot of it is thanks to aggressive marketing in the twentieth century. I spent time watching YouTube clips of Spam commercials in 1980s Australia. One campaign had the catchphrase, 'You don't say ham, you say spam!' Other adverts encouraged viewers to use the 'meat' in a wide variety of ways: adding it to fried rice; slicing it up, placing it on cream crackers and topping it with olives; and adding it to omelettes.

Spam was just so versatile and so beloved. And, to be fair, it could be stored for months or even years, which was very useful in remote towns, communities and farms across Australia.

The same goes for tins of corned beef—and yes, you guessed it, these also generally have nitro-preservative added.

In his book *Salt*, Mark Kurlansky notes that the Irish produced a salted beef in the Middle Ages that was the 'forerunner of what today is known as Irish corned beef', and in the seventeenth century, the English named it 'corned beef'.[9]

Woolworths' own branded tin, priced at around $8 (sometimes less in special deals or online), contains the same weight of meat as Spam—340 grams. The label promises it is a 'good source of protein'. The ingredient label on the back also clearly confirms the baddie in the mix:

Beef (98%), Salt, Cane Sugar, Preservative (Sodium Nitrite)

So there it was. Two of Australia's most relied upon tins of meat for the best part of a century both contained, and still do contain, preservative 250. Just how many of these tins has the average Australian—not to mention others around the world—eaten during their life, decade after decade?

My request for Spam anecdotes on social media in November 2023 garnered nearly 100 comments within an hour. It was certainly a popular yet divisive subject, with many sharing memories of hating the tinned meat as children, while others admitted to still buying Spam and cooking it just like their parents had done decades before.

'I think the price in Australia is too high for it to be as popular as it once was,' one follower told me. 'That aside I still enjoy it. I like it fried or grilled with a good amount of melted cheese on it then put it on a serving plate topping it with pineapple.'[10]

A Coles executive once told me that the company knows when Australians are facing economic pressure because Spam sales go up. 'In the food industry it's a well-known fact that a spike in Spam sales can predict a recession quite accurately,' he confided.

So who is in charge of this drive to keep Spam (and its nitro-preservative) on the dinner plates of the entire world? And who is profiting from it?

The producer and owner of Spam is still Hormel Foods, of which The Hormel Foundation owns 48 per cent. At the time of writing the largest shareholders are some of the world's major investment companies including State Street Global Advisors, Vanguard Group, Inc. and BlackRock, Inc. In theory, this means they have considerable power to influence the company's decisions. Around 10 per cent of the company is owned by the general public, through private investors.[11]

According to various financial reports, around 1 per cent of the company's shares are owned by 'company insiders', which is business-speak for figures such as board members and the CEO—who, in this case, is a chap called Jim Snee. Yes, Hormel Foods also has other food and business interests but, for the sake of this book, let's call him Spam Boss Jim.

According to a Wall Street report the precise amount of the shares owned by the CEO, who was appointed in 2015, is

0.5 per cent of the company, and in 2023 these shares were said to be worth around US$9 million. His total yearly 'compensation' is just under US$10 million, comprised of 10.6 per cent salary and the rest as bonuses, including company stock and options.

And yes, you probably know what's coming next. After feeling more and more concerned about the potential impact that Spam and Hormel Foods may be having on the health of consumers all over the world, I knew it was time to send Spam Boss Jim a letter *à la Français*. I'd done some more reading on the company, you see. I found out they also fund a cancer centre which was all rather baffling. I needed some answers.

Letter to America

After introducing myself and sharing key scientific evidence regarding nitro-preservatives, I sent the following questions to Spam Boss Jim, via his media team.

1. In light of the mounting evidence, is Hormel Foods considering using an organic preservative instead of sodium nitrite in Spam in the future?
2. In light of the cancer risks related to nitro-preservatives, is Hormel considering adding warning labels to all its Spam products? Do you think that would be fair in terms of safety of a product which is consumed globally by millions of people including young children?
3. Some health experts and bowel cancer patients like me would prefer Hormel Foods to cease production of all

Spam products in light of the links to cancer. What is your reaction to that?

4. Hormel Foods gives dividends to the Hormel Foundation, which supports the Hormel Institute, which carries out cancer research projects and studies on other chronic illnesses. While this is obviously a cause I support hugely I also ask the question whether the Foundation directors are concerned that Spam products, owned by Hormel, could be causing cancer? Does that not worry them hugely knowing how devastating cancer is through the cancer centre?

5. In 2022, The Hormel Institute's Ningling Kang, PhD, associate professor and leader of the Tumor Microenvironment and Metastasis research section, received a grant titled 'Hepatic Stellate Cell Regulation of Metastatic Growth in the Liver'. The five-year, $2 million R01 award was awarded by the National Cancer Institute (NCI) at the National Institutes of Health (NIH).

Liver metastasis is obviously a process where cancer cells that originated from a different part of the body spread to the liver.

This is the exact same cancer I have. Therefore I naturally applaud Dr Kang's research and look forward to reading the results. However, I also find it a little troubling that, at the same time Hormel Foods (and the foundation that owns it) could well be part of the high bowel cancer rates all over the world with its massive sales of Spam in multiple countries? What is Hormel CEO Jim Snee's response to this?

6. I would also be very keen for a direct comment from Hormel Foods CEO Jim Snee, in response to the following question: In the light of growing evidence of the risks of sodium nitrate in terms of bowel cancer and other health impacts, is he confident all the millions of unopened cans of various types of Spam (which all contain sodium nitrite) which are currently in Australian supermarkets, homes and in restaurants are 100 per cent safe for consumption and pose no risk at all to health?

7. Any further comment or information you'd like to share.

Many thanks in advance.

So far, I haven't heard back from Spam Boss Jim or anyone at Hormel Foods, or indeed The Hormel Foundation.

But hey, it may well be their reply is sitting in my Spam folder somewhere. I didn't have time to wait around for answers. This tinned-meat business had sparked my yearning to learn more about how Australia became so addicted to pork in the first place—a meat that isn't exactly native to this great southern land.

Yes, it's time to talk about how that cured pork ended up on your fork.

Chapter Eleven
RECIPE FOR DISASTER

> After the month, hang them up in the smoke of a wood fire for ten days. Many people in the bush just hang them in the chimney.[1]
>
> Mrs Lance Rawson on making bacon,
> *The Queensland Cookery and Poultry Book*, 1890

Blighty calling

When you bite down on a piece of pork in Australia, you are certainly consuming an intriguing part of our food history. On a recent visit to England, I explained to my children how we were likely to see many wild ponies, foals and donkeys on the side of the pretty, meandering lanes and roads. We were in the New Forest in Hampshire, where I had grown up. Drivers like us, I warned them, had to take a lot of care.

It had been so many years since we had returned, thanks to a global pandemic and cancer, that I was just as excited as they were to see the natural wonders of this glorious, historic part of the United Kingdom.

Literally the first animal we saw, however—prompting shrieks of laughter—was a large pig quite contentedly nibbling grass on the side of the road.

The New Forest still follows the ancient practice of allowing those with commoners' rights to free their domestic pigs for around 60 days a year to roam the woods, streams and grasslands.[2] It makes for beautiful scenes that delight locals and tourists alike.

There is still a useful purpose for these pigs in particular, in a season known as pannage, which occurs every September. Acorns and other nuts fall from the trees, and the pigs scour the forest to eat them up, unknowingly helping the ponies, donkeys and cattle for whom these 'pig treats' would be poisonous. Pannage was first permitted by William the Conqueror, who founded the New Forest in 1079, at a time when most rural families kept pigs and noble homes had herds of them. During the nineteenth century, as many as 6000 pigs would roam the New Forest during this season; today there are about 600 of them.

The fact that pigs still roam the forest is a link back to the time when 'every peasant [had] one or more of that useful animal', as stated in one of the most influential food books of the late nineteenth century—*Beeton's Book of Household Management*, published in 1861.[3] Not only does Isabella Beeton make an admirable effort in her brick-sized tome to instruct the readers on how to raise various varieties of pigs, but she also includes methods of curing the pork and what dishes to make with it.

In between recipes, Beeton pauses to reveal some fascinating insights:

In German Switzerland, the Tyrol, and other mountainous districts of continental Europe, though the inhabitants, almost everywhere, as in England, keep one or more pigs, they are at little no trouble in feeding them, one or more men being employed by one or several villages as swine-herds; who, at a certain hour, every morning, call for the pig or pigs, and driving them to their feeding grounds on the mountain-side and in the wood, take custody of the herd till, on the approach of the night, they are collected into a compact body and driven home for a night's repose in their several sites.

As for bacon recipes, well, they are almost endless. But making it from scratch is clearly a passion Beeton held very dear. To cure the bacon 'in the Wiltshire way', she instructs the readers to use the following recipe for the 'flitches' (the name for the meat consisting of the two sides of the pig) as follows:

Ingredients—1 1/2 lb. of coarse sugar, 1 1/2 lb. of bay-salt, 6 oz. of saltpetre, 1 lb. of common salt.
Mode—Sprinkle each flitch with salt, and let the blood drain off for 24 hours; then pound and mix the above ingredients well together and rub it well into the meat, which should be turned every day for a month; then hang it to dry and afterwards smoke it for 10 days.
Time—To remain in the pickle 1 month, to be smoked 10 days.
Sufficient—The above quantity of salt for 1 pig.

PROCESSED

The place for salting pork for bacon must always be cool and well ventilated, she goes on to tell the reader firmly: 'Confined air, though cool, will taint meat sooner than the midday sun accompanied by a breeze.'

With regard to then smoking the bacon, two precautions were necessary: 'first, to hang the flitches where no rain comes down upon them; and next, that the smoke must proceed from wood, not peat, turf, or coal'. Smoking time depended on whether a fire was burning under it—and whether that fire was large or small.

As for sausages, Beeton offers her readers a rather pure recipe compared to the mass-produced versions in supermarkets, packed with chemical preservatives, that we see on display today:

> *Ingredients*—1 lb. of pork, fat and lean, without skin or gristle; 1 lb. of lean veal, 1 lb. of beef suet, 1/2 lb. of bread crumbs, the rind of 1/2 a lemon, 1 small nutmeg, 6 sage-leaves, 1 teaspoonful of pepper, 2 teaspoonfuls of salt, 1/2 teaspoonful of savoury, 1/2 teaspoonful of pepper, 2 teaspoonfuls of salt, 1/2 teaspoonful of savoury, 1/2 teaspoonful of marjoram.

When these ingredients are thoroughly mixed, including the peppery tasting herb 'savoury', Beeton tells the reader, 'either put the meat into skins, or, when wanted for table, form it into little cakes, which should be floured and fried'. (It should be noted for safety's sake that these days it's advised to only use a tiny amount of nutmeg as it can be toxic in high quantities.)

While wild boar were native to England, domesticated pigs arrived in Europe from the Middle East region around 8500 years ago. Today DNA of many domesticated pig breeds can be traced back to both.[4] Movement of the first farmers in Europe would have been challenging. They would have taken small skin boats to make the dangerous crossing across the English Channel to ferry animals to the British Isles.[5] I find this thought extraordinary—that the sausage sizzles you munch on here in Australia can be in part traced back to this daring feat of sailing pigs across the English Channel.

In her book *Tasting the Past*, food historian Jacqui Wood explores the culinary history of Britain, looking at the traditions that were later exported here to Australia with the early colonists. The ancient Celts, who lived in Western and Central Europe (including Britain) from around 700 BC to 400 AD, ate simply. 'On the whole, Celtic food was simple and unadulterated, with lots of meat, fish, bread and butter and chunks of cheese,' Wood explains.[6] There was also preserved pork; the Celts often kept domesticated pigs, which were smaller than today's farm pigs.

It was generally these pigs, rather than the wild boars roaming ancient Britain, that provided the Celts with their ham, sausages and bacon. It's estimated that these meats would only have accounted for about 10 per cent of the Celts' total meat consumption.[7] Lamb, mutton, pigeon, rabbit, beef, duck and baked pork would have also been on the menu.

In another 'back to the future' moment of learning, I'm fascinated by my facsimile edition of *The Forme of Cury*, a collection of medieval English recipes from the fourteenth century, believed to be one of the earliest English cookery books ('cury' means 'cookery' in Middle English). In one manuscript version, it's said to be the work of 'the chief Master Cooks of King Richard II'. As a history lover, I treasure this book; it's a tangible bridge to the palates of the past.

My version was edited by Samuel Pegge in the late 1700s. He notes in his preface that British food habits were heavily influenced by invaders, and that the Romans, Vikings, Anglo-Saxons and French brought their own influences to the English table. Many ingredients that were in vogue in the fourteenth century—such as cranes, herons, seals and porpoises—are (thankfully) out of fashion as meals, but other recipes reveal a glimpse of processed-meat trends that furnish our tables today.

These include a form of sausage pie in which sausage balls are baked in pastry. The recipe has the title 'Rasyols' and, according to a modern English translation, instructs the cook as follows:

> Take swine livers and boil them well, take bread and grate it; and take yolks of eggs, & make it supple, and do there-to a little lard carved like a dice, cheese grated, & white grease, powder douce & of ginger, & wind it to balls as great as apples. Take the caul of the swine & cast ever by himself there-in. Make a crust in a pan, & lay the balls there-in, & bake it; and when they be enough, put there-in a layer of eggs with powder fort and saffron and serve it forth.[8]

It's very similar, in essence, to the meat pie, one of our nation's most beloved snacks.

We are sailing

By this stage of my research, in my own health journey I had reached a relatively high point after many, many low points. In November 2023, I marked my four-year anniversary since diagnosis, and two months earlier had undergone a course of radiation at the Olivia Newton-John Cancer Wellness & Research Centre at Melbourne's Austin Hospital. I'd been told to hold my breath multiple times inside a special machine as it worked to blast away two tiny metastatic spots on my liver.

Finally, I found myself able to work consistently and to be an engaged mother once more, and had taken up ocean swimming to boot.

The result? Unfortunately for those involved in the processed-meat industry, I was in active pursuit of the facts. I was brimming with research—and dangerous with ideas. I had miraculously survived stage-four cancer—so far, at least—against all the odds. But many of the dear and cherished friends I had made in the stage-four bowel cancer community were passing away, month by month, year by year. I had to finish this book for them.

I'd already found out a great deal and confronted a lot of the major processed-meat power-players, but I still wanted to know more about how Australia became so dependent on processed meats.

Just a few years after Samuel Pegge published his edition of *The Forme of Cury*, ships began sailing from Britain to

PROCESSED

Australia with convicts and colonists, carrying live pigs (and other animals) across the world and into our processed-meat future. When I turned to reading more about the many ships that carried these colonists from the British Isles to Australia, I found that preserved meats were very much part of their on-board diets.

In a rich and moving account, Robin Haines charts these arduous, challenging and often fatal maritime journeys, and her book *Life and Death in the Age of Sail* is a very important record of life on board those ships. After all, in the nineteenth century about 750,000 government-assisted emigrants crossed the world from the United Kingdom and Ireland to Australia.

They travelled around 24,000 kilometres, usually without stopping en route, often in cramped conditions and occasionally with up to 500 people on board a single ship. Many died of disease and malnutrition during the journey, especially babies and children.

The regimes were strict, and passengers were given set weekly rations, organised by age and gender. According to a scale from 1854, the rations for all passengers aged over fourteen included 8 ounces (about 220 grams) of preserved meat on a Sunday, Tuesday and Thursday. Foods issued on other days of the week included rice, peas, suet, oatmeal, flour and butter.[9] A detailed account by Edward Allchurch, a passenger who boarded the *Atalanta* in Plymouth Sound in January 1866, spoke of the bitter cold and how hungry the passengers were on the ship, waiting for dinner 'like hungry wolves'. He appreciated days when the passengers were given fresh meat, but was not impressed when live pigs were killed on board on a Sunday—'it was the Sabbath', he wrote with disdain.

Not only were immigrants eating cured meats on their way to Australia, but they also carried with them knowledge of how to make their favourite varieties, perhaps even bringing copies of Isabella Beeton's book with them after its publication. It's still one of the most famous cookery books of all time, and Beeton's influence on Australia's cured-meat habits remains today.

Of course, before European colonisation in 1788, Indigenous peoples had been living very successfully in a wide variety of environments, without needing the salt-laden bacons, hams and sausages that are now consumed across the country. The Indigenous people who have occupied Australia for at least 60,000 years did eat meat alongside plant foods, but the meat was far healthier, having been hunted and eaten fresh or dried in the sun.

Kangaroo meat is probably the best known in Australia and overseas as our native alternative to Western meats. The animals were often 'smoked out' by grass fires, then speared, butchered and roasted on a fire, and their meat served alongside snakes and turtles, which are still hunted by Aboriginal and Torres Strait Islander people around Australia.[10]

On a recent visit to the Northern Territory funded by the Meta Australian News Fund in partnership with the Walkley Foundation, I visited a remote Indigenous Community, Binjari near Katherine, where I noticed residents' eyes lit up when they talked about their love of going 'out bush' to hunt, fish, camp and cook. 'My dream is to live by a river,' one single mother of five young children quietly told me, speaking from inside her run-down, two-bedroom commission house. She clearly wished they could live off the land, instead of Woolworths. It was the same story when I also visited the remote beach community of Yarrabah, in Far North Queensland, where Indigenous children and teens still catch mud crabs, carefully avoiding any signs of crocodiles lurking in the shallows.

As John Newton points out in his book *The Oldest Foods on Earth*, before the British arrived in 1788 the Aboriginal populations of the tropical north alone chose from among a massive 750 different plant and animal foods:

> In more than 200 years of occupation of this continent, European Australians have turned their backs on the vast majority of the foods the Indigenous people have been eating for more than 50,000 years; ignored their sage and intricate management of the environment and its abundant foods; overlaid an alien system of agriculture which began the process of ecological imbalance the continent now finds itself in; and began exporting back to Europe the exotic foodstuffs they planted and raised. And, for around 150 years, stuck stubbornly to the diet of the first settlers. In short, we lived on and not in this continent . . .
>
> Australian native foods, foods that we've virtually ignored for the 200-plus years we've been here, are super-duperfoods.[11]

Yet hundreds of thousands of colonists, arriving year after year, brought with them many questionable food habits that would dominate our national diet. 'Food racism', says Newton, played a big part in the rejection of Aboriginal foods. 'It is only one of the many kinds of racism directed against the Aboriginal people, even today,' he adds.

Likewise, environmentalist and author Tim Flannery has argued how the Australian ecosystem, and the Indigenous peoples' way of life, seemed too 'foreign' to the Europeans. 'These factors, as much as any, account for the extraordinary lack of sensitivity of the first European colonisers of Australia to their new environment,' he wrote in his 1994 book *The Future Eaters*. 'They clearly led to enormous environmental damage and helped form the crippled environment that Australians inhabit today.'[12]

As far as food goes, Newton believes that a growing modern acceptance of native foods could help towards a 'culinary reconciliation'. Ingredients beloved by Indigenous peoples are finally beginning to be used more widely by home cooks and professional chefs. Kakadu plum, lemon myrtle and wattle seed are all ingredients that I've noticed packaged by bespoke brands, and some are even appearing in Australian supermarkets, especially in biscuits and other bakery products. Kangaroo meat, which is high in protein yet low in fat, is also on sale in most major supermarkets today.

But there's still a long way to go. As historian Bill Gammage says at the end of his impressive book *The Biggest Estate on Earth*, there is a lot more learning still to be done. 'If we are to survive, let alone feel at home, we must begin to understand our country. If we succeed, one day we might become Australian,' he concludes.[13]

PROCESSED

We were warned

For an incredible insight into Australia's historical meat trends, I turned to a copy I have of the country's first known cookery book: *The English and Australian Cookery Book*, published in 1864. Its author was the somewhat eccentric Edward Abbott, an Australian-born pastoralist, publisher and member of Tasmanian parliament.

Putting aside Abbott's directives about women providing good meals for their husbands—a tone that naturally doesn't land well in the modern era—his recipes reveal useful information on the colonial diet and the cured meats that formed part of it. Finding themselves away from their homeland and everything they had ever known, the new arrivals wanted the familiar tastes of their homeland and the familiar ingredients that had been rationed on board the ships.

Abbott, perhaps himself having learned from Beeton, includes what I believe to be Australia's oldest published bacon recipe, therefore making it important evidence of when the country's home cooks were first instructed to use a nitro-preservative—in this case, saltpetre (potassium nitrate):

> The pigs should always be hung up in the afternoon, if possible, and hung up until the next morning, when they must be cut up. If the weather will allow of their hanging a few days, so much the better. The bacon and hams must be well rubbed with coarse salt, in which a small quantity of saltpetre must be mixed, and allowed to remain twenty-four hours to drain, after which they must be put into the

following pickle: Four pounds of salt, one pound and a half of white sugar, and two ounces of saltpetre to every two gallons of water, to be boiled, and allowed to get cold, making sufficient to cover the quantity you intend to have. There is no further trouble with them, except to turn them while in the pickle, and they must remain in it, according to size, from a fortnight to three weeks. You will find them rich and fine flavoured. They can be smoked afterwards, if desired.[14]

Elsewhere, the book offers a multitude of ways to cure hams, but not just pork—mutton hams and beef hams were included too. Contrary to Newton's view some native foods do appear, including roast emu, wombat, and a mix of kangaroo recipes including the now-famous 'Slippery Bob'—kangaroo-brain fritters. But it was the ham, bacon and sausages that have survived the passage of time in terms of mass popularity.

In the same cookery book that offered us that very first Australian bacon recipe is a dark warning about sausages. Even in 1864, Abbott knew they could be bad news:

If the reader is wise he will always abstain from eating sausages, unless he knows of their manufacture, should he not be desirous of partaking of the man who, Dickens cleverly informs us, was chopped into sausage meat, and all that remained of him was his buttons. It is a positive and notorious fact in all parts of the world, that every kind of unwholesome meat is minced into sausages. Who would ever think of putting good meat into sausages when the mince and sage will effectually smother the flavour of putrid stuff?

Fair point, well made. And it still holds true more than 150 years later, in regard to the cheaper varities at least.

I managed to get a copy of another early and influential Australian cookery book, published in 1890, called *The Queensland Cookery and Poultry Book*, by Wilhelmina Rawson (writing as 'Mrs Lance Rawson'). For curing bacon, she gives a recipe that includes curing hams for more than a month in a mix of salt, sugar and—yes, there it was again—saltpetre. 'After the month, hang them up in the smoke of a wood fire for ten days,' she writes. 'Many people in the bush just hang them in the chimney.'[15]

For storing the bacon, the author recommends keeping it in an interesting place—under wood ashes. 'The white ash should be sifted and then the bacon laid in a deep case and entirely covered with the ash,' she advises.

And so it was that the early colonial population was armed with instructions—if they didn't already have them from Mrs Beeton or by other means—on how to produce and store their own bacon and other cured meats using saltpetre, just as they had done back in their homeland.

Four years later, the rather prolific Mrs Rawson offered even more tips in a book with an amusing amount of text on the front cover: *The Australian Enquiry Book: Household & General Information. Practical Guide. For the Cottage, the Villa and the Bush Home. Recipes and Information for Everything and Everybody. Refer to Me for Everything.* Snappy it wasn't. If ever an author was in need of a brutal book editor, it was Mrs Rawson, but that's another matter.

This time, her tip on 'things to bear in mind' in curing meat was to make sure 'every portion' of the meat is cured. 'Better to salt than going bad, for a little extra soaking before boiling will remedy the first, while for the last there is no remedy. There is no excuse for ill-cured bacon or hams.'[16]

It was the turn of the twentieth century that marked an upsurge in the nation's meat-eating abilities, as the domestic ice chest became a standard fixture in Australian kitchens—essentially a wooden cupboard with an insulated lining. 'Icemen' would deliver large blocks directly to the door of homes, depositing them in the ice chest if the front door was left open.[17] With this new addition to households you'd think it would mean less reliance and love for salty, preserved meats, but that wasn't the case. Once tasted, forever loved, it seems.

It was starting to become clear how a love of meat and pork-curing first emerged in Australian culinary history—and the diet trends brought over by British immigrants—but I still wanted to understand how this led to our nation's reliance on it.

From Margaret to Julie

Thankfully, I'd made an enthusiastic friend named Helena in the form of a second-hand bookseller, in a small arcade in Bentleigh, Melbourne, who made it her personal mission to help me source antique and vintage Australian recipe books for my research.

PROCESSED

'I've found another one!' she'd exclaim with glee every time I popped by her store, Helena's Curiosity Shop. She had owned the shop for over 30 years and loved history as much as I did, but Australian-born she had the upper hand: the advantage of knowing exactly which famous cook or chef had most influenced the nation's cooking, and in what era. I was also sourcing books from libraries and online, but it became a joy meeting her and seeing what gems she had found.

Together we pored over the battered, precious pages of various tomes, as she'd squeal, 'This is the one that everyone had!'

One of the most fragile books she found, with many of the pages coming loose from the spine, was the *P.W.M.U. Cookery Book of Victoria*, which was published in Melbourne in 1916—the middle of World War I. 'Compiled and issued by the Presbyterian Women's Missionary Union of Victoria', the book stated.

While the recipes inside the book certainly included some wild and wonderful meat-based offerings (scrambled brains, devilled tongues, tripe custard), there were very few recipes that involved processed meats. Most of the ingredients centred on fresh meats, vegetables, and pantry staples such as flour, bread, sugar and butter. Only four recipes inside the book involved cured meats, out of a total of nearly 200 recipes: ham balls, cold sausage rolls, sausage eggs and ham croquettes.

Towards the end, however, was a method of making bacon showing that Isabella Beeton's 'pickle' method remained, even if the crude methods involving chimneys and ash had now been dropped:

To each gallon of cold water add 2lbs salt, 1lb sugar, 1/4 oz of saltpetre; put the pork into a cask, and pour the pickle over it and move the pork every day so as the pickle will get into every part of it. At the end of 4 or 5 days draw off the pickle and boil it. Skim it very well as the skim rises. When boiled, let it stand till perfectly cold; then put it over the pork again; leave the side in for a fortnight, and the hams and shoulders a month.[18]

While this method may have been just slightly easier than the one in those early recipes, the time required—let alone the patience—was huge. Little wonder, then, that few processed meats made the final edit of this charming recipe book; home-made processed meats were one hell of a faff.

However, what I found curious was how the number of recipes including cured meats had more than doubled—to eleven—in the 1936 version of the same book. This upward trend was confirmed in another Victorian recipe book published just before the start of World War II: the *Domestic Science Handbook*, issued to 'Pupils of Girls' Schools and Domestic Art Centres by permission of the Department of Education Victoria' over the following years. This was a time, of course, when thousands of the nation's fathers, husbands and sons were serving overseas.

Australians were never rationed as heavily as civilians in Britain, but during the war there were limits on the clothing, tea, sugar, butter and meat that civilians could buy. Eggs and milk were also rationed during periods of shortage.[19] So this was a time when learning to cook without waste, by valuing each ingredient, was considered essential.

The *Domestic Science Handbook* instructs 'girls' how to make a wide variety of breakfast dishes using bacon, but each time they are urged to 'boil the bacon' for a few minutes, a method that in theory helps remove the salt and preservatives. There's even an advert for a Melbourne meat-processing brand within the pages: 'Something delicious . . . Hutton's "Pineapple" brand, Hams—Bacon—Smallgoods, look for the two blue stripes on the rind.'

One of the breakfast bacon dishes the readers were encouraged to follow has certainly not stood the test of time. It involved frying four rindless rashers of bacon, removing them from the fat and adding four halved bananas dipped in flour. 'Fry until golden brown in the hot fat from which the bacon was removed,' the recipe states. 'Serve hot with triangles of toast.'[20]

While I was delighted to be in a position to chart Australia's long-lost processed-meat history, it was with a feeling of impending doom that I saw how processed meats soon became embedded in the nation's culinary classics.

In the 1960s, it was *Entertaining With Kerr*, by popular UK TV chef Graham Kerr, that fuelled a dinner-party trend among the growing number of middle-class Australians. I examined one of Kerr's suggested recipes for the French casserole coq au vin, which included '2oz ham—cooked and pressed and cut into 1/4 inch cubes'.

Kerr, the son of two Scottish hoteliers who'd employed a number of French chefs during his upbringing, certainly brought his own unique flair to European cookery. In his recipe for 'Ham Kebabs' he gives instructions on slicing gammon rashers into cubes and threading them onto skewers with chunks of pineapple.

'This dish always succeeds,' he writes, '. . . no matter when you serve it is essential to offer a hot barbecue sauce.'[21]

I found myself giggling. Gallows humour is a must at times like these, especially when you're alone in a garden office stacked with hundreds of books collected over several years for your research, and you suddenly find a bizarre gem like this.

Just two years after the publication of this popular tome came more suggestions for home entertaining in *The Australian Hostess Cookbook*, published by *Woman's Day* magazine in Sydney. This book also has a recipe for coq au vin, but the ham is replaced with '4 ounces bacon'. Later in the book were yet more bacon offerings, including the short-and-sweet recipe for 'Prunes in bacon': 'Remove rinds from bacon; wrap strips of bacon around prunes and secure with toothpicks. Grill and serve hot.'[22]

And so it went on. Processed meats were now firmly in the mix inside more and more highly influential cookery books. These were tomes that would sit on the shelves in kitchens across the nation for decades.

The beloved recipes of prolific cookery book writer Margaret Fulton were carefully studied and made in households across Australia from the 1960s onwards. The food editor for *Woman's Day* was one of the first in the industry to be a journalist and a cook at the same time.

'Please share my enthusiasm and experience,' writes Fulton in 1980's *My Very Special Cookbook*. 'There is a lifetime of happy cooking behind this book . . . a book which is very special for me and one which I am sure will be very special to you.'

Within its pages I spotted what could well be one of the first 'recipes' ever printed in Australia for an 'antipasti platter'. 'One of the most colourful, appetising and versatile of dishes is antipasti, the splendid Italian version of hors d'oeuvre,' Fulton states. With hundreds of thousands of Italian and Greek migrants coming to Australia after World War II, giving the country's tastebuds a multicultural boost in the following decades (along with Chinese, Thai and Vietnamese immigrants, among many others), salami was now on Australia's mainstream menu too.

She also includes a simple recipe for 'Prosciutto and melon', which includes 180 grams of sliced prosciutto and two small melons. Fulton never did anything by halves.

And then there was a dish that would surely have been the ultimate crowd favourite at Christmas—'Ham baked in Guinness with spiced peaches'—whose main ingredient, 'cooked leg ham', was suggested to be a whopping 7.5 kilograms. Fulton must have had a lot of hungry friends.

'A glistening rosy pink baked ham can take star billing on a buffet table,' she writes. 'Although expensive it is an ideal choice for the busy home caterer, providing one splendid dish that is easy to serve and people will enjoy.'[23]

Joining the ranks of Australia's most beloved cooks was Stephanie Alexander, the author of the instant classic *The Cook's Companion* in 1996. It's as thick as a brick, but apparently the nation didn't seem to mind. The cook, now in her eighties, loved bacon so much she devoted a whole mini-chapter to the salty slices, including a rousing, lengthy introduction. Yes, Stephanie really loved bacon, and thanks to her even more Australians would love it too.

She concedes, at least, that she is not a fan of supermarket bacon ('too wet and flabby and the slices are too thin').[24] However, her bacon recipes are extensive, including egg and bacon pie, bacon muffins, Quiche Lorraine, chestnut and bacon salad—and so on.

Another bestselling tome which really ensured one type of processed meat in particular—ham—was eaten by the nation was the *CSIRO Total Wellbeing Diet* book, first published in 2005. According to Bookscan figures, which measure sales through mainstream Australian bookshop tills, actual total sales were well over a million copies over the two initial editions. 'In industry terms that makes it a stonking bestseller and a serious influence on the cooking and eating habits of everyday Australians in the mid-noughties and beyond,' my publisher Elizabeth Weiss confirmed.

However, media outlets and food bloggers soon had something to say about the advice in the books, written by Manny Noakes and Peter Clifton, to eat a large amount of protein, especially meat, including 100 grams for lunch and 200 grams for dinner.

Amid the lunch suggestions was 100 grams of ham with salad, which is the equivalent of a whole ten-slice pack of Primo English style leg ham.[25] The commentary at the time didn't make the link with the dangers of ham and health risks, instead focusing on another important and controversial angle—the fact the diet books were partly funded by the Meat and Livestock Industry and Dairy Australia.

'So it is no surprise the sponsors' products figure so highly in the recommended meals and weekly meal plans: beef, lamb and dairy products,' a damning article in the *Sydney Morning Herald* said.[26]

'The CSIRO's endorsement of a high-meat diet is perhaps an indication of the extent to which our scientists have taken on the role of consultants to industry in their bid to raise funds, and their willingness to deliver research findings that industry finds agreeable.

'How responsible is it, though, to be recommending such a high-meat diet in the context of concerns over the ecological sustainability and health problems associated with high meat consumption?'

Quite. The other follow-up CSIRO books didn't do nearly as well as the first one, but they were still excellent sales figures by Australian market standards. In other words, they were incredibly influential.

One of these follow-up editions I realised I even owned myself, purchased in 2009, the year after my first child was born. It's called *The CSIRO Wellbeing Plan for Kids* and I went through all the recipes, which promised on the cover a step-by-step plan for 'giving kids a healthy start in life'. I noted there were seven recipes involving ham, including pea and ham muffins. Sigh. Before my bowel cancer diagnosis I may have even made some of these recipes for my own children. Armed with the first-ever series of smartphones new mums like me were even taking pictures of the meals we were making and eating. Everyone was. Cooking started to become Instagram-cool making millions for immensely influential stars like British chefs Jamie Oliver and Gordon Ramsay, who both tapped into a wide fanbase Down Under. Oliver has always shared his loved of cured meats. He flicks the stuff into everything. In his bestselling book *Jamie's 15 Minute Meals* he tells readers to use '6 rashers of smoked pancetta' as a topping for a 'Poached chicken & salsa verde'. Of course beloved domestic goddess Nigella Lawson frequently and passionately praises bacon in her many books and TV shows too.

'Bacon is another ingredient any cook should keep in store,' she writes in her 1998 debut classic tome *How to Eat*, '. . . nothing is as good as a bacon sandwich made with white bread. There are times when you just need to have that salty-sweet curl of seared flesh pressed between fat-softened, rind-stained spongy slices.'

But it was those everyday Australians who found fame through the Australian TV series *MasterChef* who would really influence the nation's kitchen adventures. In 2009, four million Australians tuned in to watch Julie Goodwin become the show's first-ever winner. As a result of her popularity, Goodwin would go on to write multiple bestselling cookery books, including the classic *The Heart of the Home*.

Memories and family were very much at the centre of her recipes and her brand. Introducing a recipe for 'Hearty pea and ham soup', she tells her readers of its strong association to her childhood. 'My mum used to make this soup in her big orange and brown '70s crockpot,' she writes. 'The smell of it in the house reminds me of those childhood days when it was cold and grey outside, and we were so glad to be in the warmth and light of the kitchen.' The key ingredient needed is 1.2 kilograms of ham hocks, but Goodwin notes that cooks can also use 'bacon bones'.[27]

You can guess what preservative was almost certainly in both those options at the supermarkets then, just as it is now. Yes, it was another moment when processed meats were given hero status by an adored celebrity cook and crept even further into a nation's daily culinary habits.

To be fair to Goodwin, and all the other successful food writers: how were they supposed to know of the potential health risks of the processed meats they were including in their books? There was even less awareness then—possibly even close to zero awareness, considering that vital WHO classification didn't happen until 2015.

Propelled by celebrity cooks, supermarket advertising and growing numbers of fast-food chains in every town, millions of Australians were now, officially, card-carrying processed-meat addicts. The whole nation was snagged.

But it would soon get very out of hand. We weren't just eating it; we were worshipping it.

False idols

'Mummy, Mummy, what are those people eating?' asks my son, tugging at my coat. We are celebrating his ninth birthday at Melbourne's Luna Park. I look over to see a row of nine men, young and old, standing behind a long table in white T-shirts.

They are eating something I can't quite see, desperately shoving food into their mouths like starving hyenas while a crowd cheers and claps. We have inadvertently stumbled across the annual Luna Park Hot Dog Eating Competition, which attracts competitors from across the state of Victoria and beyond.

'How exciting,' I say. 'Let's watch.' What an amusing, fun spectacle for my son to see with his merry little band of classmates and his little sister.

(Yes, this was life way BBC—Before Bowel Cancer.)

The children's eyes are on stalks as the men struggle through, gulping water to try to moisten the bread, which also has to be consumed according to the rules. Behind each competitor is a marshal counting each slimy dog as it's consumed, pushed down into the competitors' already severely overstretched stomachs. As the numbers rise, the cheers become louder and now my little gang is as invested in this outcome as I am.

Devouring a total of sixteen hot dogs in ten minutes, Cal Stubbs—known on Instagram as HulkSmashFood—is victorious in the battle and we watch as he is crowned the winner of the men's event. (We're told that the women's event has already been won.) Whether they kept the sausages down or had to 'purge' in buckets behind the scenes like many food-eating champs is hard to tell. The crowd is going wild. My son and his friends are giggling and clapping.

The date was 23 July 2017. I know this because I took a photo and found it recently on a long-buried Facebook post. Oh the irony. I'd forgotten about this entire event—a pandemic and chemo can be blamed for that—but my son hadn't.

'Do you remember that hot dog event at Luna Park?' he asks, smiling, as we discuss my research for this book. 'It was really funny.'

He's sixteen now. He generally doesn't eat sausages or any other processed meats—well, not when I'm looking, anyway. But he used to. And he remembered. He remembered the day he witnessed a hero being made from eating one of the world's favourite processed meats in abundance.

It was a little off-piste but the memory got me thinking about Cal Stubbs. Was the chap okay? I felt a little worried, so I tracked him down.

He's a social media manager now, based in Melbourne, and has given up competitive eating, he admitted. 'I retired in 2022 as I put a five-year limit on competitive eating and the effects it could have on my body long term,' he told me. 'In the end I did eight years, actually, but wasn't active for the Covid years.'

I got straight to the point: had he experienced any health impacts from those years cramming endless hot dogs into his digestive system?

'Health is great,' he said, mentioning proudly that he'd also once eaten 150 bacon rashers in one go. 'No impacts, I mostly digested the food at the time although I've thrown up after a few comps due to undercooked or off food.'

But does Cal ever worry that he could still end up paying the price, in the long term, for all the processed foods he ate in extreme amounts? Without wanting to upset him, I mentioned the words 'bowel cancer'.

'Gotta die of something,' he said breezily. 'Not how I live my life, worrying about what-ifs. I've got living to do.' He didn't seem to have a care in the world about whether his stint as a competitive eater may still harm his future health.

Fair enough, I thought. *It's his attitude to choose.* I was just relieved he seemed okay, for now at least.

But for so many years as a parent I unwittingly made a hero out of processed meats. It was always somehow intertwined with happy events. Sausages around the campfire when the children were feeling their most free and alive. The bacon sandwiches as a 'treat' on a Sunday morning when the family was together and taking things slowly, in contrast to the frantic rush of the week. The juicy pieces of pepperoni on the take-away pizzas on a Friday night.

The awakening was yet to come. And when it did, it smacked me firmly around the head, as I realised the message about the link to bowel cancer just hadn't been strong enough in the public sphere for me to notice, or for us to change our ways.

Yet when I read further about the iconic hot dog a part of its history rattled me further. I spotted a headline in my research within the online archives of the *Los Angeles Times*. It appeared they once broke some bad news to a world so in love with the salty snack they just didn't want to listen; 'Hot Dogs Linked to Higher Risk of Cancers in Children', the headline said.[28]

It was June 1994, over a decade before the WHO declared processed meats to be linked to cancer, and hot dogs were firmly part of the daily diets of millions of children, particularly in the US but also around the world, scoffed in theme parks, skate rinks, cinemas and even schools. They were not only a cheap, portable fast food but beloved for their succulent, tasty savoury flavour and satisfying smell.

Reporter Thomas H. Maugh told readers that a new scientific report suggested children who ate more than twelve hot dogs per month had nine times the 'normal risk' of developing childhood leukaemia. Nitrites were the prime suspects but the researchers at that point weren't certain and also speculated the danger could be due to high fat content, bacteria or other chemicals.

In Australia, leukaemia, a cancer of the blood and bone marrow, is the most common of all childhood cancers with about 270 cases diagnosed each year.[29]

To make matters worse, the reporter went on to explain, two other reports in the very same edition of a Harvard School of Public Health journal called *Cancer Causes and Control* were suggesting that children whose mothers who were eating 'at least' one hot dog per week during pregnancy had double the normal risk of developing brain tumours, as do children whose fathers ate hot dogs before conception. Before conception? This surely should have made the world immediately ban hot dogs while more research was undertaken? Hardly. Hot dogs were, by then, just too popular and the message just didn't get heard—or accepted—which suited the billion-dollar industry just fine.

Immediately, sceptics poured scorn over the nature of the study, according to the reporter. 'Critics, as well as the researchers themselves, point out that such studies are difficult to conduct and interpret because people have a hard time recalling what they have eaten,' he said.

Over on the other side of the US, a *Washington Post* lifestyle writer and mother, wrote an exasperated opinion piece in which she dismissed the study as 'a daily dose of fear'.

'Hot dogs are, of course, the cheap trick of parenthood, the edible equivalent of Saturday morning cartoons,' Elizabeth Kastor wrote. 'They bring ease to the kitchen, peace to the dinner table, and now, apparently, guilt to the soul.

'Americans stuff down 2 billion pounds of hot dogs a year, and many parents would be willing to guess their own kids consume at least half a billion pounds themselves. And although no one ever pretended hot dogs are health food, who really wants to consider the possibility that they are sleek, fat-filled missiles of disease.'[30]

Some readers certainly seemed aghast at the report, however, leading one mother to write a letter to the *Los Angeles Times* saying she had taken action on behalf of her child.

'I have sent a letter and a copy of your article to my daughter's day-care center requesting that they stop serving nitrite-containing meats,' Linda Roberts of Pasadena wrote.[31]

'If they will not stop serving them altogether, I'll ask that she be served an alternate sandwich on those days. Peanut butter and jelly may just be the best choice after all. Other parents should consider asking their children's schools and day-care centers to stop serving nitrite-laden processed meats. We wouldn't allow our children to be cared for in an environment where second-hand smoke is present, so why should we allow exposure to another known carcinogen.'

While some readers may well have taken individual action locally, the study didn't quell the world's appetite for hot dogs which are believed to have been brought over to the US by German immigrants in the mid-1800s.'

Munching on the run continued, even with a further negative hot dog headline in January 2009. Respected global news wire agency Reuters reported that children who often ate bacon and hot dogs may have an increased risk of leukaemia.[33]

The report explained how researchers found that among 515 Taiwanese children and teenagers, both with and without acute leukaemia, those who ate cured meats and fish more than once a week had a '74 per cent higher risk of leukemia than those who rarely ate these foods'.

The findings of the study had been stated in the online journal *BMC Cancer*, but unlike the 1994 report it suggested a firmer link with nitro-preservatives.

As for hot dog sales, well they just headed onwards and upwards; in the US the hot dog and sausage market is expected to be worth a massive US$102.93 billion by 2030.[34]

In the Asia Pacific region, including Australia, financial industry projections indicate steady growth in the hot dog market owing to fast-food preferences among young people.

SBS reported in February 2024 that hot dogs were popular in Australia like the US because of their association with leisure and fun. 'These days in Australia, hot dogs are served at kid's [sic] parties, fun fairs, sporting venues and even outside some pubs and clubs,' the report said. 'That's because, over the years, hot dogs have become associated with good times.'[35]

Leukaemia in children isn't something associated with good times though, we can be certain of that. But despite the horrors the disease posed the hot dog couldn't be knocked off its pedestal as a cured family favourite. The adoration and convenience was just too deeply entrenched.

The US meat industry bodies even attempted to discredit the work of one of the experts who researched the link between hot dogs and leukaemia. A notable pioneer, Susan Preston-Martin told a French television documentary on nitrites in meats shortly before her death in 2016 how they tried to dismiss her work as the first female fellow at the University of Southern California.[36]

Another example of a ruthless and complex industry. By chance, while researching this book, I was seated at an event next to a senior food executive in charge of the Australian region for a large Asian food company.

During our conversation he reported with great pride that he'd just secured a deal to supply hot dogs to an entire franchise of well-known convenience stores based in south-east Asia. 'We're already selling 11,000 a day!' he said excitedly.[37]

He was a charming chap and asked questions about my research and cancer journey, but when I asked whether he could try to source versions which used organic preservatives (such as Cleaver's Organic beef hot dogs, a NSW brand which uses celery extract) he dismissed the idea out of hand. 'It would be too expensive, it wouldn't be worth the margins,' he admitted.

It was another revealing insight, and one which confirmed my suspicion very few in the processed meat supply or sales chain had the wellbeing of the customer in mind. This deal-making middle man was pleasing his bosses, driving profits and paying his mortgage.

PROCESSED

The famous Bunnings sausage-sizzle fundraiser is another false idol adored by millions. And I can see why.

I'll never forget my first experience of standing behind the white trestle table, sweating from the heat from the vast grill covered in dozens of sizzling sausages behind me as I tried to politely serve my next customer. It was October 2012, and the flimsy gazebo wasn't giving us enough shade in the warm spring sun. Temperatures and tempers were rising in equal measure.

I was there to help raise money for my daughter's kindergarten, a little local one that needed a lot of repairs and new toys. We'd managed to get one of the much-sought-after weekend slots, and we'd waited months for the day to come around.

This was the answer. Bunnings sausage-sizzle fundraisers are now always seen as the answer. In the end, we raised $2500 in much-needed funds.

Naturally, this was way before a bowel cancer diagnosis, and I didn't yet hold strong views about the mass consumption of processed meats. As I mentioned at the start of this book, I occasionally bought a Bunnings snag in a slice of cheap white, fluffy bread, along with onions and some mustard. It was always, without fail, utterly delicious—especially if I'd missed lunch in pursuit of some potting mix and tomato plants.

'So, after my initiation of a Bunnings sausage sizzle I know two things for a fact: Australian men are VERY serious about their Sunday snags and 50% of people like onions,' I wrote on Facebook. Later I found a photograph from that day; I'm smiling in my sunglasses, alongside another mum, as we try our best to serve hundreds of hungry hardware fans.

I remember being quite overwhelmed by the tense crowd and realising just how much the Bunnings snag was an Australian institution. I wasn't yet a citizen, and it hadn't really been something I'd noticed properly. There was the seriousness of making sure we included onions—or not. There were the precise instructions that they didn't just want one sausage—they wanted two or three. And no sauce. Or yes to the sauce—'extra please'.

In November 2020 journalist Melissa Iaria excitedly wrote in a major Australian online news platform about the sausage sizzle making a return to Bunnings after the first wave of the pandemic.[38]

'The smell of fried onion has been a notable absence from the hardware store giant after the popular community fundraiser was suspended in March due to COVID-19,' she wrote.

'The snags, slapped on thin, white bread and enjoyed with a squirt of sauce and sprinkling of onion, have become a cultural staple for many Australians.'

She's right. I could see it in everyone's eyes. Their lips pursed. Australians, I realised, adored their Bunnings snag. And it had to be just right. Just like it always was. So on-brand and unchanged like a McDonald's cheeseburger that, incredibly and cleverly, tastes the same today as it did when I was five years old.

'Certain rituals such as the sausage sizzle have deep Australian roots and are not easily overturned,' says Dr Tanveer Ahmed. 'They denote a kind of egalitarianism and to some degree a mateship around the barbecue. This can have a strong masculine air, which may not be always as relevant in the modern climate.'

The words 'modern climate' struck a chord. The Bunnings sausage sizzle may well be hugely popular, but it also encourages people of all ages to worship and consume yet more processed meat. Considering what I had learned about processed meats, it felt outdated, like some of the cookbooks I'd read telling the 'housewives' of Australia how to dress their dining table for a Saturday-night soiree.

I felt like a vibe-killer when it came to this beloved national tradition, but by this stage I felt more than comfortable in my rebellious skin.

I'd heard through an insider contact that the managing director of Bunnings, Michael Schneider, was an approachable chap. Let's just call him Hardware Mike. Armed with his personal email address, I knew that this could possibly, just possibly, be my chance to plant the idea of important change into the mind of one of the most influential figures in Australia's love affair with snags.

After all, Bunnings, owned by Perth-based Wesfarmers, who also own Kmart and Target, had made one controversial change to the sausage sizzles before. Back in 2018, when the company realised that those delicious onions were falling off the sausages and onto the ground, causing people to slip and go flying into the air, it was decided the onions should be placed under the snag, not on top of it. Surely Bunnings could make another change or two?

I had to choose my words carefully. This letter felt more important than all the rest. I had to be charming, polite, yet to the point. I have to admit I was nervous—I was taking on the

Shock news: At the age of 44 I was diagnosed with stage-four bowel cancer. The news came just seven weeks after the September 2019 launch of my debut book, *Fallen* (Allen & Unwin), where I am pictured with husband, Mike, son, Nate and daughter, Talia.

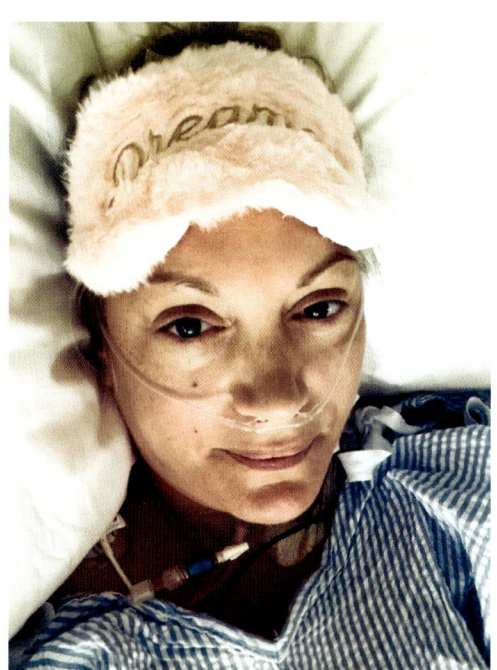

Intense times: After urgently embarking on my first gruelling rounds of chemotherapy I was treated in intensive care at Melbourne's Cabrini Private Hospital in March 2020, following the first of multiple major open surgeries.

High hopes: Shortly after I won the Walkley Book Award, late in 2020, I was told I was cancer free. However, I would soon have to begin many more years of aggressive treatment and would lose my hair again.

Close comrades: Snow entrepreneur Kieren Gaul, from Pambula, New South Wales, became one of my closest friends in the bowel cancer community. He tragically passed away from the disease in November 2023.

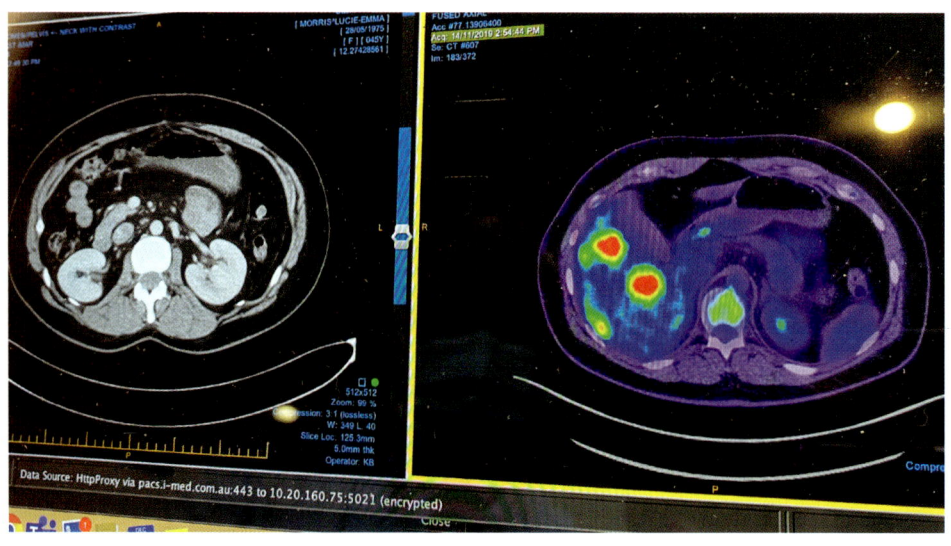

Scanxiety: Nerve-wracking waits for scan results soon became part of the routine during my long bowel cancer battle.

Mother of necessity: In the late 1970s my mother, Julia, would use her tricycle to take me and my brother, Matthew, to the local shops in Hampshire, England, where processed meats such as bacon would be a handy item on sale to last for several weeks in the fridge. The link to bowel cancer in particular had not yet been established.

Yuletide memories: Sitting wearing a dress and a blue hairband I'm pictured aged 10 in 1985 at the home of my late grandparents in Berkshire, England, after enjoying a traditional turkey lunch including pigs in blankets—the salty Christmas trimming adored by millions.

Controversial mix: Sodium nitrite and nitrate (E250 and E251) are often added to processed meats as preservatives, yet scientists warn they can create carcinogens when digested, with a particular link to bowel cancer. SHUTTERSTOCK

Salty sorrow: I believed I had followed a healthy diet but after my diagnosis I realised processed meats had played a role in my family and social life, including this processed meat platter on a winery visit in Victoria in 2017.

Bacon nation: Fried rashers of bacon, the majority of which on sale in Australia contain nitro-preservatives, are hard to resist for many, especially on camping trips, weekend brunch cafe outings or barbecues.

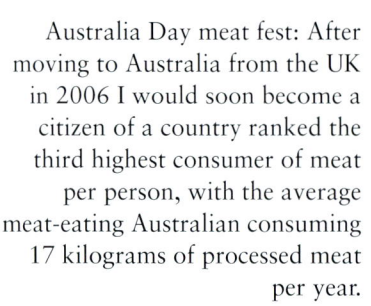

Australia Day meat fest: After moving to Australia from the UK in 2006 I would soon become a citizen of a country ranked the third highest consumer of meat per person, with the average meat-eating Australian consuming 17 kilograms of processed meat per year.

Left: Curing tastes: Such is the global love of bacon one company in the United States produces 'Bacon Candy Canes' for Christmas shoppers. BACON ADDICTS ANONYMOUS, FACEBOOK, 12 DECEMBER 2023 *Below left:* Pop culture: Bacon now comes in a wide array of forms in modern Australian supermarkets, including Popcorn Bacon containing the preservative sodium nitrite, produced by the Don mega-factory in Castlemaine, Victoria. *Below right:* Frankly speaking: Processed meat companies cleverly market hot dog style products to Australian consumers in major shops and supermarkets—however, many shoppers are unaware of the bowel cancer risks and other health implications.

Deli devils: During my investigation I soon discovered how controversial nitro-preservatives lurk in a large majority of deli counter meats, including bacon, pepperoni and salami.

Grazing the risks: With a surge in popularity of grazing platter foods, processed meat companies are creating a higher number of products such as these 'Snackertaining' salami and cheese sticks by company San Marino.

As of 2022, Domino's had almost 20,000 stores worldwide. In Australia, the company does not make public the precise ingredients in its products, instead only providing nutritional tables and potential allergens. But where are the missing ingredients that go into its popular processed-meat pizza toppings such as salami, ham and pepperoni?

Plant dilemma: Amid an explosion of new plant-based 'meat' products nutritionists warn they can often be heavily processed with large amounts of salt and an extensive ingredient count.

Spammed: First gaining popularity among troops in the Second World War, tins of Spam, which contain sodium nitrite preservative, are still popular in Australia and overseas.

Ancient tastes: Curing meats, particularly pork, can be traced back thousands of years when food sources were scarce, or to sustain families during lean times or long winters. They are now entrenched in daily Western diets, cultural traditions and feasts. Some traditional meats such as Parma ham contain no nitro-preservatives and cure using only salt. FRANCESCO DE MARCO/ SHUTTERSTOCK

Tiny targets: Major Australian supermarkets such as Coles stock processed meat snack packs containing nitro-preservatives, heavily marketed for consumption by toddlers, pre-schoolers and school-aged children.

Snag nation: The Bunnings sausage sizzle, famously sold outside the hardware stores by local schools, community groups and charities, has become one of Australia's beloved fast-food snacks.

Wrapped risk: On Bacon Addicts Anonymous, a popular US-based Facebook group with over 116,000 members, users share their creative homemade recipes including this bacon-wrapped mashed potato stuffed meatloaf. @BACONUNIVERSITYFRIEDWITHPRIDE, FACEBOOK, 29 NOVEMBER 2022

Mouths of babes: A small baby eating a rasher of bacon became a popular image on Bacon Addicts Anonymous, where consuming the cured meat in regular abundance is celebrated by its members. @THEBACONEXPERIMENT, FACEBOOK, 22 JANUARY 2024

Winning vote: State and federal elections in Australia have witnessed a surge in popularity of what is dubbed the 'Democracy Sausage', increasingly sold between white bread at voting stations by schools and community groups. PETER A. COMENSOLI, TWITTER, 26 NOVEMBER 2022

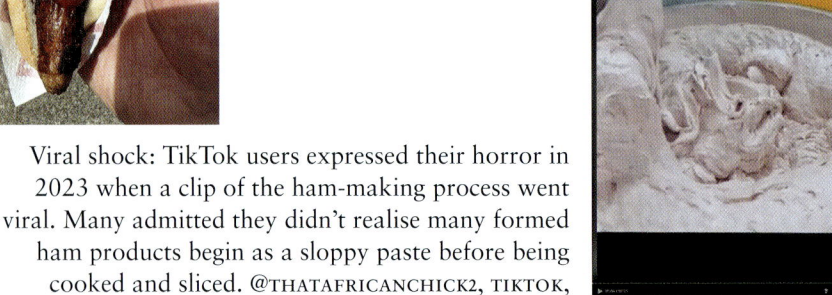

Viral shock: TikTok users expressed their horror in 2023 when a clip of the ham-making process went viral. Many admitted they didn't realise many formed ham products begin as a sloppy paste before being cooked and sliced. @THATAFRICANCHICK2, TIKTOK, 13 AUGUST 2023

iconic Bunnings sausage sizzle, for christ's sake. Bunnings snags aren't just a snack, are they? They are a religion. I took a deep breath and pressed send. Then I ran for cover.

Hi Michael,

Hope you're well.

My name is Lucie Morris-Marr and I'm a freelance investigative journalist and author based in Melbourne.

I was keen to touch base with you as managing director of Bunnings regarding the current book I'm writing for publishers Allen & Unwin regarding processed meat.

As a stage-four bowel cancer patient and advocate I have a keen interest in this subject due to the large number of respected global reports linking, in particular, processed meat to cancer—in particular the cancer which I'm still fighting since my diagnosis in 2019 aged 44.

This link is a good summary of the evidence.
https://www.wcrf.org/the-politics-of-processed-meat/
Over 15,000 Australians are diagnosed with bowel cancer every year. In 2015 the World Health Organization classed them as a Group 1 carcinogenic alongside tobacco.

Naturally, I'm mentioning the cultural influence of the Bunnings sausage sizzle in my book.

I will state how I greatly admire what it has become in Australian society. It's sociable, feeds many and raises millions for small community organisations across the country. Many of which literally depend on it for their survival.

That said, the popularity of the Bunnings 'snag' increases the amount of processed meats consumed by Australians, including children, whose diets in their early years dictate their future health.

What would be my ideal scenario, as someone who has suffered in ways I never want any other Australian to suffer—including four open surgeries and over 1000 hours of chemotherapy, plus a year with a colostomy bag—is for Bunnings to help play its part in making a change to improve the future for all of your customers and their health outcomes.

Of course I'd love you to announce the end of selling all processed sausage offerings outside your stores.

But I'm being realistic. You're a commercial operation with a huge number of employees and stakeholders. Your customers would be up in arms and protests would be held. There could even be civil unrest!

So here is my suggestion; could you possibly think about creating a new policy, just how you did with ensuring the slippery onions need to go under the meat.

That policy being to request that all organisations running a Bunnings sausage sizzle do two small but significant things:

1. Make sure the sausages they purchase are free of nitro-preservatives, commonly found in cured hot dog type products.

2. Make sure they also always offer a vegetarian sausage as an option. (Which is also important for those in this culturally diverse nation who don't eat meat and especially pork such as Jews and Muslims etc.)

If Bunnings made this announcement you would be a leading light as a brand and as a company operating with integrity. You would be setting a positive example. You could save countless lives.

As you know the media LOVE a Bunnings sausage sizzle story. The onion story went viral.

Yes, it would be a brave move, but also a bold and positive move. And a fair move for both your company and your customers—and the organisations who may even get more customers as a result.

It's a small step for your company. But a huge one for the future health of your customers and Australians as a whole.

Just by making those tiny changes Bunnings would gain positive headlines—and even better it would make the Australian public read those headlines and stop and think. They would learn about the possible health impacts of consuming too much processed meats.

And that would mean the world to bowel cancer patients like me who want to try to help make this country better. Healthier. Happier.

I'm happy to discuss this suggestion further with you if you have time.

And if you'd also like to give a general comment for my book on the Bunnings sausage sizzle I'd be delighted to talk to you.

Many thanks in advance
Lucie Morris-Marr

After sending the Bunnings email I felt quite empowered, as I had when I sent the email to Cartoon Bob and the other power-players. If this was my calling—to send Hardware Mike a direct, emotive letter about my concerns about the snags sold at the doors of his stores—then so be it.

Someone had to do it. I was proud I'd gained so much momentum.

As with the other emails I'd sent to companies involved in this processed-meat business, I didn't expect a reply. I was just happy I'd made my point.

To be fair, Hardware Mike isn't responsible for the whole nation's devotion to the snag; as we all know, sausage sizzles have become a popular side-show at polling booths at Australian elections and nicknamed 'democracy sausages'. Widespread media coverage of this began in the 2013 and 2016 Australian federal elections, with the hashtag '#democracysausage' trending on Twitter at the time. Twitter, now known as X, also included a sausage-in-bread emoji to the '#ausvotes' hashtag on the day of the 2016 election.

In short, our society makes false idols of processed meats, especially in the context of children. After footy and cricket matches, soccer games, Little Athletics sessions and Scouts meetings, and at every school fete, there's usually a sausage sizzle. There's rarely a veggie option. You either take part and fit in, or you don't. That pressure is immense.

But there is a lack of responsibility at play here. It's just accepted that this is the menu choice, as it always has been. End of discussion.

Indeed, when I approached multiple sporting organisations that work with children, suggesting that they could possibly issue guidelines for parents and organisers to at least offer alternative choices, most of them chose not to respond. Those who did told me that the food choices around their sporting events or activities had nothing to do with them.

A spokesperson for NSW Rugby League made their feelings on the matter quite clear; they said they were 'not responsible' for any canteens or food vendors at sporting events and venues. 'These are the responsibility of individual venues, clubs, and/or event organisers,' they said curtly.

One thing is certain. Australia's beloved meat sausage or hot dog—is one hell of a slippery snag to try to catch.

But at least I'd given it a good Aussie go.

Chapter Twelve
BEYOND THE SNAG

> Not everybody has the geography, the finances, the knowledge to make better choices every meal of every day . . . The important moment isn't when you don't have the choice. The important time is when you do have the choice . . . that's the time when you have the chance to change the world.[1]
>
> Matthew Evans, *On Eating Meat*, 2019

Swap shop

Ikaria, a small Greek island located in the Aegean Sea, is known for its natural beauty but also for being one of the few areas in the world identified as 'Blue Zones'—places where people live longer and healthier lives than the average.

The reason?

Exercise and social environment certainly help, but the diet on the island is also credited with the population's longevity. It is a variation of the Mediterranean diet that emphasises fruits, vegetables, olive oil, cereals and legumes; a low consumption of meat products; and a moderate consumption of wine.

Processed meats don't tend to be on the menu. Protein sources on Ikaria are focused on legumes such as beans, chickpeas and lentils, plus fish like sardines, salmon, trout and herring. The people there use a lot of herbs and spices to inject flavour and health benefits into their foods.

Of course it's impossible to identify a diet that will suit all humans on the planet, and recommending one is not the purpose of this book. But as author David A. Sinclair says in his *New York Times* bestseller *Lifespan*, eating more vegetables, legumes and whole grains, while consuming less meat, dairy products and sugar, is 'a great place to start'.

'There is no best diet; we're all different enough that our diets need to be subtly and sometimes substantially different, too,' Sinclair points out. 'But we're also similar enough that there are some very broad commonalities: more veggies and less meat; fresh food versus processed food.'[2]

We all know this stuff, he says, though applying it can be a 'challenge'. He's right about that.

Another inspiring 'Blue Zone' of the world is Okinawa, a region on a group of islands called the Ryukyu Islands in the south of Japan. Okinawans are among the world's longest living people and follow a mostly plant-based diet that is based on sweet potato, leafy greens, yellow root vegetables, soy and low-GI grains that don't spike your blood sugar levels. Apparently the Okinawa diet is rich in vitamins and minerals and packed with antioxidants, which help fight free radicals and reduce the risk of age-related chronic diseases.

Other health commentators agree that the main dietary principles of these Blue Zones—more plant food, less animal food, and fewer refined carbohydrates and ultra-processed foods—are the way forward.

In his book *The Reducetarian Solution*, US author Brian Kateman states the costs of a poor diet plainly: 'One thing we know for sure: the way Americans are eating today has resulted in a sickly, medically dependent society, with healthcare costs that are unsustainable and needless suffering and tragedies.'[3]

Personally, ever since my bowel cancer diagnosis, it is the overall principles of the Mediterranean diet I've generally turned to. I did go through an initial vegan phase but I found it too strict.

In the week after each round of chemotherapy, I also sometimes craved red meat, perhaps as a sign my body needed iron, so I went with it and occasionally had an organic, grass-fed steak. We all need to do what we feel is right and it's fine to change how we eat according to your changing needs and health status.

The Mediterranean diet consistently tops the lists of 'Best Diets' compiled by experts, which isn't surprising: numerous studies have found the diet can reduce the risk of many health issues such as diabetes, high cholesterol, dementia and cancer. Most pertinently, meals from the Mediterranean diet have been linked to a longer life, which is something I now try to encourage my teens to think about with their food choices. As a family we eat a lot more fruit and vegetables, and we swap meat in meals for legumes in dishes like a rich, chilli-infused lentil bolognaise. When we do eat meat it is free range, low fat and the best quality we can find. And I know not everyone can afford that, especially in a cost-of-living crisis.

I don't buy any processed meats anymore but if it came to it, I'd choose the nitrate-free or organic nitrate versions of processed meat over any products with nitro-preservatives.

As well as the small organic nitrate cured pork offerings in Woolworths, at the time of writing there are a few Australian organic farms which will also deliver organic nitrate pork products, including Cherry Tree Organics in South Gippsland in Victoria.

The ingredients listed in their 'chemically nitrite free ham' state they use 'pork from certified organic pigs, sea salt, pepper, parsley, rosemary, honey, tapiaco [sic], carrot, celery, and Australian hardwood smoke'.[4] The Australian Organic Meat Co based in Queensland also deliver a range of nitrite-free products including 'bourbon streaky bacon', costing $10.99 for 250 grams.

From a farm business in New Zealand called Naturally Organic you can order 250 grams of 'Matakana gourmet bacon dry cured loin' made with 'sea salt and a blend of herbs & spices, including native botanicals, then smoked with real Manuka'.

As much as I applaud this trend, it's important to remember that the jury is still out on whether 'natural cures' come without risks.

Oh, and then there's the cost. 'Celery powder is double the price to use, so the meat industry isn't using it,' Leah, another local butcher, tells me.

So yes, this is another reason why billion-dollar meat companies are all incredibly touchy and nervous. They know if public awareness about their nitro-preservatives starts to impact demand, the entire business could be under threat because there may not be economically or practically viable, healthier alternative preservatives. The coming years will prove if they are businesses that are actually built on sand.

A few times during my research I've seen chat group suggestions that consumers can 'boil away' added nitro-preservatives in cured items such as bacon. However, it's impossible to measure what remains deeply embedded in the tissues of the meat.

As for the 'fake-meat' options in our supermarkets, I started off hoping they could be a good replacement for processed meat. Now I view them as culinary trapdoors.

Investors were initially enthused with the trend for plant-based meat alternatives. The groundbreaking Beyond Meat brand in the US, made famous through the Beyond burger, started the whole upsurge. The Beyond burger is a highly processed affair, however, made of pea protein and a massive list of other complex 'plant-based' ingredients.

In Australia, the trend set off a wave of investment in plant-based meat start-ups. However, the CSIRO reported in 2023 that the Australian market had stagnated, and in the US sales have declined since their high point in 2021.[5]

A couple of times, during the course of my research, I've used my children as guinea pigs for some of the fake meats on offer in our supermarkets. It has never turned out well. Once I chopped and fried small strips of a meat-free bacon from the Made with Plants brand, which I purchased from Woolworths. The wording on the pack promised 'Mouth-watering, streaky bacon that crisps like the original! Made with plant-based protein.'

Personally, when it was cooked really well to the point of making it crispy, I didn't think the taste was too bad, and it certainly had those famous bacon flavours. I scattered little pieces on top of my children's favourite macaroni cheese and let matters unfold.

'Oh yuck? What's this, Mum? This is *not* real bacon!' they both shrieked.

To be fair, there was an apt question within their dismay. What is in this 'plant protein' exactly?

Well, it turns out there are just as many ingredients in 'meat-free bacon' as there are in some of the cured meats I'd found. It is an ultra-processed product. The ingredient label reads:

> Water, Soybean Oil, Textured Soy Protein (Non-GMO Soy Protein Isolate, Wheat Starch, Wheat Protein, Stabilisers (170, 516), Modified Starch (1414), Salt, Yeast Extract, Sugar, Hydrolysed Vegetable Protein, Vegetable Extracts (Pea, Carrot), Flavours, Smoke Flavour, White Pepper, Colour (172))

When I looked at the ingredient labels for other fake meats, the labels were all very similar. They certainly weren't 'clean' alternatives, which is causing concern among nutritionists.

In one brief, horror anecdote I saw on a Facebook video reel, someone had undergone a colonoscopy and their doctor had asked if they consumed fake-meat products. When the man said he did, and quite often, the doctor replied: 'I could tell as there is some of it in your colon—the body doesn't know what to do with it.' As with all such social media clips, you have to be wary of its validity but I wanted to note it in these pages because for me it raised a really good question. Perhaps our bodies struggle with 'invented protein' and not clean protein, and literally don't know how to handle it?

Keeping this in mind, I focused instead on homemade veggie burgers, made of ingredients such as chickpeas, breadcrumbs, egg, herbs, spices, lentils and corn. These sort of burger patties are also in supermarkets, often alongside the fake meats, but I still find you have to check the labels and make sure the list of ingredients is more of a brief note than an essay.

'I don't recommend people swap from processed meats to fake meats because fake meats are still highly processed and often high in salt,' says Jemma O'Hanlon, the dietician who gave me so much expert advice during this investigation. 'Instead, we need to encourage people to choose healthy proteins like fish, seafood, legumes, nuts and seeds.'

Another danger Jemma also says people should be wary of is protein-fad diets such as keto, Paleo and Atkins. All three encourage people to focus on a heavy-protein diet, with some recipes often including processed meats such as bacon.

I can't deny that it's a challenge, day to day, to eliminate processed meats totally. It's also not cheap. Here in Australia I know all too well how hard it is to make changes when bacon, sausages and frankfurts are so abundant and lower in price than, say, fresh beef or pork meat.

When I'm at a cafe for breakfast or brunch and I order my favourite poached eggs, grilled tomato and spinach, that's when I miss bacon the most. My go-to solution? Realising that it's that meaty, salty bite that goes so well with the soft egg and moist vegetables, I've recently turned to grilled halloumi as a side dish. A good-quality version grills or fries beautifully, and brings both a crunch and a softness that is delicious—all for around the same price as a side of bacon. Mushrooms, when cooked well or with added flavours and herbs, can also provide that satisfying, harder bite between the teeth that complements the soft egg.

In recipes, I find it's easy to replace bacon with onion and garlic, perhaps with smoked paprika for that smoky, earthy flavour. If you do decide to keep eating bacon, remember to try and source nitrite-free or organic nitrate versions and it might help if you gently fry it on a low heat using a healthy avocado or flax seed oil, or lower oven or grill temperatures.[6]

Instead of making a traditional Quiche Lorraine with bacon or ham, I love to make quiches with red capsicum, feta, zucchini and broccoli, topped with organic eggs, milk and vintage cheddar. If it's a large minestrone-type veggie soup or my favourite zucchini and leek soup, I often add a few crumbs of feta cheese just before serving for the saltiness that bacon bits would provide.

That said, I'm not advocating adding too much salt of course, or trying to match the amount of salt you'd find in processed meats. As we know, salt can have many negative health impacts, especially centred on blood pressure.

I've learned that what we humans really seek is flavour, and that doesn't have to come from salty ingredients. You can use an array of herbs, lemon, limes, ginger, lemongrass and chilli, with our tastebuds soon adapting after a few weeks.

PROCESSED

Friday is still pizza night in the Morris-Marr household, of course, as it is for millions of others all over the country, indeed the world. This was one of the hardest meat habits for my husband and children to change. But now they are happy with homemade margherita pizza, sometimes topped off with marinated red capsicum and spinach. And we treat ourselves to one of those large, fresh balls of mozzarella instead of the bag of grated, more tasteless offerings which contain anti-caking agents.

For me personally, I also add goat's cheese, mushrooms and halved cherry tomatoes for a taste-and-health hit.

If you still find life challenging without processed meat, these are some of my own personal tips:

- veggie sausages or falafel
- sides of mushrooms, fried halloumi or roast vegetables with your eggs
- make sure you read the ingredient labels or use an app such as Yuka which gives label information and avoid items with nitrites listed
- instead of deli processed meats on your grazing platter try sundried tomatoes, olives, white anchovies, marinated capsicum strips, avocado, fruits, salad items, cheeses and dips
- for main meals or lunch box ideas choose other protein sources such as eggs, cottage cheese, tofu and hummus.

As Australian lawyer-turned-food-author David Gillespie says, the most important thing of all is to choose 'real food'. 'This doesn't mean you have to start haunting farmer's [sic] markets, being on first-name terms with the staff at the local bio-dynamic health-food store, keeping chooks, milking cows and breeding your own yeast (unless you want to),' he writes in his book *Eat Real Food*. 'Real food is also still available in the average supermarket; you just have to walk past a lot of food-like substances to get to it.'[7]

Some high-profile figures are taking a rather more public and hard-hitting approach, however, when it comes to meat. Back in 2016, *Avatar* director James Cameron joined a campaign called '5 to Do Today' to encourage people to eat less meat. 'The number one thing that you can do is to just stop eating or cut down on your consumption of meat and dairy. Meat and dairy are not good for your body, and they're not good for the environment,' Cameron says in a behind-the-scenes video, sitting alongside actor and former California governor Arnold Schwarzenegger. Cameron and Schwarzenegger are then seen standing on a set depicting a deforested world. 'If they tell you to eat more meat to be strong, don't buy it,' Schwarzenegger says. 'Less meat, less heat, more life.'[8]

It was a clever tactic to tap two Hollywood legends. It meant people would listen.

Bringing in new rituals, which don't spark the same need for the same foods, can also help.

'This is why it is important that we often update traditions, where we keep elements of the past but possibly update them,' Dr Tanveer Ahmed says. 'It is also important to keep bringing in new rituals over events such as Christmas as times change. This includes not just food but also the types of activities or even the people who are invited. Some things that are quite unhealthy are fine if they occur quite rarely, but they can require changes to make things more inclusive.' This is especially true today when we have a wide range of eating habits, such as vegan or gluten-free, that need to be accommodated in a ritual that may be quite meat-centric.

When it comes to advising my own children, I tell them they don't need to choose a fixed identity around food. But I do tell them the facts I've uncovered. I also repeat the mantras: 'No label is the best label' and 'eat food that loves you back'.

I've also mentioned how inspired I am by Brian Kateman's 'Reducetarian' solution, a term he coined when he realised that many people struggled to stop eating meat altogether.

'Reducetarianism is inclusive,' he says in his book. 'This new perspective provides everyone with a platform to make small choices to eat less meat in their own lives and collectively to make huge differences in the world.'

Dear Santa

As I was nearing the end of writing this book, I have to admit that my energy was waning. It was early December 2023 and I'd had some bad news about my health; while the radiation on two tiny liver tumours had worked seven small new ones had now appeared. I feared I was losing the cancer-version of the game Whac-A-Mole. I'd given this investigation my all, body and soul. And now Christmas was coming and between restarting targeted anti-body infusions I was about to get on a plane for my first UK Christmas in nearly fifteen years. I felt a deep Yuletide yearning.

I just wanted to be lying down on a sofa by a log fire, nibbling mince pies, not spending yet more days imprisoned in my increasingly hot Melbourne garden office.

Not that I hadn't enjoyed the process. It had been a fascinating and important project to work on, in between my various cancer treatments. I felt incredibly grateful to have had the opportunity to follow my instincts, go off on my mission, and report back and share it with the world.

But there was something niggling me as I completed the final pages. Remember Chef Miguel and his new range of cured-meat products, right at the start of this book? The celebrity had certainly been enjoying himself at that bacon festival in Queensland. Then there was Gilded George, the CEO and uber-rich heir of Associated British Foods, the UK umbrella company that owns George Weston Foods in Australia, which in turn owns the Don KRC mega-pig-palace in Victoria.

I knew I needed to write them both a little letter—or, rather, a 'Dear Santa'.

As the temperatures rose in Melbourne, I knew I would have to dig deep to get these final wish lists written. To be frank, I was longing to just press 'send' on the manuscript document and jump into the sea.

But I was determined to make Professor Corpet proud. And I was feeling more confident. Bolder. Braver. Cheekier. Because now, at this stage, I knew a lot more about what was at stake and, more importantly, who was responsible for what. Using all the information I had gained in the research and writing, I was able to speak an even blunter truth to power.

PROCESSED

Gilded George would get my first note. I'd already tried to get a response from the Sydney PR company that held a contract for his Australian meat businesses. The brands didn't want to 'contribute' to the book, they'd said.

Again, it was very few words to a journalist, in return for what was likely to be a very expensive monthly retainer. It really didn't seem like George Weston Foods, who own Don KRC, were getting good value for money from these PR folk, just as the Aldi Albrechts didn't seem to be getting their money's worth from Ogilvy PR. It was all very confusing. I needed a show and tell, not a game of hide and seek.

Anyway, my Yuletide letter to Gilded George would hopefully get a response. After all, as we know he is the top boss of an entire processed pyramid and capable of helping to change Australia's cured-meat landscape with one touch of his iPad.

Dear Mr George G. Weston,

My name is Lucie Morris-Marr and I'm an investigative journalist and author based in Melbourne, Victoria, Australia.

I'm currently completing my manuscript for my new narrative non-fiction book which will be published by Allen & Unwin.

I'm seeking to give you the opportunity, as CEO of ABF, to respond to some questions regarding your products made by your business Don KRC, owned by George Weston Foods (and therefore ABF), here in Australia.

I'm also giving many other meat companies and brands mentioned in the book the same right of reply.

I'm aware GWF has many brands here, however I'm particularly interested in your large meat business Don KRC based in Castlemaine, Victoria.

I will be mentioning your family business and career in the book, including how you know the meat business here well and worked expanding it while running George Weston Foods in Australia.

As well as a journalist I'm also a bowel cancer patient advocate, after being diagnosed with stage-four bowel cancer in late 2019, so naturally I have a personal interest in any foods or preservatives that could risk others also suffering from this devastating disease.

My questions to you, as CEO of ABF, are as follows;

1. Don KRC produces multiple products, including ham, bacon, luncheon meats and salami, all of which, apart from a small 'Naturals' range (of ham and bacon), contain sodium nitrite (preservative 250). Is the company looking at using organic preservative compounds in all your products in the future considering the growing body of evidence regarding health impacts of nitro-preservatives in processed meats? The EU, for example, recently declared meat companies in member states need to reduce their sodium nitrite levels in meat, while many leading scientists including Professor Denis Corpet in France and Professor Chris

Elliott, of Queen's University Belfast, are calling for them to be banned completely due to their cancer risk. They have made these calls based on studies which proved processed meat containing sodium nitrite can directly cause bowel cancer.

2. I personally feel some of Don's packaging is misleading consumers in terms of the actual product (as do other meat companies).

    It may well fall just within the Australian labelling laws but calling some items certain names such as 'English style leg ham' etc. and 'Honey leg ham' I feel is misleading as the meat is manufactured meat and ultra processed. I expect a lot of consumers of Don's products have no idea that the product starts as a raw mix/paste of bits of meat which is removed from the leg with high-pressure water and then all sorts of additives, preservatives are added to the mix. The 'flavour' mentioned on the ingredient label also does not fully describe the many chemical flavours which could be being added. I would like your personal reaction to this please? Do you and fellow ABF executives believe you are treating Australian consumers fairly?

3. Do you understand why, as a bowel cancer patient, I feel troubled by the current marketing slogan 'Is Don. Is Good.' considering the ingredients of most of your ultra-processed-meat products, in particular sodium nitrites?

4. Does ABF, GWF and Don KRC stand by the slogan that their products are 'Good' for Australian children esp. in regard to many of their products [that] are aimed for school lunch boxes? I'm particularly referring to Don's 'minis range' and the snack range which all contain sodium nitrite and overall are ultra-processed products.
5. Do you think it's appropriate that your staff at Don KRC in Castlemaine, Victoria, are given discounted and free processed-meat products from the Don meat ranges which (apart from the Naturals range) contain sodium nitrite, in light of the growing concerns from experts I have mentioned? And especially as these workers are likely to have children and may place these products in their meals and lunch boxes?
6. I'm aware that nitro-preservatives are allowed in set amounts according to the safety code in place with the Food Standards Australia New Zealand (FSANZ), but as a major supplier of processed meat to Australians do you agree that it's also your place, especially as the ultimate CEO of the ABF business chain, to be able to answer these questions directly about your products in the spirit of transparency and care for your consumers?
7. Any other comments/information.

Best wishes
Lucie Morris-Marr

PROCESSED

I may well have ruined the office Christmas party for Gilded George and his media advisers. But that's what you get paid millions per year for as the top gun, I suppose. Unexpected missiles.

And yes, you guessed it, I sent a very similar letter to another handsome fella, the always-smiling Chef Miguel. I told him I had questions about his relatively new own-brand of cured meats because many of the products in the range contain sodium nitrite.

I won't repeat the entire tome. You know the score. Except I did add one extra question, considering he is someone with direct cultural influence in Australia and the star of his very own meat offerings.

'Would you be prepared to consider alternative preservatives in the future,' I asked him, 'to help try to safeguard the future health of your consumers who perhaps are not fully aware of the use of nitro-preservatives and their potential health risks?'

Surprisingly, his wife Sascha, who works with him on his meat brand, immediately replied, saying they did intend to respond. But so far, so silent.

I also then decided to tie a neat little red Christmas bow around this entire investigation and also fire off letters to the Australian health minister at the time, Mark Butler; the industry body Australian Pork Limited; the Australian Meat Industry Council; and FSANZ.

Importantly, I also asked Meat & Livestock Australia for a progress status after that illuminating 2020 CSIRO review I unearthed which made it clear they were aware of nitrite risks, the one which they funded jointly with the government.

So, would they move to recommend the widespread use of organic preservatives and additives in processed meats rather than chemical preservatives? Could high-pressure processing (HPP) or high-pressure thermal processing (HPTP) be viable solutions too? What about making all cured meat nitrite-free and selling it from freezers instead of fridges?

And, pressingly, did they intend to bring in labels warning of possible nitrosamine formation from preservatives on the ingredient labels—and also warn of the PAH content in smoked goods and advise on safer processed meat cooking methods?

I also dropped a line to the education minister and Independent Schools Australia regarding my concerns over processed meats being sold in school canteens.

And I hadn't forgotten that tense interaction with Hospital Harry over my intensive-care ham sandwich, so I sent the Australian Medical Association a letter too and fired off one to the CEO of Private Healthcare Australia, just for good measure.

I also had a few choice words to say to Murray Watt, the federal agriculture minister at the time, who issued a media release on 4 December 2023 demanding supermarkets to freeze the price of Christmas hams. 'The traditional ham is a staple of any Christmas lunch in Australia,' he said. 'And we know families are doing it tough at the moment and the cost of a lot of things is going up.

'It's time for supermarkets to do their part and say one thing we won't put up is the price of a Christmas ham.'[9]

Ostensibly he was making a fair point in terms of high supermarket prices and the cost-of-living crisis, but in my view he'd picked on the wrong Christmas protein favourite to stand up for.

'Can you understand that as a bowel cancer patient who has researched the subject of processed meats extensively that this stance concerns me?' I immediately wrote to his media team in an email, as his release began to make Yuletide media headlines.

'Are you also aware that nearly all Christmas hams on sale in the main three supermarkets—Coles, Woolworths and Aldi—contain Sodium Nitrite? The levels used are likely to adhere to levels issued by the FSANZ however there is a growing body of evidence which shows that even tiny amounts of Sodium Nitrites still pose a potential risk.

'Therefore are you not concerned that more people eating Christmas hams increases the risk of Australians getting bowel cancer in particular?'

Surprisingly, the reply was swift, but the contents rather confusing. 'This kind of enquiry generally wouldn't be handled by the Agriculture team as we tend to manage the raw products more than food manufacturing standards, unless they pose a biosecurity threat,' the senior media adviser told me in her email. 'Can I suggest, if you haven't already, to reach out to Food Standards Australia New Zealand.'

Hang on, so the minister was able to make headlines making demands about a common processed meat, but when questioned about it further his team effectively refused to respond?

I wasn't going to let it end there. It was time to go 'nuclear', as my teenage son likes to joke.

'These processed meats using Australian meat are very much part of Australian agriculture,' I fired back. 'I'm keen for

Minister Watt to please see and consider my questions as his role is still influential and if he's making public statements on processed meats such as ham (and they are processed as they are cured with Sodium Nitrite) the questions are important.'

The silence that followed was deafening. Maybe the minister was busy rushing to his local supermarket to buy his Christmas ham before they sold out, after all he'd single-handedly given the product a rather large publicity boost. He'd soon move on from his role anyway, being made minister of employment and workplace relations a few months after I wrote to him.

When I found out that a lengthy review of the 2013 Australian Dietary Guidelines was taking place, overseen by the federal government's National Health and Medical Research Council (NHMRC), I also sent them a note.

As it stands, processed meats are included on the famous 'pie chart' of foods issued by the NHMRC as part of those 2013 guidelines. You may have seen the chart on a large, colourful poster in your doctor's waiting room or even on the walls of hospitals. Currently, there is an image of a sausage along with lollies, meat burger, cake and so on; these are in a little side group called 'sometimes' or discretionary foods.

The NHMRC's review, as we learned earlier, will take years to conclude but they are accepting public submissions. So I asked them if they would please change the guidelines and advise the Australian public to stop eating processed meats and make it clear why. I really hope they do.

And just when I thought I'd never get a reply from any of the big hitters and major decision makers, a message pinged in my inbox. It was from Bunnings. I nearly fell over. I had almost forgotten that long and emotive letter I'd sent to Hardware Mike. What did he have to say?

Hi Lucie,

Thanks for reaching out, Mike has asked me to respond on his behalf.

We appreciate you taking the time to get in touch about our sausage sizzles and sharing your experience as a bowel cancer patient. I'm sorry to hear how difficult and lengthy the treatment has been since your diagnosis, and I applaud your work in raising awareness of bowel cancer in the community.

Bunnings is committed to supporting the communities we operate in, including through our popular fundraising sausage sizzles. They give community groups the opportunity to raise money while promoting their cause and engaging with their local community—and as you say, Australians feel particularly passionate about the iconic Bunnings sausage sizzle.

To streamline the operation of the sausage sizzles and make them as successful as possible for the host community groups, we have a uniform set of guidelines that include a set price for sausages. Community groups make the decision on the type of sausages they offer at the sizzle and purchase the supplies themselves. This allows groups to consider options that cater to the dietary, lifestyle and religious preferences of the community they operate in, such as vegetarian, vegan, organic, Kosher or Halal.

On the back of your email, we'll be taking the opportunity to remind our store teams to reinforce the importance of community groups considering alternatives for customers who still want to take part in a sizzle but prefer not to consume a traditional snag.

In addition to community groups having the flexibility to offer a product selection that responds to the needs of the local community, our store cafes also provide food options that cater to a range of dietary requirements and preferences.

Wishing you all the best for your future advocacy work and upcoming publication of the book.

The response from Bunnings meant at least the company wasn't afraid to engage with me and my questions, unlike the other mega-companies. Most importantly, I was delighted the email had prompted Hardware Mike to remind the store teams about telling community groups to offer other choices. I'd rather it was a strict rule but it was a start; I'd planted a seed in the store that sells a hell of a lot of seeds and it felt like a win.

I may never get a full reply from any of the others. Who knows? But, like a child who posts their 'Dear Santa' letter into their nearest postbox without an exact address, I know it's the dream that counts.

My nitrite-free Christmas gift list was out in the ether.

PROCESSED

The bottom line

I'll never forget when I first entered journalism in a London newsroom in the late 1990s. Newspapers had long since left their traditional base of Fleet Street and had slowly moved to various modern offices and tower blocks scattered across London.

But there was one Fleet Street habit that remained: heavy smoking, either from the comfort of office chairs, in special smoking rooms or in communal areas. As a wide-eyed work-experience reporter on *The Guardian* in London, I remember hoping to sneak a glimpse of a well-known crime reporter, maybe even talk to him. All I ever saw of this mysterious figure were spirals of cigarette smoke circling above his desk, his face blocked from view due to the various books and papers stacked up all around him in his personal ash-covered fortress.

Less than ten years before, in 1989, I'd excitedly taken my first long-haul flight, aged thirteen, from London to Orlando, Florida. I have vivid memories of coughing due to all the cigarettes being lit by the passengers in the special smoking section at the back. Nobody raised an eyebrow. Smokers had rights.

Looking back, it's hard to believe this was all part of normal daily life. In a relatively short time, awareness about the undeniable cancer risk from smoking and secondary inhalation saw huge attitude shifts, changed personal behaviour, and led to the introduction of new policies and laws that banned smoking on transport, in workplaces and in restaurants.

Governments, health campaigners and consumers themselves all played their part, in the end, to bring about radical change that has saved millions of lives. Of course smoking is still a major public health issue worldwide, but it's far less a 'crisis' than it was.

Globally, smoking has declined by 27.2 per cent for men since 1990, and by 37.9 per cent for women. Declines have been higher in wealthier countries, falling by more than 40 per cent in some, and also quite dramatically in several Latin American countries, notably Brazil, where the habit has dropped by 70 per cent since 1990. The number of female smokers in particular has declined in some countries, including Nepal, Holland and Denmark, and remains low throughout Asia and Africa.[10] In Australia, 11 per cent of people smoked in 2019, down from 24 per cent in 1991.[11]

So, in short, patterns of behaviour that seem ingrained and unmovable are capable of changing.

What we've created here in Australia, through false idols such as the Bunnings sausage, the democracy sausage and the post-sport snag, is an adoration of processed meat. It's become part of our daily lives. And at one point, I have to admit, I was part of this humongous processed-meat party. But no more.

Though it may seem impossible, I truly believe our society is capable of changing this obsession with processed meats, just as the world decided to break up with smoking. We've seen similar impressive changes in the past few decades, like the shift from cage eggs to free-range eggs, along with a bigger demand for free-range meats, as people became aware of the cruelty and suffering involved in restrictive factory farming.

Consumers wouldn't tolerate it and made food choices that drove sales in a new economic direction. The industry altered its practices. Laws were changed. In regard to processed meats, a joint government, industry and consumer shift may be required; if just one of my many dreams comes true and the government orders the food industry to switch to frozen nitrite-free meat products for example, the public will hopefully soon adapt.

It heartens me to know change is already being seen in some parts of the world when it comes to processed foods, and in some cases processed meats. It has to start somewhere.

One shining example happened in 2017, when the American Medical Association demanded that hospitals should serve more plant-based meals and totally drop processed meats such as bacon and hot dogs. It may not have been implemented yet, but at least it was the official policy of an organisation that represents 200,000 doctors in the US, and it helped to raise awareness among the US public. The policy also called for hospitals to reduce sugar-sweetened drinks, including in vending machines.[12]

Since then, Lithuania has imposed limits on the levels of salt and sugar permitted in hospital food, which means that salty processed meats may be targeted. Interestingly in Brazil, the country that is home to meat giant JBS, there is a guideline that any food sold or served in the country's Ministry of Health facilities 'requires minimal use of processed food, including processed meat'.[13]

One of the largest studies ever carried out into the long-term impacts of modern-day diets certainly adds weight to these changes.[14] Just as I was completing the manuscript for this book Harvard University revealed the results of studying the diets of more than 114,000 Americans over three decades. While there had been many probes into ultra-processed foods in the past, what made this study stand out was that the researchers from the Harvard T.H. Chan School of Public Health focused on food-subgroups. It didn't surprise me that they found the highest risks of mortality were associated with those who regularly ate processed meats, with a 13 per cent higher chance of dying during the time they were tracked for the study.

While we've seen the powerful impact of marketing and deeply entrenched cultural food habits, as consumers we can play our part too in helping to change the status quo. Voice by voice, we can be a powerful force. If you still choose to consume processed meats every time you're at the deli counter or butcher, perhaps ask if they do nitrite-free or organic versions of your favourite items. If enough people ask, the message will get through. And, if you wish, start replacing processed meats with the other healthier protein options I've mentioned. When you are with friends and family, tell them what you've learned.

If you're a parent, you can help future generations by encouraging fellow parents to stop putting ham sandwiches in lunch boxes. And maybe, just maybe, if you wish, you can be bold and politely suggest to your kids' footy club, school or Scout group to offer other alternatives to the sausage sizzle.

In May 2024 it was reported one brave Melbourne mother did just that. Sheena Chhabra asked her son's football club to stop serving snags at their post-match Auskick barbecue, primarily on the grounds of animal cruelty allegations against their meat-supplier. She wrote emails to the South Melbourne District Sports Club saying she was unhappy there had been no vegan options available.

She told *The Age* newspaper she was also concerned about the health impact of children consuming sausages. 'We need to evolve the foods being given to children to reflect modern values of inclusivity, animal welfare, health and sustainability rather than the cultural tradition of a sausage sizzle,' she said.[15]

It really isn't a difficult change. The alternative options are endless. What about halloumi and red capsicum kebab sticks on the barbecue, with homemade corn-and-chickpea burgers, rolls and some tomato relish? If there is still a need for meat, homemade beef burgers or chicken skewers are easy to put together. None of it has to be expensive or complicated. With a little more thought and planning, it can be done.

Conversation is the start of everything. One voice can cause a chain reaction among your whole network of friends and family.

It doesn't mean the road ahead will be an easy one. Far from it. Most tobacco smokers for example, would admit the habit is smelly and dangerous, but the difficulty of giving up comes from a physical addiction to nicotine. That's a different beast from the deeply held love of bacon. And there isn't an obvious chimney of doom filling the room every time it's eaten.

I researched whether a meat tax could help in the same way that high taxes on cigarettes have aimed to reduce tobacco consumption. It's a subject that is being discussed in Germany and the Netherlands, and is actually focused on issues such as animal welfare and climate change, rather than health.

But according to Rebecca Taylor of the World Cancer Research Fund, if implemented, meat taxes could indeed have the knock-on effect of reducing processed-meat consumption. 'Marketing restrictions and other fiscal measures could also cut processed meat consumption,' she says. 'But there are few marketing restrictions in place that target highly processed food, including processed meat. Brazil, which has banned advertising of highly processed foods within Ministry of Health premises, is a rare example.'

Restrictions on advertising junk food might also help, Taylor adds, noting that the UK has restrictions coming into force in October 2025 after initial delays. 'The restrictions will prevent online and TV advertising of food that is high in salt, sugar or fat before 9pm to help tackle childhood obesity—and so processed meat, which is frequently high in salt and fat, would be covered.'[16]

Financial measures that target processed meat specifically don't yet exist, but I passionately hope they will. In the meantime, I'll keep shouting what I've learned from the rooftops.

On Twitter a few years ago, I asked the following question: 'Processed meats, including bacon, salami, hot dogs etc, have been defined in multiple respected medical reports as a cause of bowel cancer. Out of interest, does that info motivate you to give them up for good?'

I was fascinated to see the responses. More than 360 people took part in my little survey and 63 per cent said no. Only 37 per cent said yes.[17]

This disengagement from the issue is a problem. 'Just about everything gives you cancer in the current environment' said one user. That's been a common response, as you may have noticed.

When I interviewed one of the world's leading bowel cancer surgeons and researchers, Dr Yuman C. Fong, during his visit to Melbourne in 2022 from his usual post at the City of Hope in Los Angeles, he agreed it was hard to tell the public to avoid certain food groups. He accepted he had immense influence in the health arena globally and didn't want people to be disengaged.

But I pushed him, mostly because I wanted to know his view. 'But would you prefer people didn't eat processed meats?' I asked.

He hesitated. 'Yes, I would.'

I hope I won't be part of that disengagement by writing this book. In sharing my personal story and investigating the subject, my aim was always to show, not tell.

I have been heartened by the public response to impressive Australian books on other areas of the food industry, including *Sweet Poison* by David Gillespie on the health risks of sugar, and *Toxic* by Richard Flanagan, who exposed the destructive practices of the Tasmanian salmon industry.

I still eat sugar sometimes, and very occasionally have red meat or a celebratory glass of French champagne. We are human. And imperfection makes us more so. Once a year I may even still have a small bite of a Christmas pig in a nitrite-free blanket, if I'm feeling homesick. As one specialist told me, 'You've fought hard to live, Lucie, so live and have a drink around the campfire now and then.'

But what gives me hope is knowing the seismic changes that have gone before. With just with a few lifestyle tweaks, we can still be sociable and enjoy quick hot snacks, whether they are outside hardware stores or after Little Athletics.

After the investigation for this book however, I'm left with a lot of deeply troubling questions. Did my grandfather pass away too soon because of processed meats?

Did my dear friend Kieren, who passed away in November 2023, leaving behind three beautiful daughters, get bowel cancer because of eating bacon, even if it wasn't very often? What about my other lost beloved friends in the bowel cancer community?

What about the cause of my cancer?

As the French author Guillaume Coudray points out, the global number of bowel cancer cases is predicted to reach 2.2 million per year in 2030. Personally I find this devastating, knowing the pain, suffering and potential loss of life involved.

Yes, we know these figures will not all relate to the consumption of processed meats. But, as Coudray quite rightly asks, 'Why contribute to this catastrophe, when specialists in bowel cancer constantly recommend that we introduce a genuine prevention policy relating to food?'

He also suggests that we should be introduced to meat that isn't made pink and long-lasting by nitro-preservatives. It would be greyer and duller looking but it would have far fewer risks.[18] I'm confident we could all adapt.

We need to process these risks further and demand change. We all deserve the chance to live our best lives. Long lives. For our future, and for the future of our children. We need to consider the environmental impact too, and ensure the animals we kill for a protein source in this salty mix are treated ethically and humanely.

It distresses me greatly to imagine anyone in the future, from any country, facing the horrors of bowel cancer because of what is added to processed meats. I don't want a single soul to suffer like I have, or to pass away too soon like my dear friends have. I've experienced it, and now I've shared it here in this book for the greater good, to try my best to bring the message home.

I try to stay positive and seek out emerging treatments and experts, but the truth is I may still not survive my cancer. As this book was being edited I was still waiting for a liver transplant, and doctors have warned me the metastatic bowel cancer could still occur elsewhere. I can barely utter the words, amid my usually strict day-to-day mantra of I Will Survive positivity, but my life may turn out to be far shorter than I'd hoped. That's just my reality. And I'll never know if it's because of the mass-produced processed meats I naively consumed in the decades before my shock diagnosis at age 44.

One of the other key questions I've been left with is a simple one: Is nature telling us not to do weird things with meat? From what we've clearly seen in my investigation there are major questions over the safety of many elements of smoking, preserving, curing and flavouring the flesh of animals for human consumption.

These questions come at a time when there are pressing ethical and health concerns surrounding the rapid global development of cell-based meats, also known as lab-grown meat. While sales are currently illegal in Australia, an initial framework for permission is being examined by the US regulatory bodies among others. Such meats would surely need to have clear advisory labels.

I personally think at the very least laws should be introduced to have warning labels placed on processed meats, clearly stating, in particular, they contain nitro-preservatives or PAHs that can cause cancer, just like the hard-hitting labels on cigarette packets. My loyal French penpal Professor Corpet agrees: 'In my opinion, in a democracy like Australia, these should be clearly labelled and I am surprised it is not the case.'

As for surprises, well, you may have experienced as many as I have in the course of my journey through these pages. And I thank you hugely for reading and coming on this wild, terrifying and fascinating ride with me.

We've seen why our government, like many others, needs to do major public health awareness campaigns. Donald Trump famously declared, 'They're eating the dogs!' during a heated pre-election TV debate with Kamala Harris, creating viral memes all over social media. If only somebody so powerful could make such a statement, complete with exclamation marks, about the health risks of eating hot dogs. After all, we've seen why they should—ideally—ban the use of nitro-preservatives in meats altogether, or at least reduce them as the EU has done. We need our government to commission further research into whether organic preservatives make a healthy alternative—or not—and also look into banning certain smoke flavourings just as the EU has done. The meat industry, fast-food companies and supermarkets, the ones getting rich from processed meats, need to be made to take responsibility too. This needs to happen now, in my view, and urgently, in order to prevent further suffering, deaths and grief.

I conclude this book stunned by what I've uncovered in the course of my research, most pertinently that processed meats have been linked in studies to more than ten serious illnesses and conditions, some of which can be fatal. I didn't expect to form such a long and abhorrent list on this journey but, as a reminder, here it is:

- Bowel cancer
- Breast cancer
- Prostate cancer
- Upper GI cancers (including pancreatic, stomach, oesophagus)
- Renal (kidney) cancer and diseases
- Heart disease
- Obesity
- Leukaemia
- Type 2 diabetes
- Dementia
- Mental health issues

It's also become clear that convincing consumers and law makers of the risk processed meats pose is complex, especially because measuring consumption of individual foods and their potential health impacts can be such a challenge for scientists.

So go ahead, still eat that 'Is Don. Is Good.' bacon sandwich if you want to. Put those Primo *Paw Patrol* snack packs in your child's lunch box. Because it's clear to me, as I emerge from this complicated maze, that in fact your next move is quite simple.

You just need to decide where to place your trust.

Is it with respected experts such as Denis Corpet and Chris Elliott, along with all the thousands of underpaid university researchers and clinical biologists from Harvard to Oxford?

Or does your trust lie with the cashed-up captains of industry, including Gilded George, Cartoon Bob, McChris, Domino Don, Spam Boss Jim, Subway Neal, the Aldi Albrechts, Chef Miguel and the Billionaire Brothers of Brazil?

Who cares most for your health? The shareholders or the scientists?

What 'risk' is worth taking?

Is a lifetime of pepperoni on your pizza worth a colostomy bag, or worse?

Ultimately, the choice is yours—to get snagged or to break free. Just please remember to check your poo.

And that's my bottom line.

Afterword

TRANSPLANTED

On a warm, breezy day, there were two packages being prepared with my name on them.

One I was writing on at the post office counter in Mentone, Melbourne. It was going to Sydney. It was the final proofs I'd been sent of this book.

'Make sure you add some sellotape. Really make sure it's sealed down, please,' I said to the lady behind the desk as she took the package from my hand. The biggest, most important book of my life. The destination: Allen & Unwin, Crows Nest, Sydney. Sender: Lucie Morris-Marr.

As I walked outside, it was the first time I'd had no tasks for quite some while. Breathe. It was time to swim, rest, be a mum and continue waiting for news of my liver transplant.

Naturally, I wasn't to know that somewhere in Australia, in a hospital, the location of which I will never know, there was another package soon to be carefully, carefully put together with my name on it. Someone in Australia was in that moment losing their life. Male, female, young, old, I'll never know. All I know is their blood type.

As I carried on my day, unaware that it would be my last before major surgery, I relished the freedom that every writer feels after completing such an epic project.

The rest of the day had a stillness to it. I'd done my usual swim at a different time, lunchtime instead of suppertime, when my daughter was at a dance class. So when darkness began to fall, I found myself at home, feeling a little restless.

It was a beautiful night. I opened the front door and just walked down our street, our little court. My cavoodle and two ginger cats followed, as has been our custom since our lockdown walks, and there was no traffic and no birds swooping at us.

By the light of the moon, we walked a couple of hundred steps. I remember feeling how still it was amid the weather systems that had been battling as the spring had turned to summer, and the storms coming across the Tasman, across Port Phillip Bay, would have furious clashes with the warmth and red dust that sometimes come from the north and hit Melbourne, causing upset, rain and high winds.

Tonight was silent. The universe had paused around me. My mind paused.

I strolled back to the house, went through the front door and sat back down on the sofa. Almost immediately, my mobile rang with a number I didn't recognise.

'Hello?' I said.

'Oh, hello. Is that Lucie Morris-Marr?'

'Yes.'

'Good news. We have a liver for you.'

For a moment I had no words. I'd waited for this call for six months, started to wonder whether it would ever come in time.

They were holding back the tumours in my liver with targeted antibody infusions every two weeks. I was stable, but the cancer was there. We had run out of options. A major surgery just for the sake of removing the tumours for a third time would be traumatic and pointless, because we knew they were coming back. Radiation was not possible: I'd had as much as I could. The drugs, which were keeping the cancer at bay, would have a shelf life. I'd been warned of that. A transplant was my only chance.

But even this was an extraordinary option that came from a clear, blue sky earlier in the year. A series of incredible coincidences, luck, and new, emerging treatments and research coming together to make the Austin Hospital in Melbourne change their liver transplant protocol, just to try to safe my life.

You see, metastatic cancer patients aren't given transplants in Australia—in very few countries around the world, for that matter. It's very new. It worries even the surgeons. Because the livers are naturally such a previous resource they cannot risk giving them to anyone who might not be able to bear them for long, when it could give someone else an entire lifetime. They have to make strict ethical decisions.

The reason it came to pass was last Christmas, as described earlier, I had been told I had seven new liver tumours just before I flew to England. Thankfully, I dropped a line to a cancer friend, a young barber named Mitch, who lives in Gippsland, Victoria.

By chance, a few years earlier, he'd got in touch because I wrote an article during Melbourne's stage-four lockdown about what it was like trying to also deal with stage-four cancer. It was the exact advanced bowel cancer Mitch had. He was also battling to survive with similar treatments.

For some reason, I just wanted to know how he was. 'How's it going?' I wrote to him in the Instagram message. 'How are you?'

Thankfully, he's a young chap and quick to respond. 'Oh, Lucie, great to hear from you. I'm amazing. I've just become the first man in Australia to have a liver transplant with stage-four bowel cancer.'

I nearly dropped my phone. I'd asked about transplants before many times, and was told patients like me, with my condition, weren't candidates. It wasn't an option. All I could say to Mitch, with some urgency, was, 'Mitch, please tell me who your surgeon was.'

I then contacted his surgeon, Associate Professor Carlo Pulitano, based at Royal Prince Alfred Hospital in Sydney, who had been allowed a special clinical trial to give liver transplants to the right candidates with colorectal cancer. So far, he'd only done one. Soon, he'd have done two.

By extraordinary coincidence, Mitch had gone to his local post office in Gippsland and mentioned he'd had a transplant. The post office lady had said, 'Oh my gosh, there's a young mother in this village called Amanda. She's got four children under ten. She's got advanced bowel cancer.'

Amanda became the second person in Australia to have a liver transplant with advanced bowel cancer. I would be the third.

In my case, Dr Niall Tebbutt, the head of medical oncology at the Olivia Newton John Centre at the Austin Hospital, Melbourne, had become my new oncologist. I said, in our first meeting, 'Niall, please can you send my notes to this surgeon in Sydney. I'm going to have to live there and wait for a transplant. They've offered me one.'

And he said, 'Hang on a minute. Let me just speak to our team here.'

By 6.30 that evening, the team at the Austin, acknowledging that Victorian patients shouldn't have to travel to New South Wales for a procedure they could do, agreed I would be the first to have a transplant in a Victorian hospital—whereas the other two patients were Victorians but they went to New South Wales.

When you get phone calls like that, the jubilation is overwhelming, but it's quickly followed by immense fears. I would go through weeks of intensive testing, counselling. Everything to check there wasn't a speck of cancer outside my liver. That was the rule. That was the protocol they were sticking to. And also, the cancer could only have been in the one place for at least a couple of years. Mine wasn't unstable. It hadn't been anywhere else since the primary tumour in my colon had been removed via resection in April 2020.

I fit the bill. I was young. It had been made clear to me again and again during the process that a transplant may not be a cure, that the metastatic cancer could return, often in the lungs. The immune suppressants could also cause skin cancer, plus kidney issues. All these, however, would be treatable matters and with careful monitoring I felt I could deal with any blips.

'My alternative is guaranteed death, so I'll take it,' I said to surgeon Marcos Perini, who had been placed in charge of developing the new colorectal cancer transplant protocol, as I signed the transplant permission forms.

He told me to stay active and keep my phone on. And then everything fell silent.

As I got up from the sofa, I saw my daughter walking towards me in the kitchen. In that split second, she didn't yet know. It was hard. She was so young. She'd already had five years, a third of her life, with a mother with serious cancer and going through so many treatments. I had to tell her she had to be brave. I had to go through one more surgery. Tears welled in her eyes.

My son, beautifully dressed in his air force cadet uniform, came through the door so handsome, dazzling, from his evening parade. I led him to my room, and we sat and we cried and we laughed. I said it was time. I would have to go in an hour. We had an hour together.

I'd already been told I had a three per cent chance of dying on the operating table. The pain and tears—as a mother, you just want to solve it. You just want to do anything to resolve that pain when it's your child. You don't want to leave them. It's the last thing you want to do.

I had to reassure them, but I also gave them a choice. I said, 'Either I can stay now, and you don't have to go through the darkness. You won't cry for most of the night. But you may only get one more trip, maximum two, around the sun with me. If you let me go, you're going to have to spend a night or so in the darkness. Be brave and tell me to go, you may get forty years of trips around the sun with me. What should we do?'

'Do it, Mummy,' my son uttered. My daughter just nodded, more tears welling.

I wanted them to feel that they were part of the decision, because this is why I was doing it. I was doing it for them. I knew of the risk. It was a massive risk. Part of me just wanted to stay with them, investigate trials at Peter Mac, or stay tracking as I was. There are so many trials going on around the world. Surely someone could cure cancer. After all, someone quickly found the vaccine for Covid.

But I knew deep down I'd done the risk calculations. I'd spoken to other transplant patients. I'd actually had other consultations, opinion consultations, with liver surgeons who had no skin in the game. No possible competitive ego motivations, which can happen between hospitals, between men, between humans. They said, 'Do it. Take the chance.'

I mentioned it to Betsy Post, a community leader of Colontown—the biggest colorectal cancer forum in the world, which I'd been very much a part of in mentorship of other patients—whose sister died of colorectal cancer. When I said here in Australia the transplant was free and I shouldn't have to wait more than a few months, she couldn't believe it. She said, 'Do it. Take it. Here in America, you'd have to sell your house because the insurers don't always pay.' And of course, some people aren't insured. She said, 'To wait for a deceased donor in America could take one to two years, when it's too late anyway.'

With no stone left unturned I even met with Derryn Hinch, now eighty, who'd famously had a successful liver transplant thirteen years earlier, led by surgeon Bob Jones, now the head of the Liver Transplant Unit at the Austin. 'You've got this, go for it and don't look back,' Derryn said. The one thing the Human Headline certainly knows about more than most is staying alive. His words were like rocket fuel.

It made me feel so lucky to have this option, and I knew the surgeons were experts.

My children walked me out into the front garden, my husband pulling the suitcase towards our car in the street. We hugged for a final time in the driveway, in the darkness. I knew there'd be tears as soon as I went. A dear friend, thankfully, had dropped everything to be with them for the night. She was waiting for them inside with hot tea and toast. I knew they were safe.

Again, they talk about cancer patients being brave, but I've never felt brave before. I've simply got on with it. Because you do what you have to do. But even I admit, walking away from my children felt like I needed every brave bone in my body to just get out the gate.

As we got to the car, I could see their shadows waving. I'd like to say the bright moon that night lit up their faces, to make the perfect Rembrandt-style image for you. But the trees were in the way as we drove off, and I couldn't see my children. They were already alone in the dark.

PROCESSED

We drove away in silence. All the way north, north through the suburbs of Melbourne to reach Heidelberg. Through Camberwell, along Burke Road, up through Ivanhoe and Kew. We pulled up outside the emergency department, where I'd been told to present myself.

The waiting room was packed with probably forty or fifty people, but I was whisked straight in and taken away to a ward—a ward I would soon know very well: Ward 8 West, on the eighth floor. It's where the transplant patients go.

They x-rayed me. They did bloods. It was just after midnight. I would be asleep by six. And incredibly, those hours went very fast. My husband holding my hand, dozing slightly in the chair. Me, sending messages to family in England, informing them of what was happening. And of course, messages to my children for when they woke up.

With word spreading among my family and friends, I was told in messages that multi-faith prayer vigils were already beginning all over the word. My dear friend Tessa Sullivan, Honorary Consul for Thailand in Melbourne, had informed the Thai Buddhist monks based in the Buddha Bodhivana Monastery, deep in the forest of the Yarra Ranges near Warburton. They knew of my fight, having recently given me a personal blessing at Tessa's home. Further afield friends of the Jewish, Muslim, Catholic and Anglican faith would spend the entire night, UK time, praying for the duration of my operation. I could not have had more support, and willingly opened my heart to their prayers and kindness.

The porter came. 'It's time to go.'

My bed was wheeled along the corridor to the lift and down to Level 2, to where surgery was and where I would be in intensive care.

Sooner than I hoped, we turned a corner and they said, 'This is where you say goodbye to your husband.'

We just looked at each other, held hands, and I told him, 'I'll be okay. See you later.'

He said, 'You will be okay, and I will see you later,' before my journey continued to the small side room where I could see them busy prepping the theatre. Bright lights, metal. Technical workers were already prepping me. The surgeons would not be there until perhaps seven. They wanted me asleep, to set me up, to make sure I was stable, to be ready for the operation to begin.

For the package that had my name on it was now in the theatre. A liver on ice in an Esky, possibly having been flown in by private jet. By now, it had been placed in a machine perfusion device, which keeps the liver pumping and alive. The contents of the package was waiting.

'You're going to go to sleep now, Lucie,' the anaesthetist said. I don't remember any more.

'Lucie, you're on a ventilator. Just breathe.'

This had been my worst fear out of the entire procedure. They warned me I would have to be woken up and ventilated, which is rare, very rare. They have to do it. They have to 100 per cent know that you can breathe on your own when you're awake. My nine-hour surgery had been a success, but then they'd kept me asleep on the ventilator for my body to stabilise and relax for another seven hours. And now it was time to make sure I could breathe on my own.

'We'd like you to stay on it as long as possible,' the anaesthetist said calmly.

It's funny how the phrase 'It's never as bad as you think it will be . . .' is so often true. It wasn't one of those facemask type of ventilators. It was a tube that went in my mouth and down my throat.

I breathed calmly over it, and she said, 'If it's getting bad, just let me know.'

I managed a few more minutes of just breathing, focusing on the Yarra Valley campsite and the river I love so much, and floating down it with my children. The light was coming in, dappling on the surface. My hand went into the cold water. I was there. I wasn't in intensive care.

'I think that's all I can do now,' I said to the anaesthetist.

'That's fine,' she said, and with one movement it was removed very easily.

I was breathing on my own. I was alive. The operation had worked.

I asked to call my husband. They put the phone to my ear. 'I did it. I did it,' I said down the line. 'We did it.'

'I'm so happy,' he said. 'They let me in earlier. They let me hold your hand briefly when you were still under. I'm so happy.'

That's all I could manage. I just wanted him to know, from me, I was okay.

I would eventually call Mitch too; his openness about his pioneering transplant had now played a serendipitous role in saving not just one mother, but two.

———

Of course, even though I was okay, there was still a long way to go to really fully come back to life.

In the following days, I would remain in intensive care. Tubes, a mainline in my neck, a massive drain around the wound. Other tubes in my hand. Multiple medications and infusions happening at all times.

Amazingly a physio, even on that first day, helped me to a chair with all the tubes as part of the protocol to make sure your body doesn't clot, to keep moving. I even managed, with the help of a frame, to walk some steps around intensive care, and then straight to bed again.

The next days are now quite a blur, but they involved a lot of pain, a lot of sickness, as my body tried to grapple with the surgical assault.

At one point, they wheeled me out into the terrace just off intensive care, and I felt the sun on my cheeks. It was the first time I was able to pause and take in this incredible, miraculous gift—the result of an Australian passing away and being so generous, thinking of someone else. Having signed up to the organ-donation program, possibly, and either way their family would have been asked if they gave permission. I put my hand over my wound for the first time and said, 'Thank you.'

PROCESSED

As I lay on the terrace, the sun and the breeze, things I would never, ever take for granted again, were so healing.

I'd be soon moved back to Ward 8 for further recovery. But on the second night, I called out for the nurse. My heart was beating rapidly.

'I'm sure it's fast,' I said.

'No,' he said. 'Your heart's been quite fast for a while, but not in a dangerous way.'

I said, 'Please check.'

He leaned over to put the heart monitor on my finger, and then he looked at the machine and went, 'Oh, my gosh.'

Before I could ask why, he pressed the emergency button. A MET call was declared. Doctors and nurses and specialists, whoever was there at that 2 a.m. shift and part of the MET team protocol, came rushing to my room.

'Her heartbeat's 171. I've just done an ECG,' the nurse said to the team when they came in.

They busily talked. I felt so frightened. I'd got through the operation, but maybe, just maybe, all the cancer treatments had weakened the internal structures of my heart. Chemotherapy can do that. Had I made the wrong decision? Should I have simply waited? Was this all a huge, ambitious, ridiculous mistake? I wouldn't even get to say goodbye to my children. They would never know I was thinking of them.

I turned my head to the left. I saw a lady, beautifully dressed. She wore wedge shoes, a necklace, a white top, cream jeans. She was looking.

I then saw a man in a baseball cap. He was circling the room. He wasn't one of the nurses in the MET team.

They were ghosts. I didn't know either of them. Had they come for me? Was this my time? Were they donors looking for their livers? Was I now hallucinating? Was it the drugs? The high heartrate? Was I dead? Was I alive? I didn't know anymore.

The next day, when I woke up, my heart was back down to 110. I was alive. I'd survived the night. It turns out that if you're very sick for a week and you don't eat, magnesium levels can drop. Every cell in our bodies needs magnesium. The doctors had soon worked it out, and as I'd drifted off to sleep they'd given me IV packs of magnesium and pumped them urgently into my body, along with phosphates and potassium. It was simply a chemical imbalance that my heart was struggling with. Though still serious, at least there was a solution.

Then, another patient had got their call and had their liver transplant. My private room was needed. I didn't mind, naturally. I was taken to a ward with other patients with varying conditions, and there began to improve.

But the worst wasn't over. There would be another MET call that night, too. The panicked looks. The pale faces. The worry. Was it the same thing? Why wasn't the heart coping? Again, I feared for my life in that moment, but I felt so helpless. There was nothing I could do.

PROCESSED

Thankfully—such world experts—they again found the right solutions, the right drugs, the right IV drips. I survived again and I was getting stronger. The wound was getting less painful. I was beginning to have special sustenance drinks with minerals. A few bites of fruit. Slowly, slowly healing.

I would also face a fever from an unknown source. Scans followed and more discomfort. Each day though I was grateful for the positive words of encouragement from the dynamic Dr Avik Majumdar, consultant gastroenterologist and hepatologist, on his daily rounds.

'This is brutal, Avik,' I moaned one morning.

'I know, but just remember recovery doesn't always go in a straight line and you're tracking incredibly well overall.'

It gave me great strength to get a social visit from a smiling Professor Vijayaragavan Muralidharan, known to all as Murali. Murali, a veteran consultant surgeon at the Austin and a senior lecturer in the University of the Melbourne Department of Surgery, performed my second complicated liver resection in 2022, keeping me alive long enough to become a transplant candidate. The amusing, perpetually elegant Sri Lankan, with a penchant for silk scarves and bespoke suits, had been an essential part of the journey.

My two lead surgeons would be frequent visitors. 'Less talking, more walking,' Brazilian-born surgeon Marcos Perini would prescribe frequently, served with a wry smile. A man of few words with tremendous drive and genius-level skills, he was the liver unit's very own Ronaldo.

The extremely talented surgeon Graham Starkey would sweep in with his assistants, serious and focused. With his *Game of Thrones*–style name and princely, strong physical deportment, he would be well deserving of the Iron Throne.

Fellow consultant surgeons Dr Eunice Lee and Dr Ruelan Furtado also took great care with my recovery. Ruelan's beaming smile each morning showed off his world-class teeth, matching the team's world-class brains.

The huge group of dedicated nurses were vital comrades too, deep in the trenches alongside me twenty-four hours a day.

I was also listening to powerful and rousing ballads through my AirPods to give myself strength and help my body vibrate with life and energy: 'Beggin'' by Måneskin, 'Cuff It' by Beyoncé, 'About Damn Time' by Lizzo, 'Caruso' by Pavarotti, 'Girl on Fire' by Alicia Keys, 'We Pray' by Coldplay (and others), 'Jai Ho' by A.R. Rahman, 'The Edge of Glory' by Lady Gaga, 'Diamonds' by Rihanna, 'Carmina Burana' by Carl Orff, 'Skyfall' by Adele and 'Don't Blame Me' by Taylor Swift. My unique cheer squad playlist I'd named 'Transplanted'.

I would be further uplifted when I was informed of the pathology report on my now 'old liver'. We knew there was some active cancer in the liver from the scans, but they had discovered a whopping 3-centimetre-wide golf-ball-sized tumour deep within, with at least one other marble-sized tumour nearby. It didn't take a genius to tell me I had been well below par. I may have only had months to live without the transplant.

I would move wards once more, this time sharing with two other women. Started to have my first conversations, to think outside my own afflictions and ask about theirs. That was me. I was coming back.

Late on the second night on the ward, in the darkness, the door opened. A large Greek family walked in, pushing the matriarch, in her eighties, through the centre of the room, their faces lit up by the small side lights. There was the son, his wife. There was even a child, two others.

The matriarch had literally just been told in the emergency downstairs that it was suspected she had pancreatic cancer that had already spread to her liver. My blood froze. Was it because of processed meat? I'd already found out pancreatic cancer was linked. Did her diet contain those beloved southern European dry-aged salamis, hams, bacons? There is the reality of the risk. Could it be linked to her case? As we know, it's impossible to be certain.

They surrounded the matriarch with tears, with cuddles, with drinks, with food.

'I'm sorry, but you can't all stay the night,' the nurse said to them quietly in the darkness. 'It's policy.'

'But she could be dying,' the son said. I could hear the pain in his voice.

'We don't think she is. She's stable.'

'But she has cancer,' he said. I knew the pain. When you first get diagnosed, it puts everyone into a spin, a panic. You think the world's crashing in. You think you're going to die *now*. You certainly don't want to let your loved ones go in that moment when they've been told the worst news of their life.

'Okay. We'll just stay a bit longer,' her son agreed.

Slowly the other family members slipped away, and he literally lay next to his mother, with her in his arms, until she fell asleep.

I've never seen such beauty from a man. It was something that healed me after writing this book, where men's behaviour, in business especially, had been so ruthless. I'd started to become a bit anti-man, to be honest. I was worrying about male behaviour, and recent disturbing allegations against powerful male cultural role models Andrew Tate and Sean 'Diddy' Combs, denied by both, had added to my concerns. Were there any good ones left? Here he was. He was one of the good ones who reminded me there were so many more.

I watched this moving, ancient scene, of this man being so strong. He was so strong for her, as she wept and wept in his arms, and he never let her go until she was sound asleep. It really did look like a painting, a biblical painting, the values that we all should hold.

He left around midnight to sleep in his car and returned in the light of the dawn. Just as my nurse was taking my temperature he quietly slipped back into the exact same position and was there when his mother woke up.

After nearly two weeks in the hospital, I was finally, finally okay. I had to be mobile. I'd proven I could walk around the corridors. All my liver numbers were going in the right direction. My wound was healing and my magnesium levels had at last, after many days of infusions, come back to normal.

PROCESSED

'Yes, you're fine,' said the doctor on the Sunday morning. 'But we can't let you go, because we don't really like discharging people on a Sunday. It's just hard with the pharmacy, wanting to leave early. We'd rather let you go tomorrow.'

I tried to be calm. 'I've done everything I've been asked to for the last two weeks,' I said. 'I fought to get to this position. I've walked to get fit. I have to see my children.'

My daughter had not been allowed in because she'd had a cold. I'd seen my son only briefly. I couldn't spend one more hour in the wards in discomfort, watching more trauma. I'd known I had to go in, but I also knew when I needed to come out to heal further.

Thankfully, they agreed.

My husband arrived. I was very quiet. Having to negotiate my departure had taken the final bit of fight that I had left. I didn't want to fight anymore. It had taken every ounce of my past experiences and skills to somehow wriggle free from a terminal cancer diagnosis, including the awkward firing of three oncologists along the way in pursuit of new ideas, new solutions. My time at Leighton Park, a Quaker boarding school in Reading, England, had given me the confidence to always think independently, and my challenging time in Fleet Street as a young reporter gave me the street-wise ninja skills to keep chasing the scoop of a cure, no matter how ambitious.

Now though, I was exhausted.

I was taken by wheelchair down to our car by a porter and put in the front seat.

As we drove out of the car park, up past Heidelberg Station, destination home, I let out a scream. The seat was back. The tears began to flow. I was free. I was alive. I'd been through hell, fighting for my life for five years. I was crying in the most primal release I couldn't control. It was the first time I'd cried in two weeks.

'Don't worry about me. I think it just needs to come out,' I said to my husband, pale at the wheel. 'This is okay. Let me release it.'

I was laughing. I was alive. I was upset. For the trauma, for every injection, for every temperature, for every fear, for every time I'd vomited. For everything. It was every emotion that had to come out. I had to express it. I was crying and screaming, crying and screaming. It was so bizarre. It was like an exorcism—but it was needed.

Soon we had to stop to wedge a cushion under my back. We pulled into a church car park.

'Would you also like a lorazepam?' my husband said with a little smile.

They'd given us a bag, a paper bag like you get from Woolworths, full of the medication I required. I said, 'Give one to me.'

My husband is a saint. He does everything. But even saints can't drive down Burke Road with a hysterical hyena in the passenger seat. It was time for some quiet.

When we reached home, he said, 'I'll open the gate so we can drive up.'

I said, 'It's okay. I just desperately want to get inside. Let me walk.'

PROCESSED

I stepped out, my slippers left behind. It was wonderful to feel the grass as I walked up the garden. The earth. Only a few metres to the front door.

I'd been informed that the package I'd sent to Allen & Unwin had been safely delivered to their offices in Crows Nest. I was now delivering my own package, safely inside me, to its new address in Bayside, Melbourne. My home.

There would be no return to sender, but the sender will be celebrated and remembered every day for the rest of my life. By law I'm not allowed to ever know who they were, but I am allowed to write their family an anonymous letter in coming weeks, also devoid of any facts which could identify me. Thankfully, I've had a bit of practice with letters recently, but this one will be the most important I will ever compose: a moment to thank their departed loved one for saving a nameless mother's life and bringing two children back into the light, for hopefully decades of trips together around the sun.

ACKNOWLEDGEMENTS

Unlike a dry-aged prosciutto this book wasn't meant to be cured for quite so long, the delivery of the manuscript delayed multiple times due to cancer treatment.

So I'm beyond grateful to my Allen & Unwin publisher Elizabeth Weiss for always being so supportive, patient and understanding each time I called her with news of yet another reoccurrence, prompting yet another long manuscript delay.

Elizabeth's enthusiasm for the importance of this book was always so energising and motivating, especially during the times when I wondered if I'd ever have a long enough gap between treatments to finally finish it.

This is the second investigative book we've now worked on together and Elizabeth's wisdom, humour and insight is so valuable. I'm so fortunate to have such a talented figure as a mentor and friend.

ACKNOWLEDGEMENTS

I'm also hugely indebted to the brilliant expertise of Tom Bailey-Smith, senior editor at Allen & Unwin, and forensic copyeditor Emma Driver.

Their advice and suggestions really helped elevate this book during the editing process, ensuring its impact and significance. I'm also very lucky to benefit from the entire, wider team at Allen & Unwin in Sydney, including the publicity, sales and marketing teams. Thanks also to the wonderful agent Alex Adsett for her seamless literary consultation services.

I'm hugely grateful to Professor Denis Corpet for not only sharing so much of his own personal family story, work history and expertise but for also authoring the foreword to this book.

To have such frequent encouragement from afar, from a leading global expert on this complex subject matter, gave me the confidence to keep bashing on powerful, salty doors and asking impertinent questions.

I'm also very thankful to other industry experts and insiders, many of whom wished to remain anonymous, who helped me gain a deep understanding into a business often shrouded in mystery and dark manipulation. You know who you are and I thank you. Thank you to my editorial research assistant, Julie Laurent, who helped me compile the endless articles, studies and reports to ensure facts came first.

With huge, long-term projects like *Processed* there is also an army of family and friends who have not only been my treasured, loyal cheerleaders during my cancer fight but have also often found themselves being asked baffling questions about their processed-meat consumption and shopping habits.

ACKNOWLEDGEMENTS

Thank you for all the love and support from my 'lifers'—always there to catch me when my bravado and strength recedes and cancer treatments intrude. The phone calls, fish pies for the freezer, ocean swims and beach walk chats have meant the world to me.

There are so many incredible, strong female friends in my life but I'd like to say a special thank you to the following: Natalie Galsworthy, Tessa Sullivan, Patricia Simmonds, Deborah Golden, Shemaine Van de Wiel, Anne Foster, Fiona Rose, Ella Pigott, Belinda Wanis, Preeti Krishnan, Rebecca Tanner, Sharon Bourke, Tiffany Middleton, Sarah Asome, Alison Weavers, Bec Tatman, Kirstie Seton, Chantal Cain, Yvonne Stinson, Kylie Mustow, Sarah Chicott, Katherine Tutt, Lauren Sadler, Kirsten Wilcox, Casey Gill, Julia O'Donnell, Mary Knight, Tina Richmond, Mascha Nieweg, Kim Harper, Jools Magools, Emma Dewhirst, Dianne King, Nicola Carter and Samantha Welford.

There are also some dear and brave comrades in the cancer community whose friendships have formed a welcome silver lining in this whole journey: Mitchell Snow, Amanda Calder, Brad Glover, Krystal-Kate Meacham and those on the Meaningful Movement and Colontown Facebook forums.

Thank you to my family in England and Wales, Julia and Kurt Newman, Matthew and Simone Morris, David Rolfe, Sophie Breakenridge, Sarah Morris, Jenny Marr, Ruth, Paul, Alex and Sam Irvine. And a special mention to my half sister Haidi in Canada. I'm so happy we found out about each other in 2020.

ACKNOWLEDGEMENTS

For my husband, Mike, son, Nathaniel and daughter, Talia, thank you for taste testing all the various fake bacons and the rest, sometimes unknowingly, always with good humour. And thank you for giving up your pepperoni on your Friday night pizza.

You are doing me proud, just as you do every day with your love for life and adventurous spirits. You have lifted me up and given me a reason to go onwards and upwards when aggressive treatment has, at times, made me go downwards. Recuperating with you and our precious tribe of ginger pets, Maggie, Pookie and Edwardo, has always given me more strength than you'll ever know.

A special mention to the world-class individuals in my current health team, including Professor Niall Tebbutt at Darebin Street Specialist Centre, who is also director of the Department of Medical Oncology, Olivia Newton-John Cancer Wellness & Research Centre. And to all the wonderful staff at the Liver Transplant Unit at the Austin Hospital, including Professor Avik Majumdar, Professor Bob Jones, Angela Vago and Tracey Hughes.

It may take a village to raise a child but over the last five years it has taken the entire city of Melbourne, across multiple clinics and hospitals, to give this patient the best chance of surviving and hopefully being cured.

Thank you to every nurse, oncologist, specialist, GP, radiologist, scan technician, department manager, surgeon, anaesthetist, theatre technician, pathologist, physio, dietician, pastoral care worker, cleaner and administrator who have cared for me in the precarious trenches of stage-four bowel cancer.

ACKNOWLEDGEMENTS

The birth of this book, a miracle in many ways, is a testament to the care I have received from possibly hundreds of health workers in Victoria and I thank them for their dedication, sacrifice and expertise.

Lucie Morris-Marr
Melbourne, August 2024

NOTES

Epigraph
1 www.wcrf.org/our-blog/the-politics-of-processed-meat

Introduction Intensively caring about ham
1 www.statista.com/forecasts/758709/per-capita-volume-sales-in-the-meat-products-and-sausages-market-worldwide-by-country
2 www.wcrf.cancer-trends/

Chapter 1 In plain sight
1 www.sciencedirect.com/science/article/abs/pii/S0306919222000173#:~:text=The%20Global%20Burden%20of%20Disease,deaths%20(IHME%2C%202019b)
2 www.just-food.com/news/uk-abf-names-george-weston-as-new-ceo/
3 www.independent.co.uk/money/rich-list-2023-who-are-the-wealthiest-people-in-the-uk-b2341903.html
4 inherit.dplh.wa.gov.au/public/inventory/printsinglerecord/783b1a3a-5a01-49a7-b46f-43e7f6fedd60
5 amp.smh.com.au/national/is-don-is-not-so-good-for-640-workers-20080730-3nfz.html
6 www.watoday.com.au/national/western-australia/220-meat-packing-jobs-to-go-20080730-3n89.html
7 www.mirror.co.uk/money/city-news/uk-greed-list-champagne-lifestyle-1944817

8 www.abf.co.uk/content/dam/abf/corporate/AR-and-RR-website-updates-2022/AR2022%20Remuneration%20Report.pdf
9 Anonymous Don KRC employee, interview with the author, October 2023
10 isdonisgood.com.au/naturals/
11 According to Don KRC ingredient labels, checked by the author in visits to leading Australian supermarkets, November 2023
12 www.watoday.com.au/national/western-australia/220-meat-packing-jobs-to-go-20080730-3n89.html
13 amic.org.au
14 bmcmedicine.biomedcentral.com/articles/10.1186/1741-7015-11-63
15 pubmed.ncbi.nlm.nih.gov/26063472/
16 www.reuters.com/article/health-meat-idUSL8N12Q20K20151026
17 canceratlas.cancer.org/risk-factors/human-carcinogens/
18 www.mdpi.com/2072-6643/16/1/132#:~:text=For%20diet%20high%20in%20processed,to%202019%20(Table%20S10)
19 www.mdpi.com/2072-6643/16/1/132#:~:text=For%20diet%20high%20in%20processed,to%202019%20(Table%20S10)
20 www.reuters.com/article/health-meat-idUSL8N12Q20K20151026
21 www.cancerresearchuk.org/about-cancer/bowel-cancer/risks-causes#:~:text=Eating%20too%20much%20red%20and%20processed%20meat&text=It%20is%20estimated%20that%20around,canned%20meat%20or%20chicken%20nuggets
22 www.wired.com/2015/10/who-does-bacon-cause-cancer-sort-of-but-not-really/; www.theguardian.com/news/2018/mar/01/bacon-cancer-processed-meats-nitrates-nitrites-sausages
23 www.futureoffood.ox.ac.uk/article/dont-go-bacon-my-heart-what-do-we-mean-when-we-talk-about-processed-meat
24 www.mpi.govt.nz/dmsdocument/21407-Sulphur-dioxide-sulphides-in-meat.pdf
25 www.infiniumglobalresearch.com/reports/global-processed-meat-market
26 www.theage.com.au/lifestyle/health-and-wellness/all-the-research-says-it-s-not-good-for-you-what-do-we-replace-bacon-with-20230501-p5d4qv.html

NOTES

Chapter 2 Toxic bites

1. www.theguardian.com/society/2022/dec/27/too-much-nitrite-cured-meat-brings-clear-risk-of-cancer-say-scientists
2. www.qld.gov.au/health/staying-healthy/food-pantry/food-labelling/food-product-guides/meat-and-meat-products
3. www.theguardian.com/lifeandstyle/2015/oct/26/processed-meats-how-are-they-made
4. www.mblsa.com.au/327378/SODIUM-DIACETATE-25KG/pd.php
5. www.ncbi.nlm.nih.gov/pmc/articles/PMC3278747/
6. additivefreelifestyle.com/flavour-v-natural-flavour/
7. www.foodstandards.gov.au/business/labelling
8. papandrea.com.au/products/black-garlic-piccolo-salami
9. edition.cnn.com/2024/09/16/health/food-packaging-chemical-toxins-study-wellness/index.html
10. 'Inaugural episode', open.spotify.com/show/19MJsJIsNbega1DvzGEMzA?si=f00669711e044841
11. Joanna Blythman, *Swallow This*, 4th Estate, 2015
12. Guillaume Coudray, *Who Poisoned Your Bacon Sandwich?*, Icon Books, 2021
13. www.sciencedirect.com/topics/agricultural-and-biological-sciences/saltpeter
14. www.theguardian.com/food/2023/sep/18/the-truth-about-nitro-meats-my-seven-year-search-for-better-bacon
15. www.sciencedirect.com/science/article/pii/S2666154323001527
16. www.sciencedirect.com/science/article/pii/S2666154323001527
17. www.ncbi.nlm.nih.gov/pmc/articles/PMC7464959/
18. clinical-nutrition.imedpub.com/nitrates-nitrites-and-nitrosamines-from-processed-meat-intake-and-colorectalcancer-risk.php?aid=21326
19. Interview with the author, August 2024
20. www.mla.com.au/globalassets/mla-corporate/research-and-development/program-areas/food-safety/pdfs/guidelines-for-the-safe-manufacture-of-smallgoods_2nd-edition.pdf
21. www.foodstandards.gov.au/sites/default/files/consumer/additives/nitrate/Documents/Survey%20of%20nitrates%20and%20nitrites.pdf
22. www.ncbi.nlm.nih.gov/pmc/articles/PMC6068531/

NOTES

23 https://www.mla.com.au/globalassets/mla-corporate/research-and-development/final-reports/2020/v.rmh.0110-final-report.pdf
24 Teresa Mitchell-Paterson, interview with the author

Chapter 3 Swallowing the bait
1 invasives.com.au/our-solutions/tools-products/hoggone-feral-pig-baits/
2 www.abc.net.au/news/2021-07-17/feral-pigs-kangaroo-island-sa-eradication/100293826
3 pestsmart.org.au/toolkit-resource/poisoning-of-feral-pigs-with-sodium-nitrite-hoggone/
4 animalcontrol.com.au/products/hoggone
5 www.coronerscourt.wa.gov.au/_files/inquest-2021/Wani%20finding.pdf
6 www.semanticscholar.org/paper/Rising-incidence-and-high-mortality-in-intentional-McCann-Tweet/6ed3312e1d0994dd7504e6fb102c63d82d193da1
7 www.judiciary.uk/wp-content/uploads/2022/07/Gillchrest-Linda-2021-0002_Redacted.pdf
8 www.judiciary.uk/wp-content/uploads/2020/12/Jason-Thompson-2020-0246_Published-1.pdf
9 www.judiciary.uk/wp-content/uploads/2020/12/2020-0246-Response-from-Ebay-UK-Ltd-Redacted.pdf
10 arstechnica.com/tech-policy/2022/10/amazon-suicide-kits-have-led-to-teen-deaths-according-to-new-lawsuit/
11 www.nyc.gov/assets/doh/downloads/pdf/han/advisory/2022/sodium-nitrate-ingestion-poisonings.pdf
12 onlinelibrary.wiley.com/doi/10.1111/1556-4029.15350
13 Guillaume Coudray, *Who Poisoned Your Bacon Sandwich?*, Icon Books, 2021
14 www.asiaplustj.info/en/news/tajikistan/incidents/20120225/accidental-use-sodium-nitrite-instead-table-salt-causes-fatal-food-poisoning-kulob
15 Quotes from Denis Corpet in this section are from an interview with the author, October 2023
16 pubmed.ncbi.nlm.nih.gov/24769880/
17 pubmed.ncbi.nlm.nih.gov/7192376/

NOTES

18 www.foodnavigator.com/Article/2003/03/21/Triumph-for-Denmark-in-food-additive-case
19 www.theguardian.com/tv-and-radio/2022/nov/28/matt-hancock-was-meant-to-fail-on-im-a-celebrity-heres-what-went-so-horribly-wrong
20 www.reuters.com/world/europe/end-pink-ham-france-cut-use-nitrite-cured-meats-2022-02-04/
21 www.just-food.com/news/france-to-cut-nitrites-in-food-because-of-cancer-risk/
22 www.ncbi.nlm.nih.gov/pmc/articles/PMC9797476/
23 www.theguardian.com/society/2022/dec/27/too-much-nitrite-cured-meat-brings-clear-risk-of-cancer-say-scientists
24 www.theguardian.com/society/2023/jul/11/nhs-hospitals-in-england-serve-meat-with-chemicals-feared-to-cause-cancer
25 www.foodsafetynews.com/2023/10/eu-to-tighten-rules-on-use-of-nitrites-and-nitrates-as-additives/
26 Coudray, *Who Poisoned Your Bacon Sandwich?*
27 Deborah Blum, *The Poison Squad*, Penguin, 2018
28 Coudray, *Who Poisoned Your Bacon Sandwich?*
29 www.foodstandards.gov.au/consumer/additives/nitrate/
30 Joanna Blythman, *Swallow This*, 4th Estate, 2015

Chapter 4 Club billionaire
1 John Robbins, 'Foreword', in T. Colin Campbell & Thomas M. Campbell (eds.), *The China Study*, BenBella Books, 2006
2 www.woolworthsgroup.com.au/content/dam/wwg/investors/reports/2023/f23-full-year/Woolworths%20Group%202023%20Annual%20Report.pdf
3 www.hsph.harvard.edu/nutritionsource/2015/11/03/report-says-eating-processed-meat-is-carcinogenic-understanding-the-findings/
4 www.woolworths.com.au/shop/productdetails/110534/primo-mini-mix-ups-paw-patrol-chicken-breast-cheese-cookie
5 www.facebook.com/photo.php?fbid=689286746571740
6 www.woolworthsgroup.com.au/content/dam/wwg/investors/reports/2023/f23-full-year/Woolworths%20Group%202023%20Annual%20Report.pdf

7   pubmed.ncbi.nlm.nih.gov/37174864/#:~:text=Globally%2C%20the%20latest%20estimates%20showed,overweight%20or%20obese%20in%202016
8   Jemma O'Hanlon, interview with the author, November 2023, www.jemmaohanlon.com
9   www.foodsafetynews.com/2024/04
10 www.abc.net.au/news/2022-04-25/jbs-meat-company-australia-four-corners-investigation/100997044
11 www.abc.net.au/news/rural/2022-01-05/jbs-seals-the-deal-on-rivalea-pork/100738828
12 www.foodsafetynews.com/2024/04
13 deadline.com/2023/03/paramount-global-ceo-bob-bakish-pay-executive-compensation
14 ir.paramount.com/static-files/7ac26e99-e03e-4d20-a4cf-6f49415db119
15 Dr Tanveer Ahmed, interview with the author, November 2023
16 www.dailymail.co.uk/news/article-12777977/Woolworths-ham-cheese-sandwich-cost-living.html
17 Moby & Miyun Park (eds.), *Gristle*, The New Press, 2010
18 www.colesgroup.com.au/investors/?page=reports
19 societyachievers.com/indian-origin-business-leaders-are-taking-on-the-world/
20 www.macrotrends.net/stocks/charts/COST/costco/gross-profit

Chapter 5 Take away this
1   www.instagram.com/chrisk_mcd/reel/CupMna0MOBF/
2   www.newscientist.com/article/mg23230980-600-every-human-culture-includes-cooking-this-is-how-it-began/
3   www.smithsonianmag.com/science-nature/why-fire-makes-us-human-72989884/
4   lithub.com/who-were-the-first-humans-to-start-cooking-meat-and-why/
5   time.com/5295907/discover-fire/
6   Guy Crosby, *Cook, Taste, Learn*, Columbia University Press, 2019, excerpted at lithub.com/why-and-how-exactly-did-early-humans-start-cooking

NOTES

7 Marta Zaraska, *Meathooked*, Basic Books, 2016
8 theconversation.com/bacon-how-you-cook-it-could-partially-lower-cancer-risk-152723
9 www.cancer.org.au/cancer-information/causes-and-prevention/diet-and-exercise/meat-and-cancer-risk
10 www.mla.com.au/globalassets/mla-corporate/research-and-development/final-reports/2020/v.rmh.0110-final-report.pdf
11 www.bunnings.com.au/oklahoma-joe-s-longhorn-combo-charcoal-gas-smoker-and-grill_p0411761
12 health.clevelandclinic.org/is-smoked-meat-bad-for-you
13 www.researchgate.net/publication/369595408_Smoked_Fish_Consumption_and_Health_Effects
14 ec.europa.eu/newsroom/sante/items/827828/en
15 www.subway.com/~/media/Australia/Documents/Nutritionals/Aus-Ingredient-Summary%20.ashx
16 www.wsj.com/business/deals/subway-sandwich-chain-nears-sale-bd776623
17 www.bbc.com/news/articles/c4nnz3ze3l7o
18 mcdonalds.com.au/sites/mcdonalds.com.au/files/Aus%20Core%20Food%20Menu_November%202023_0.pdf
19 mcdonalds.com.au/sites/mcdonalds.com.au/files/CH2_McDonalds_CR&S_OurBusiness.pdf
20 www.macrotrends.net/stocks/charts/MCD/mcdonalds/gross-prof
21 financialpost.com/executive/mcdonalds-new-ceo-eats-at-the-chain-twice-a-day-but-runs-50-miles-a-week-to-burn-it-off
22 www.statista.com/statistics/207118/number-of-dominos-pizza-stores-worldwide/
23 investors.dominos.com.au/don-meij
24 www.theguardian.com/lifeandstyle/2023/may/21/should-i-worry-about-eating-too-many-takeaways
25 www.australianpork.com.au/industry-facts
26 www.farmtransparency.org/media/34-15-animal-activists-charged-over-april-slaughterhouse-occupation-as-pig-wel
27 www.abc.net.au/news/2023-03-27/pork-industry-carbon-dioxide-stunning-hidden-cameras-730/102094548
28 Matthew Evans, *On Eating Meat*, Murdoch Books, 2019

NOTES

29 www.abc.net.au/news/rural/2021-09-18/consumers-want-aussie-bacon/100464348
30 Jonathan Safran Foer, *Eating Animals*, Penguin Random House, 2009
31 kb.rspca.org.au/knowledge-base/what-are-the-animal-welfare-issues-associated-with-pig-production
32 Evans, *On Eating Meat*
33 australianpork.com.au/sites/default/files/2022-03/APL%20Sustainability%20Framework_Web.pdf
34 www.farmbiosecurity.com.au/wp-content/uploads/2022/01/Pork-Biosecurity-Manual-Update.pdf
35 www.aph.gov.au/DocumentStore.ashx?id=c97c0d64-9aaf-4e0c-b762-d2cdfcd0e210
36 www.agriculture.gov.au/biosecurity-trade/import/goods/food/type/cooked-meat
37 www.peta.org.au/issues/food/truth-cattle-food/
38 Anonymous former worker, interview with the author, October 2023
39 www.pbs.org/newshour/show/cow-burps-are-a-major-contributor-to-climate-change-can-scientists-change-that
40 unearthed.greenpeace.org/2021/12/15/australia-beef-deforestation-climate-brexit-trade-deal
41 www.abc.net.au/news/2022-06-11/gannawarra-council-decision-on-western-plains-pork-at-kondrook/101141620
42 Tim Flannery, *The Future Eaters*, Reed New Holland, 1994
43 Joseph Ponthus, *On the Line*, trans. Stephanie Smee, Black Inc., 2021
44 www.smh.com.au/business/workplace/abattoir-boss-threatens-chinese-workers-visa-status-in-abusive-tirade-20210625-p58470.html
45 www.peta.org.au/news/killing-for-a-living
46 www.news.com.au/national/slaughterhouse-workers-are-more-likely-to-be-violent-study-shows/news-story/f16165f66f38eb04a289eb8bd7f7f273

Chapter 6 Gut instinct

1 David A. Johnson (ed.), *The GUT Microbiome: New Understanding and Potential Translational Applications for Disease Management*, Nova Science Publishers, 2015

NOTES

2. emedicine.medscape.com/article/1690010-overview
3. www.cancer.org/cancer/types/colon-rectal-cancer/causes-risks-prevention/risk-factors.html
4. www.hopkinsmedicine.org/health/conditions-and-diseases/colon-cancer/apc-i1307k-and-colorectal-cancer
5. www.futureoffood.ox.ac.uk/article/dont-go-bacon-my-heart-what-do-we-mean-when-we-talk-about-processed-meat
6. www.cancerresearchuk.org.health-professional
7. www.cancer.org.au/cancer-information/types-of-cancer/bowel-cancer
8. www.9news.com.au/national/call-for-bowel-cancer-test-kits-to-be-sent-to-younger-australians-lucie-morris-marr/d66e9824-744b-44ee-a399-1931022fd6e9
9. www.9news.com.au/national/bowel-cancer-screening-age-lowered-amid-surge-in-young-onset-cases/3cfaedbc-e87a-4b26-9b17-948e700c2c59
10. ew.com/movies/2018/02/14/black-panther-chadwick-boseman-emotional/
11. www.theguardian.com/society/2022/jun/28/podcaster-deborah-james-dies-of-bowel-cancer-bowelbabe
12. www.bowelcanceraustralia.org/modifiable-risk-factors#meat
13. https://www.dailymail.co.uk/health/article-13830089/doctor-healthy-foods-fueling-colon-cancer-crisis-young-people.html
14. Giulia Enders, *Gut*, Greystone Books, 2015
15. www.healthline.com/health/how-long-does-it-take-to-digest-food#digestion-process
16. www.news-medical.net/health/What-Does-the-Large-Intestine-Do.aspx
17. Bill Bryson, *The Body*, Black Swan, 2020
18. Mike McRae, *Unwell*, University of Queensland Press, 2018
19. www.nytimes.com/2022/06/29/well/eat/processed-meats.html
20. www.reportlinker.com/clp/country/475268/726390
21. Isabella Beeton, *Beeton's Book of Household Management*, S.O. Beeton, 1861
22. www.wcrf.org/cancer-trends/colorectal-cancer-statistics/
23. www.oecd-ilibrary.org/sites/1ff286c9-en/index.html?itemId=/content/component/1ff286c9-en

NOTES

24 www.jpr.org.uk/countries/how-many-jews-in-slovakia
25 www.statista.com/forecasts/758709/per-capita-volume-sales-in-the-meat-products-and-sausages-market-worldwide-by-country
26 aacrjournals.org/cancerres/article/68/9_Supplement/1055/546472/Nuclear-radiation-age-and-cancer-incidences-
27 www.sciencedirect.com/science/article/abs/pii/S1212411717300879; State of health in the EU, European Commission, 2019

Chapter 7 Meat me in the cells
1 www.theguardian.com/food/2022/jul/08/nitrites-in-bacon-scientists-mps-call-for-uk-ban-cancer-fears
2 www.cancer.org.au/cancer-information/types-of-cancer/breast-cancer
3 www.breastcancerfoundation.org.nz/breast-awareness/breast-cancer-facts/breast-cancer-in-nz
4 onlinelibrary.wiley.com/doi/10.1002/ijc.31848
5 www.bcna.org.au/resource-hub/articles/your-breast-cancer-risk/
6 www.who.int/news-room/fact-sheets/detail/breast-cancer
7 www.sciencedirect.com/science/article/pii/S0002916523017215?via%3Dihub
8 www.acrf.com.au/news/ovarian-cancer/ovarian-cancer-statistics
9 Ross Dobson, *King of the Grill: The Bumper Book of No Nonsense Barbecuing*, Allen & Unwin, 2014
10 bjui-journals.onlinelibrary.wiley.com/doi/10.1111/bju.16001
11 www.ncbi.nlm.nih.gov/pmc/articles/PMC9365633/
12 www.pcfa.org.au/news-media/news/prostate-cancer-in-australia-what-do-the-numbers-tell-us/
13 www.pcfa.org.au/media/24ndvdz3/pcf13465_-_08_-_understanding_health_and_wellbeing_28_pg_booklet_4-pdf.pdf
14 www.pancare.org.au/about/cancer-statistics/
15 www.cancerresearchuk.org/about-cancer/causes-of-cancer/diet-and-cancer/does-eating-processed-and-red-meat-cause-cancer
16 journals.plos.org/plosone/article?id=10.1371/journal.pone.0070955
17 www.canceraustralia.gov.au/cancer-types/stomach-cancer/statistics
18 www.wcrf.org/wp-content/uploads/2021/02/stomach-cancer-report.pdf

357

NOTES

19 www.sciencedirect.com/science/article/abs/pii/S0027510702001690
20 www.cancer.org.au/cancer-information/types-of-cancer/pancreatic-cancer
21 www.ncbi.nlm.nih.gov/pmc/articles/PMC8537381/
22 academic.oup.com/eurpub/article/31/Supplement_3/ckab165.230/6406225
23 www.canceraustralia.gov.au/cancer-types/oesophageal-cancer/statistics
24 www.cancervic.org.au/research/vcr/cancer-fact-sheets/oesophageal-cancer.html
25 theconversation.com/bacon-how-you-cook-it-could-partially-lower-cancer-risk-152723
26 www.canceraustralia.gov.au/cancer-types/oesophageal-cancer/awareness

Chapter 8 Salty sorrow
1 www.washingtonpost.com/wellness/2023/03/09/salt-excessive-diet-who/
2 www.hsph.harvard.edu/nutritionsource/salt-and-sodium/
3 www.deloitte.com/au/en/services/economics/analysis/changing-chronic-kidney-disease-landscape.html
4 www.actiononsalt.org.uk/salthealth/salt-and-the-kidneys/
5 www.actiononsalt.org.uk/salt-surveys/2020/bacon/
6 www.bloodpressureuk.org/news/news/astonishing-amounts-of-salt-in-bacon-exposed.html
7 www.washingtonpost.com/wellness/2023/03/09/salt-excessive-diet-who/
8 www.who.int/news/item/09-03-2023-massive-efforts-needed-to-reduce-salt-intake-and-protect-lives
9 www.bloodpressureuk.org/your-blood-pressure/how-to-lower-your-blood-pressure/healthy-eating/fats-and-cholesterol-and-your-blood-pressure/
10 www.heartfoundation.org.au/Bundles/For-Professionals/coronary-heart-disease-key-stats
11 www.heartfoundation.org.au/healthy-living/healthy-eating/protein-and-heart-health

NOTES

12 www.uclahealth.org/news/the-effects-of-processed-meats-on-your-heart-health
13 www.healthdirect.gov.au/stroke
14 strokefoundation.org.au/about-stroke/prevent-stroke/overweight-and-obesity
15 www.ahajournals.org/doi/full/10.1161/STROKEAHA.115.010693
16 www.reuters.com/article/idUSKBN0TE2I9

Chapter 9 Painful reality

1 Edward Abbott, *The English and Australian Cookery Book*, Sampson Low, Son, & Marston, 1864, nla.gov.au/nla.obj-9562000
2 arthritisaustralia.com.au/what-is-arthritis/fastfacts/
3 www.medicalnewstoday.com/articles/foods-to-avoid-with-arthritis#foods-to-avoid
4 www.ncbi.nlm.nih.gov/pmc/articles/PMC6746966/
5 www.dementia.org.au/statistics
6 theconversation.com/dementia-is-processed-meat-another-risk-factor-157713
7 www.hopkinsmedicine.org/news/newsroom/news-releases/2018/07/beef-jerky-and-other-processed-meats-associated-with-manic-episodes
8 pubmed.ncbi.nlm.nih.gov/35807749/
9 pubmed.ncbi.nlm.nih.gov/31561370/
10 ajcn.nutrition.org/article/S0002-9165(22)00297-0/fulltext
11 metro.co.uk/2024/08/23/microplastics-found-brain-linked-alzheimers-cases-21475758/
12 Lisa Mosconi, *The XX Brain*, Allen & Unwin, 2020
13 www.thenewdaily.com.au/life/health/2024/08/06/bacon-carries-dementia-risk
14 www.diabetesaustralia.com.au/about-diabetes/what-is-diabetes/
15 journals.plos.org/plosmedicine/article?id=10.1371/journal.pmed.1004149
16 www.dailymail.co.uk/health/article-12648205/TWO-bacon-sandwiches-week-raises-risk-type-2-diabetes.html
17 www.hsph.harvard.edu/news/press-releases/red-meat-consumption-associated-with-increased-type-2-diabetes-risk/

NOTES

18 Garth Davis, *Proteinaholic*, HarperOne, 2015
19 www.who.int/news-room/fact-sheets/detail/obesity-and-overweight
20 www.calories.info/food/ham-sausage
21 www.calories.info/food/poultry-chicken-turkey
22 www.aihw.gov.au/reports/cancer/health-system-expenditure-cancer-other-neoplasms/
23 www.aihw.gov.au/reports/heart-stroke-vascular-diseases/hsvd-facts/contents/impacts/expenditure-cvd
24 www.agrifood.info/review/1995/Kriven.html
25 www.abc.net.au/news/2011-11-22/garibaldi-e-coli-contamination-legal-case/3686838
26 www.who.int/news-room/fact-sheets/detail/botulism
27 www.mcgill.ca/oss/article/history-you-asked/what-saltpeter-used-and-it-true-it-reduces-certain-carnal-urges
28 www.health.qld.gov.au/newsroom/news/listeria-listeriosis-what-you-need-to-know-food-poisoning
29 www.sciencedirect.com/science/article/pii/S0168160522004044

Chapter 10 Memory addicts
1 open.spotify.com/episode/1En5HPDC86cwkLp3SXywaJ?si=b87f0b25ed8849a6
2 www.wcrf.org/the-politics-of-processed-meat/
3 Interview with the author, November 2023
4 Jonathan Safran Foer, *Eating Animals*, Penguin Random House, 2009
5 x.com/TheFoodGranny/status/1727901233078555095?s=20
6 www.eater.com/2014/7/9/6191681/a-brief-history-of-spam-an-american-meat-icon
7 www.spam.com/what-is-spam-brand
8 www.healthline.com/nutrition/is-spam-healthy
9 Mark Kurlansky, *Salt*, Random House, 2011
10 twitter.com/Ultimateqestion/status/1727824267138757069
11 finance.yahoo.com/news/while-institutions-own-42-hormel-160323736.html

NOTES

Chapter 11 Recipe for disaster
1. Mrs Lance Rawson [Wilhelmina Rawson], *The Queensland Cookery and Poultry Book*, W. Hopkins, 1890
2. www.forestryengland.uk/new-forest/pannage-pigs-and-acorns#:~:text=The%20pannage%20season%20usually%20lasts,the%20Forestry%20Commission%27s%20Deputy%20Surveyor
3. Isabella Beeton, *Mrs Beeton's Book of Household Management*, S.O. Beeton, 1861
4. www.nhm.ac.uk/discover/news/2019/august/understanding-the-origins-of-european-domestic-pigs.html
5. James Dyer, *Ancient Britain*, Guild Publishing, 1990
6. Jacqui Wood, *Tasting the Past*, History Press, 2020
7. www.roman-britain.co.uk/the-celts-and-celtic-life/farming-in-celtic-britain/
8. www.godecookery.com/mtrans/mtrans09.htm
9. Robin Haines, *Life and Death in the Age of Sail*, UNSW Press, 2003
10. www.environment.sa.gov.au/topics/plants-and-animals/sustainable-use-of-animals-and-plants/hunting-information/aboriginal-hunting-gathering
11. John Newton, *The Oldest Foods on Earth*, NewSouth, 2016
12. Tim Flannery, *The Future Eaters*, Reed New Holland, 1994
13. Bill Gammage, *The Biggest Estate on Earth*, Allen & Unwin, 2011
14. Edward Abbott, *The English and Australian Cookery Book*, Sampson Low, Son, & Marston, 1864, nla.gov.au/nla.obj-9562000
15. Rawson, *The Queensland Cookery and Poultry Book*
16. Mrs Lance Rawson [Wilhelmina Rawson], *The Australian Enquiry Book*, Pater & Knapton, 1894
17. Jacqui Newling, *Eat Your History*, NewSouth/Sydney Living Museums, 2015
18. Presbyterian Women's Missionary Union of Victoria, *The P.W.M.U. Cookery Book of Victoria*, Brown, Prior & Co, 1916
19. www.awm.gov.au/articles/encyclopedia/homefront/rationing
20. Department of Education of Victoria, *Domestic Science Handbook*, Osboldstone & Co., 1938
21. Graham Kerr, *Entertaining with Kerr*, A.H. & A.W. Reed, 1963

NOTES

22 Hanna Pan (ed.), *The Australian Hostess Cookbook*, Thomas Nelson, c. 1965
23 Margaret Fulton, *My Very Special Cookbook*, Octopus Books, 1980
24 Stephanie Alexander, *The Cook's Companion*, Viking, 1996
25 www.woolworths.com.au/shop/productdetails/544696/primo-english-style-sliced-leg-ham
26 www.smh.com.au/national/not-enough-science-behind-scientific-diet-20050829-gdlyol.html
27 Julie Goodwin, *The Heart of the Home*, Penguin, 2012
28 www.latimes.com/archives/la-xpm-1994-06-03-mn-29-story.html#:~:text=Children%20who%20eat%20more%20than,in%20a%20cancer%20research%20journal
29 www.ccia.org.au/about-childhood-cancer/leukaemia#:~:text=How%20common%20is%20leukaemia%20in,0%2D19%2Dyear%20olds
30 www.washingtonpost.com/archive/lifestyle/1994/06/04/hold-the-relish-a-wurst-case-scenario/dabaf608-6d75-49d9-96e7-6ea50932f5d3/
31 www.latimes.com/archives/la-xpm-1994-06-15-me-4257-story.html
32 edition.cnn.com/travel/article/hot-dog-classic-american-summer-food/index.html
33 www.reuters.com/article/idUSTRE50R781/
34 www.coherentmarketinsights.com/market-insight/hot-dogs-and-sausages-market-1471#:~:text=The%20hot%20dogs%20and%20sausages,US%24%20102.93%20billion%20by%202030
35 www.sbs.com.au/food/the-cook-up-with-adam-liaw/article/hot-dog-history/im311s8r1
36 www.youtube.com/watch?v=nX1KUPZC3Ck
37 Conversation with the author, November 2022
38 www.news.com.au/lifestyle/food/eat/aussie-icon-returns-as-bunnings-sausage-sizzles-back-on-menu/news-story/a8bf4342d9094a31c0b30d9c9203c396

Chapter 12 Beyond the snag
1 Matthew Evans, *On Eating Meat*, Allen & Unwin, 2019
2 David A. Sinclair with Matthew D. LaPlante, *Lifespan*, Atria Books, 2019

NOTES

3. Brian Kateman (ed.), *The Reducetarian Solution*, TarcherPerigee Books, 2017
4. www.cherrytreeorganics.com.au/collections/ham-bacon/products/certified-organic-nitrate-free-ham
5. www.afr.com/technology/plant-based-meat-on-the-turn-as-start-ups-struggle-for-customers-funding-20230810-p5dvfu
6. theconversation.com/bacon-how-you-cook-it-could-partially-lower-cancer-risk-152723
7. David Gillespie, *Eat Real Food*, Pan Macmillan, 2015
8. news.mongabay.com/2016/06/less-meat-less-heat-arnold-schwarzenegger-james-cameron-call-for-less-meat-consumption-to-combat-climate-change/
9. minister.agriculture.gov.au/watt/media-releases/hands-off-our-ham
10. tobaccocontrol.bmj.com/content/31/2/129
11. www.aihw.gov.au/reports-data/behaviours-risk-factors/smoking/overview
12. www.livescience.com/59539-doctors-group-wants-unhealthy-foods-out-of-hospitals.html
13. www.wcrf.org/the-politics-of-processed-meat/
14. www.hsph.harvard.edu/news/hsph-in-the-news/ultra-processed-foods-some-more-than-others-linked-to-early-death/
15. Vegan mum's war on footy sausage sizzle, *The Age*, May 18 2024
16. www.wcrf.org/the-politics-of-processed-meat/
17. twitter.com/luciemorrismarr/status/1383948802009169926?s=20
18. Guillaume Coudray, *Who Poisoned Your Bacon Sandwich?*, Icon Books, 2021

INDEX

abattoirs 145–6, 151–2, 155–9
Abbott, Edward 214, 260–2
ABC Radio National 18
Aboriginal foods 257–9
accidental poisonings 65
acid reflux 205
acidity regulators 31–2, 38, 92, 95, 132, 137
Acland, Sir Antony 7
Action on Salt (UK) 208
Additive Free Lifestyle 34
additives 31–41, 81
Adelphi 6
adipose tissue 222
advanced glycation end products 126–7, 205, 218
Africa 123–4
African Americans 169
The Age 27–8, 158, 314
AGEs 126–7, 205, 218
Ahmed, Tanveer 113, 238–40, 281, 297–8
Ajmera, Rachael 242
Alaska Native people 169
Albrecht, Anna 119
Albrecht, Beate 119

Albrecht, Karl Jr 119
Albrecht, Karl Jr (son of Karl Jr) 119
Albrecht, Karl Sr 119
Albrecht, Theo 119
Aldi 77, 89, 118–20, 300
Alexander, Stephanie 268–9
alimentary canal 182–3
Allchurch, Edward 256–7
Alzheimer's disease 216–19
Amazon 62–3
American Cancer Society 26
'American cure' 83
American Indians 169
American Institute for Cancer Research 26
The American Journal of Clinical Nutrition 193–4, 211
American Meat Packers Association 82
American Medical Association 312
amino acids 188
Andriukaitis, Vytenis 69, 73–5
Animal Control Technologies Australia 58
animal welfare activists 17, 145–6, 151, 158

INDEX

antibiotics, in meat 150–1
antioxidants 36, 289
anxiety 218
Armitage, Michael 227
Aronson, Neal K. 134–5
arthritis 215
Arthritis Australia 215
ascorbic acid 33, 55
Asda 77
Ashkenazi Jews 169
Association British Foods 5–6, 299–303
Atalanta (ship) 256–7
Atkins diet 294
Auskick barbecues 313–14
Austin Hospital, Melbourne 255
Australasian Meat Industry Employees Union 8
Australian Competition and Consumer Commission 103
Australian Dietary Guidelines 194–5, 307
The Australian Enquiry Book: Household & General Information. Practical Guide. For the Cottage, the Villa and the Bush Home. Recipes and Information for Everything and Everybody. Refer to Me for Everything (Rawson) 262–3
The Australian Hostess Cookbook 267
Australian Institute of Health and Welfare 225–6
Australian Meat Holdings 102
Australian Meat Industry Council 304
Australian Medical Association 305
Australian Organic Meat Co 291
Australian Pork Limited 146, 150, 304
Avatar (film) 297

bacon
  advanced glycation end products in 205
  alternatives to 294–5
  as a processed meat 24, 26
  'boiling away' preservatives in 292
  carcinogenic nitrosamines in 191
  deliciousness of xix
  frying and grilling of 126–7
  IARC report on link with bowel cancer 15–16
  in Australian cookbooks 260–6, 269, 271
  in McDonald's products 137–9
  in Subway products 133
  in the WHO classification of meats 20
  in Woolworths 90–1
  Kingaroy BaconFest 3–5
  link with risk of stroke 212
  marketing of 40–1
  'meat-free bacon' 293
  nitro-preservatives in 41–3, 47–9, 71–2, 90
  salt in 208
  salting of 251–2
  saturated fat in 209
  scepticism about cancer risk of 51
  smoked bacon 130, 252
Bacon Addicts Anonymous (Facebook site) 21–2, 24
bacteria 43, 45, 182, 227–8
Bakish, Bob 106–8, 112
Banducci, Brad 96
barbecue smokers 128
barbecued meat 127, 202–3
Barrett's oesophagus 205
Batista, Joesley 101–2, 108, 110
Batista, Wesley 101–2, 108, 110
Bayonne ham 44
Beating Cancer Plan (Europe) 80
beef industry 144–5, 150–3

INDEX

beef mince 25
beef salami 223
Beeton, Isabella 250–2, 257, 264
Beeton's Book of Household Management (Beeton) 250–1
Belarus 187
Belgium 140
Benton, Elizabeth 51
Berg 119
Bertocchi 100
best-before dates 42
Better Naked 79
Beyond Meat 292
The Biggest Estate on Earth (Gammage) 259
Bill & Melinda Gates Foundation 14
biltong 24
Binjari 257
Biobank 216
BJU International 197
black pudding 223
BlackRock, Inc. 245
Blue Zones 288–9
Blum, Deborah 81
Blythman, Joanna 42, 85
BMC Cancer 278
boar stalls 148
The Body (Bryson) 182
bologna 24
Boseman, Chadwick 172–3
Botswana 123–4
botulism 44
botulism poisoning 228
bowel cancer
    author's personal experience of xiii, 8–11, 13, 161–8, 179, 255, 290, 298, 318
    Corpet's research into 66–8
    government expenditure on 225–6
    in Australia 169–70
    in the United States 169
    incidence of xviii, 169–70, 183, 317

international comparisons 185–7
KRAS wild-type cancer 168
link with processed meat vii, xviii, xx, 11, 15–17, 19, 26–7, 67–8, 70–3, 76, 78, 109, 169–70, 238, 242, 247–8, 315–20
link with sodium nitrite 46, 109, 302
nature versus nurture 168–9
symptoms of 171, 174
Bowel Cancer Australia 167, 170–1, 179
the brain, and diet 218–19
Branca, Francesco 206, 208
Brazil 101–2, 311–12, 315
breast cancer 72, 115, 188, 191–3, 198, 225, 320
Breast Cancer Foundation NZ 192
Breast Cancer Network Australia 193
Brexit 69
brines 46
Britain *see* United Kingdom
browning, of meat 218
bryndzové halušky 184–5
Bryson, Bill 182
Buck, Peter 134
Bulchandani, Devika 120
Bunnings sausage sizzles 280–6, 308–9
burgers 25
Butler, Mark 304

cabanossi 20
calcium chloride 39
calories 223–4
Cambodia 140
Cameron, James 297
Campbell, Denis 79
Canadian Meat Council 17
cancer
    government expenditure on 225–6
    incidence of in Australia xviii

366

INDEX

link with processed meat 14–17, 19, 26–7, 53, 67–8, 70–3, 76, 78, 108–9, 178, 185–6
link with smoked meat 129–30
see also specific cancers, e.g. bowel cancer
Cancer Australia 205
Cancer Causes and Control 276
Cancer Council 19–20, 127, 192
Cancer Research UK 20, 170, 201
cardiovascular disease 210–11, 226
Cargill Incorporated 154
Cargill Ltd 17
Castelló-Pastor, Adela 198
Castlemaine 7, 35
Catholics 238
cattle industry 144–5, 150–3
celery powder 46, 291
cell-based meats 318
Celts 253
Central Europe 184–6
champagne leg ham 25, 30–1, 34, 90
Chapman's 6
Charlie's Angels (television series) 174
cheese, smoked 130
The Cheesecake Factory 135
'chemical method' 83
chemicals, in pork 150–1
chemotherapy 163–4, 166, 191, 290
Cherkizovo Group PJSC 154
Chernobyl nuclear accident 187
Cherry Tree Organics 291
Chhabra, Sheena 313–14
chicken, calories in 224
chicken nuggets 25
children
    consumption of processed meat by 8, 40, 72, 74, 92–4, 96, 100, 104–11, 114–17
    lack of alternatives to processed meat for 286–7
    leukaemia in 276, 278–9

link to cancer risk from hot dogs 275
    obesity in 100, 315
China 44, 64, 138, 185
cholesterol 209–10
chorizo 20, 24, 223
Christie Hospital, Manchester 79
Christmas 233–9, 298
Christmas hams 305–6
chronic kidney disease 207
Churchill, Winston 163
chyme 181
Cinnabon 135
citric acid 39
Clifton, Peter 269
Clostridium botulinum 43, 228
cold smoking 129
Coles 31, 35, 38, 89, 98–100, 102, 104, 117–18, 245
colon cancer *see* bowel cancer
colonial recipes, for bacon 260–3
colorectal cancer *see* bowel cancer
colostomy bags 167–8
comminuted meat 24
Commonwealth Scientific and Industrial Research Organisation 52, 127, 130, 270, 292, 304
ComRes survey 72
Conagra Foods Inc. 154
consumer behaviour 310–16
The Conversation 205, 216
Cook, Taste, Learn (Crosby) 125
cookery books 260–72
cooking, of food 124–8
The Cook's Companion (Alexander) 268–9
Cooper, Nicole 175–7
corned beef 25, 244
coronary heart disease 211, 226
Corpet, Denis 66–76, 79–80, 84–5, 96, 114–15, 301, 319, 321
Corsican charcuterie meats 44

367

INDEX

Costco Wholesale Corporation 89, 121–2
Coudray, Guillaume 82–3, 317
Countdown 96
Covid-19 pandemic 75, 165–6, 281
Crosby, Guy 125
CSIRO Total Wellbeing Diet 269–70
The CSIRO Wellbeing Plan for Kids 270
Culbertson, Gillian 129–30
culture, role of processed meats in xix, 12, 40, 131–2, 233–41, 260–72, 275, 281–2, 311, 313–14
curing 22, 31, 39, 44–5, 47, 49

Daily Mail 221
Daily Mail Australia 114
Dairy Australia 270
Davis, Garth 222
deforestation 152–3
Delforce, Chris 146
DeLuca, Fred 134
dementia 216–20, 320
Dementia Australia 216
Denmark 67–8, 311
depression 218
devon 20, 24
diabetes 220–2, 242, 320
Diamond Valley Pork Pty Ltd 103
diet 194–5, 218–19, 288–9
digestive system 180–3, 201
Dobson, Ross 196–7
domestic pigs 249–51, 253
Domestic Science Handbook 265–6
Domino's Pizza 139–43
Don KRC 6–8, 35, 119, 299–303, 320
'Don't Go Bacon My Heart' (study) 23
D'Orsogna 91
drinking water, nitrates in 52
Dupuy, Chantal 66, 80

E. coli 227
Easter 238
Eat Real Food (Gillespie) 297
Eating Animals (Foer) 147, 239
eating habits 100, 115–16, 297–8, 313–16
eBay 62
Elliott, Chris 29, 77–8, 109, 191, 301–2, 321
emulsifiers 179
Enders, Giulia 180–1
The English and Australian Cookery Book (Abbott) 260–2
Entertaining with Kerr (Kerr) 266–7
EPIC 197–8
Essen, Germany 119
Estonia 187
European Commission 79, 185
European Common Market 83
European Food Safety Authority 73–4, 77–8, 130
European Heart Journal 212
European Prospective Investigation into Cancer and Nutrition 197–8
European Union 69, 79–80, 109, 319
Evans, Matthew 148, 288

fake meats 292–4
Falconio, Peter 206
Farm Transparency Project 146
farming practices 154–5
fast-food industry 131–44
fats, in processed meats 209–10, 223
Fawcett, Farrah 173–4
feral pigs, culling of 56–9
fermenting 22
feta cheese 295
Financial Post 138
Findus 77
Finkel, Alan 18
Finland 67
Finnebrogue 72

INDEX

fire, for cooking 124–8
fish, smoked 130
Flanagan, Richard 316
Flannery, Tim 154, 259
flavourings 33–4
Fleet Street journalism 310
Foer, Jonathan Safran 147, 239
Fong, Yuman C. 316
food insecurity xxi
food poisoning 227–9
Food Standards Australia New Zealand 23–4, 31, 33, 35, 50, 83–4, 97–8, 303–4, 306
food technologies 53–4
Foodwatch 75–6
forever chemicals 40
The Forme of Cury 253–4
formed ham 25, 30
Four Corners (television program) 101–2
France 72, 75–7, 140
frankfurts 11, 20, 24, 90, 119, 211, 223
free radicals 45
frontotemporal dementia 216
Fry, Joanne 34
Fry, Tracey 34
F*** You Cancer (James) 175
Fulton, Margaret 267–8
fungi 43
The Future Eaters (Flannery) 154, 259

Gammage, Bill 259
Garibaldi Smallgoods 227–8
Gaul, Kieran 177–8
genetics 168, 172
genotoxicity 130
George Weston Foods 6, 301–3
George Weston Limited 5
Germany 140
Gillchrest, Londa 61–2

Gillespie, David 296–7, 316
Global Burden of Disease Study 3, 14, 70
global greenhouse gas emissions 152
Globe 6
glyphosate 17
Goodwin, Julie 271–2
Goodyer, Paula 27–8
gout 215
grape seed extract 47
Grazia 148
Green, Brian 78
green tea polyphenols 47
Greenpeace 153
grilling, of fish and meat 126–7, 202–3
Gristle (Moby and Park) 115
Growth Truth Adventure Love (Gaul) 177–8
Gu, Xiao 221
Guam 243
guar gum 39
The Guardian 20, 32, 44, 75, 78–9, 143, 310
Guidelines for the Safe Manufacture of Smallgoods 49
gut bacteria 217, 227
Gut (Enders) 180

haemolytic uraemic syndrome 227
Haines, Robin 256
halal meat 152
halloumi 295
ham
  as a processed meat 20
  calories per 100 grams 223
  Christmas hams 305–6
  in Australian cookbooks 269–70
  labelling of 35
  manufacture of 29–32, 302
  marketing of 30–1
  off the bone 25, 90

369

INDEX

ham *continued*
   preservatives and additives in 31–5, 43, 67, 71–2, 90, 95, 115
   Primo as a manufacturer of 100–1
   types of 25–6
Hamilton, Leslie 62
Hancock, Matthew 68–9, 74–5
Harris, Kamala 319
Harskamp, Samantha 239
Harvard T.H. Chan School of Public Health 91, 184, 312–13
Harvard University 219, 221
Hawaii 243
Haynes, Graeme 8
HCAs 126–7, 129, 203, 211
head cancer 204
heart disease 209–11, 226, 320
Heart Foundation 210
The Heart of the Home (Goodwin) 271–2
Helena's Curiosity Shop 264
Herta ham 72
heterocyclic amines 126–7, 129, 203, 211
high-pressure processing 54, 305
high-pressure thermal processing 54, 305
high-protein diets 222, 294
Hinchcliffe, Stirling 4
Hoffman, Richard 126, 205, 216–17
HOGGONE® 56–8
honey ham 25, 223
Hormel Foods 245–8
Hormel Foundation 245, 247
Hormel Institute 247
hormones, in meat 150–1
horsemeat scandal (2013) 77–8
hospitals, serving of processed meat in xv–xviii, 78–9, 312
hot dogs 15–16, 24, 26, 40, 51, 272–9

hot smoking 129
How to Eat (Lawson) 271
Hu, Frank 184
humectants 242
Hungarian salami 90
Hungary 185
Huon Aquaculture 103

Iaria, Melissa 281
IGA 102
Ikaria 288–9
I'm a Celebrity . . . Get Me Out of Here! (television program) 75
Improvac 150
Independent Schools Australia 305
India 44, 133
Indigenous Australians 257–9
Indigenous food 257–9
Instagram 175
International Agency for Research on Cancer 15–18, 26, 68, 70–1, 169
International Journal of Cancer 192
International Journal of Epidemiology 198
Ireland 134
ischaemic strokes 212–13
ISO Group 154
Italian salami 223
Italian sausages 223
Italy 138

Jackson, Peter 5
James, Dame Deborah 79, 174–6
Jamie's 15 Minute Meals (Oliver) 271
Japan 138, 140, 185
JBS Australia 101, 104, 108, 153–4
JBS Brazil 101–5, 108, 110, 154, 312
JBS Canada 17
JBS USA 154
Jenkins, Michael 61

INDEX

jerky 24, 212
Jews 169, 186, 238
Johns Hopkins University 71, 217
Johnson, Boris 69
Johnson, David A. 160
Journal of Forensic Sciences 64
Joyce, Barnaby 17–18

kabana sticks 25
Kaiser, Rebecca 21
Kang, Ningling 247
Kangaroo Island, South Australia 56–8
kangaroo meat 257, 261
Kastor, Elizabeth 277
Kateman, Brian 290, 298
Kempczinski, Chris 123, 137–9
Kerr, Graham 266–7
keto diet 294
Key, Tim 27
kidney cancer 207, 225, 320
kidney disease 207–8
Kidney Health Australia 207
King of the Grill: The Bumper Book of No Nonsense Barbecuing (Dobson) 196–7
Kingaroy BaconFest 3–5
Kitasamycin 150
Kmart 282
Knüppel, Anika 211
kosher meat 152
KR Castlemaine 7
kransky 20, 24
Kubersky, Sara 115
Kurlansky, Mike 244
Kyriakides, Stella 80

La Ligue contre le cancer 75–6
lab-grown meats 318
lactic acid 39
large intestine 181–2
Latvia 186–7

law, on processed food 31, 35
Lawson, Nigella 271
Lederer, Andrew 100
Lees, Joanne 206
leg ham 32–3, 90
leukaemia 276, 278–9, 320
Lewis, Ronny 157
Lewy body disease 216
L'Express 155
Life and Death in the Age of Sail (Haines) 256
Lifespan (Sinclair) 289
listeria 43, 54, 228–9
listeriosis 228–9
Lithuania 312
liver cancer 247
longevity 288–9
Los Angeles Times 275, 277
Luna Park Hot Dog Eating Competition 272–4
luncheon ham 25
luncheon meat 24, 242
Luxembourg 140
Lynch syndrome 169

Made with Plants 292
Maestre, Miguel 4, 299, 304
Maillard reaction 126, 129
Malaysia 140
maltodextrin 179
mania 217–18
Māori people 192
Maple Leaf Foods 17
Marvel films 172–3
MasterChef (television series) 271
Maugh, Thomas H. 276
Mauvigney, Joël 77
McCartney, Paul 157
McDonald's 135–40, 281
McRae, Mike 182
'Meat consumption and mortality' (report) 13–14

371

INDEX

meat industry *see* processed meat industry
Meat & Livestock Australia 49, 52–3, 127, 270, 304
meat pâté 25
meat pies 25
meat, reducing consumption of 294–8
meat taxes 314–15
Meathooked (Zaraska) 126
Medical News Today 215
medieval cooking 253–4
Mediterranean diet 198, 288–90
Meij, Don 139–42
Melosi 6
men, consumption of processed meat by 195–9
mental health 217–18, 320
Meta Australian News Fund 257
methaemoglobinaemia 58, 63
mettwurst 227
microplastics 218
migrant workers, exploitation of 157–8
Minimal Disease pigs 148–9
The Mirror 7
Mitchell-Paterson, Teresa 55
Moby 115
Monty Python's Flying Circus (television series) 243
mortadella 25
mortality 14–16, 185–6, 193, 313
Mosconi, Lisa 218–19
M&S 79
mushrooms 295
Muslims 238
My Very Special Cookbook (Fulton) 268

N-nitroso compounds 45, 67, 71, 91, 127
Naked Bacon 72
Naked Ham 72

National Art Gallery, New Zealand 157
National Beef Packing Company LLC 154
National Bowel Cancer Screening Program 170–1
National Cancer Institute 247
National Health and Medical Research Council 194, 307
National Institutes of Health 247
National Party 17
native food 257–9
'natural flavours' 33–5
Naturally Organic 291
neck cancer 204
Nepal 311
Nestlé 72
Netherlands 140, 311
New Forest, Hampshire 249–50
The New York Times 184
The New Yorker 65
New Zealand 96, 140, 192
Newton, John 258–9
NH Foods Ltd 154
Nickelodeon 94, 105–6, 108–11
nitrates 44–5, 50–2, 198
nitric oxide 45
nitrite-free products 291
nitrites
  as poisons 64
  in processed meats 40–55, 72–4, 76–7, 79, 82–4, 90–9, 104–5, 109, 220–1, 278
  link with bowel cancer 67–71, 78
  link with breast and prostate cancer 198
  nitrite-free products 44, 48, 79, 90–1
  see also potassium nitrite; sodium nitrite
nitro-preservatives *see* nitrates; nitrites; preservatives

INDEX

nitrosamines 45, 52, 55, 71, 188, 305
Noakes, Manny 269
North American Meat Institute 17
Norway 67
NSW Rugby League 287

obesity 100, 187, 222–4, 315, 320
The Observer 70
oesophageal adenocarcinoma 204–5
oesophageal cancer 204–5, 320
oesophagus 181
Ogilvy 120, 300
O'Hagan, Toby 115, 196
O'Hanlon, Jemma 100, 116, 294
Okinawa 289
The Oldest Foods on Earth (Newton) 258–9
Oliver, Jamie 271
Olivia Newton-John Cancer Wellness & Research Centre 255
On Eating Meat (Evans) 148
On the Line (Ponthus) 155–6, 159
oral cancer 203–4
organic meat 291
Osbourne, Sharon 174
osteoarthritis 215
ovarian cancer 194, 224

Pacific Islanders 192
PAHs 129–31, 203, 211, 319
Paleo diet 294
pancetta 24
pancreatic cancer 15, 188, 201–3, 320
panic attacks 162–3
pannage 250
Papandrea 37
paprika 295
Paramount Global 106–7, 110–12
parents, as role models 116
Park, Miyun 115
Parma ham 44, 71, 223–4
pastrami 25, 223

pâté 25
Paw Patrol packs 91–2, 94, 99, 104–5, 109, 320
Paylean 150
Pearson, Kim 143
Pegge, Samuel 254
People for the Ethical Treatment of Animals 17, 151, 158
pepperoni 25, 43, 131–3, 160–1, 209–10
pesticides 32
PETA 17, 151, 158
phytophthora 57
Pierre, Fabrice 67, 76
pig-farming industry 145–51, 153–4
pig in a blanket 235–6
pigs, domestic 249–51, 253
pit barbecuing 129
pizza 296
plant-based diets 26
plant-based meats 53, 292–4
The Poison Squad (Blum) 81
polycyclic aromatic hydrocarbons 129–31, 203, 211, 319
Ponthus, Joseph 155–6, 159
porcine somatotropin 150
pork industry 145–51, 153–4
pork salami 223
Portugal 186
potassium bisulphite 43
potassium lactate 32
potassium metabisulphite 43
potassium nitrate 43–4, 198, 260
potassium nitrite 43, 81
potassium sulphite 43
potassium tripolyphosphate 32, 39
preservative 250 *see* sodium nitrite
preservative 252 *see* potassium nitrate
preservatives 23, 31–55, 73–86, 100, 115, 292, 319
  see also nitrates; nitrites; sulphites
Preston-Martin, Susan 279

373

INDEX

Primal Potential (podcast) 51
Primo Foods 30–1, 92–5, 99–101, 103–5, 108, 320
Private Healthcare Australia 305
processed meat industry
    cost of alternative preservatives 291–2
    current worth of 13, 26
    JBS 17, 101–5, 108, 110, 154, 312
    pressures government to allow saltpetre 82
    Primo Foods 30–1, 92–5, 99–101, 103–5, 108
    profit margins in 279
    reliance on chemical preservatives 49
    response to IARC report 17
    use of nitrites 52–4
processed meats
    alternatives to 294–7, 314
    as comfort food 237–8
    consumption of by children 8, 40, 72, 74, 92–4, 96, 100, 104–11, 114–17
    consumption of by men 195–9
    consumption of per capita xviii
    contamination of 227–9
    defined 23–4
    digestion of 182–4
    effect on heart health 211, 226
    in Australian culture xix, 12, 40, 131–2, 233–7, 260–72, 275, 281–2, 311, 313–14
    in English culture 237–8, 240–1
    in supermarkets 90–8, 104–5
    in the Australian Dietary Guidelines 194–5
    industry guidelines for making 49
    international consumption statistics 185–7
    law regarding 31, 35
    link with arthritis 215
    link with bowel cancer vii, xviii, xx, 11, 15–17, 19, 26–7, 67–8, 70–3, 76, 78, 109, 169–70, 238, 242, 247–8, 315–20
    link with breast cancer 192, 320
    link with cancer generally 14–17, 19, 26–7, 53, 67–8, 70–3, 76, 78, 108–9, 178, 185–6
    link with dementia 216–20, 320
    link with diabetes 220–2, 320
    link with mania 217–18
    link with mortality 14–16, 185–6, 313
    link with obesity 222–4, 320
    link with ovarian cancer 194
    link with pancreatic cancer 201–3, 320
    link with prostate cancer 197–9, 320
    link with risk of leukaemia 276, 278
    link with risk of strokes 212–13
    link with stomach cancer 201–2, 320
    nitrites in 40–55, 72–4, 76–7, 79, 82–4, 90–9, 104–5, 109, 220–1, 278
    popularity of 28
    products comprising 24–5
    public perception of 23–4
    regulation of 312, 315, 319
    salt in 207–9
    saturated fats in 209–10
    serving of in hospitals xv–xviii, 78–9, 312
    shelf-life of 41–2, 48
    WHO classification of 19, 53, 108, 178, 272, 283
    see also preservatives; *specific processed meats, e.g.* bacon, ham, salami
prosciutto 24, 268

INDEX

prostate cancer 15, 188, 197–9, 225, 320
Prostate Cancer Foundation for Australia 199
Proteinaholic (Davis) 222
Protestants 238
Prudent diet 198
Pure Food Movement (US) 81
P.W.M.U. Cookery Book of Victoria 264–5

Oliquindox 150
quail, calories in 224
Queensland 152–3
The Queensland Cookery and Poultry Book (Rawson) 262
quiches 295

racism 259
Ramadan 239
Ramos, Richard 76
Rawson, Wilhelmina 249, 262
recipe books 260–72
red meat
  effect of consuming unprocessed red meat 216–17
  grilled and barbecued red meat 203
  IARC report on 16–17
  link with bowel cancer 19, 27
  link with breast cancer 130, 192
  link with diabetes 221
  link with heart disease 210–11
  link with pancreatic cancer 15, 203
  link with prostate cancer 15, 130
  link with risk of stroke 212–13
  WHO classification of 19, 53, 108, 272, 283
The Reducetarian Solution (Kateman) 290, 298
rheumatoid arthritis 215

rituals 297–8
Rivalea Holdings Pty Ltd 102–3, 147
Roark Capital Group 134
Robbins, John 89
Roberts, Linda 277
Robinson, Nikki 227–8
Rolfe, George 199–201, 240
Royal Marsden Hospital, London 79
RSPCA 147–8
Ruxton, Carrie 32

salami
  additives and preservatives in 36–7, 42–3, 90, 104
  alternatives to 100
  as a processed meat 24
  calories per 100 grams 223–4
  Don KRC products 35–6
  effect of migration on consumption of 268
  emulsifiers in 179
  in Coles 98–9
  in Subway products 133
  in Woolworths 90–2
  manufacture of 35
  Primo products 101
salmon industry 316
salmonella 43, 54, 77
salt *see* sodium chloride
Salt (Kurlansky) 244
salting 22, 31
saltpetre 44, 81–2, 260–2, 265
saturated fats 42, 209–10
sausage pie 254–5
sausage rolls 25
sausages
  Abbott's warning about 261–2
  as processed meat 24
  Bunnings sausage sizzles 280–6, 308–9
  calories per 100 grams 223–4

375

INDEX

sausages *continued*
   in Australian culture 40, 281–2, 311, 313–14
   link with bowel cancer 15
   link with risk of stroke 212
   mass-produced sausages 38–9
   Mrs Beeton's recipe for 130
   nitrite-free sausages 91
   risk of botulism poisoning 228
   smoked sausages 130
   sulphites in 43
   traditional sausages 37, 39
   ways of cooking 128
SBS 278
Schneider, Michael 282–3, 309
school canteens 116
Schwarzenegger, Arnold 297
Scott, Andrew C. 125
Sellers, Phillip 41, 233
serrano ham 223
shelf-life, of processed foods 41–2, 48
ships, diet aboard 256–7
The Simpsons (television series) 209
Sinclair, David A. 289
Singapore 138, 140
The Sizzle (podcast) 41, 233
Skydance 112
slaughterhouses 145–6, 151–2, 155–9
Slovakia 184–7
small intestine 181
smallgoods market *see* processed meat industry
Smee, Stephanie 155
Smithfield Foods 154
smoke roasting 129
smoked bacon 130, 252
smoked brats 24
smoked ham 223
smoked meat and fish 22, 31, 128–31, 195
smoked pork hocks 25
smoked sausages 130

smoked speck 24
smoking, of tobacco 16, 310–11, 314
Snape, Joel 143
snatch farrowing 149
Snee, Jim 245–8
Sobrinho, José Batista 102
social media 21–2
sodium alginate 39
sodium bisulphite 43
sodium chloride 35, 42, 207–9, 244, 295
sodium diacetate 32
sodium lactate 32
sodium metabisulphite 43
sodium nitrate 36, 43–5, 60, 132–3, 188
sodium nitrite
   alternatives to 46–7
   approval of as a preservative 82–4
   as a poison 49–50, 56–65
   characteristics of 46
   in bacon 41–3, 47–9, 90
   in Don KRC products 8, 301
   in ham 31, 33, 95
   in hot dogs 40
   in McDonald's products 137
   in pepperoni 132–3
   in processed meats generally 43–55, 67–80, 99, 172
   in products for children 92–3, 100
   in salami 36–7
   in Spam 241–2, 244, 246–8
   in supermarket products 90–3, 96–7, 99, 104–5
   link with bowel cancer 46, 109, 302
   link with cancer risk 302
   link with prostate cancer 198
   reaction with amino acids 188
   use of in suicides 59–64
   use of to kill feral pigs 56–9
sodium phosphate 33
sodium pyrophosphate 32

INDEX

sodium sulphite 43
South Melbourne District Sports Club 313
sow stalls 147
Spain 197–8
Spam 25, 239–48
Spanish chorizos 44
Spurlock, Morgan 136
Staples, Linton 58
State Street Global Advisors 245
the stomach 181
stomach cancer 16, 127, 201–2, 320
stomas 167–8
Straif, Kurt 16
Strasbourg 24
Stroke Foundation 212
strokes 212–13, 226
Stubbs, Cal 273–5
Subway 131–5, 140
sugars 223, 316
suicide 60–5
sulphites 38, 40, 43, 92
sulphur dioxide 43
Super Size Me (film) 136
supermarkets 13, 89–99, 102, 259, 292, 305–6
see also Aldi; Coles; Costco Wholesale Corporation; IGA; Woolworths
Swallow This (Blythman) 85
Sweden 67
Sweet Poison (Gillespie) 316
Swift 102
Switzerland 251
Sydney Morning Herald 27–8, 158, 270

Taiwan 140
Tajikistan 65
Target 282
Tasman Group 102
Tasting the Past (Wood) 253
Taylor, Nik 159

Taylor, Rebecca vii, 237–8, 314–15
Tesco 77, 98
Therapeutic Goods Administration 60–1
Thompson, Jason 62
Thorne, Frank 206–7
Time 125
tinned meat 239–48
tobacco smoking 16, 310–11, 314
Toxic (Flanagan) 316
Travers, Richard 62
Trump, Donald 319
trust 117–18, 320–1
turkey, calories in 224
turkey ham 223–4
twiggy sticks 25–6
type 1 diabetes 242
type 2 diabetes 220–2, 320
the Tyrol 251
Tyson Foods Inc. 154

umami 37
United Kingdom 5–6, 20, 41, 62, 69–73, 77–9, 134, 170, 315
United States 62–5, 80–3, 169, 185, 312
University of Leeds 216
University of New Mexico 218
University of Oxford 27
Unwell (McRae) 182
upper gastrointestinal cancers 201–5, 320

Vachris, Ron 121–2
Vallat, Bernard 77
Vanguard Group, Inc. 245
vascular dementia 216
Vazquez, Tina 64–5
Vienna sausage 24

Wagyu beef bresaola 25
Waitrose 79

377

INDEX

Walkley Foundation 257
wall saltpetre 44
The Wall Street Journal 134
Wani, Elia 59–61
The Washington Post 208, 277
Watson Foods 6–7
Watson, William 6
Watsonia 6
Watt, Murray 305–7
Weckert, Leah 117–18
Weddington, Brian 19
Weiner, Russell 139
Weiss, Elizabeth 21, 85, 269
Wesfarmers 282
Western diet 198
Western Plains Pork 153
Weston, Garry 5
Weston, George Garfield 5–7, 119, 299–300, 304
Weston, Katharine 7
Who Poisoned Your Bacon Sandwich? (Coudray) 82–3
wiener 24
Wiley, Harvey 81–2
William the Conqueror 250
Wired 20
Woman's Day 267

Wood, Jacqui 253
Woolworths 4, 31, 35, 89–98, 102, 104, 108, 244, 291–2
Working Men (exhibition) 157
World Cancer Research Fund International xviii, 185, 202
World Health Organization
  Andriukaitis becomes envoy for 75
  Benton sceptical of claims of 51
  classification of red and processed meat 19, 53, 108, 272, 283
  IARC report on processed meat 15–16, 26, 68, 71, 169
  obesity rankings 187
  on obesity 100, 222
  report on salt in diet 208
Worthington, Joachim 171
Wu, Kana 91

X (formerly Twitter) 114, 286
The XX Brain (Mosconi) 218–19

Yarrabah 258
You, Me and the Big C (James) 175

Zaraska, Marta 126